Fashion Packaging Now

Edited by Chris Huang

images
Publishing

Contents

Why Packaging Design Is Necessary for Fashion

In this age when time is measured in nanoseconds, consumers may find it hard to keep up with the trends, and nowhere is this more obvious than in the fashion industry, which is nothing if not trendy. In order to maintain and grow their positions in the ever-changing fashion marketplace, fashion manufacturers and retailers must establish strong brands that resonate with consumers through the "complete package" experience—from attracting shoppers with storefront designs and advertisements to them falling in love with a dress, trying it on, peeking at the price tag, and paying for it, then walking out of the store smiling, carrying a specially designed shopping bag.

Whereas many stores may think the sales process is over post-purchase, savvy marketers continue to promote brand exposure after the fact. They influence shoppers to not only love the merchandise itself, but also to appreciate the decorative packaging, which can include bottles, tubes, boxes, shopping bags, or other imaginative containers. So after removing or using the merchandise, shoppers can reuse that leftover packaging for other purposes: empty shoe boxes become storage containers or decorative pieces for the home, cool shopping bags a fashion accessory. This extra after-sales usage puts additional, invisible value on top of the merchandise. Studies show that more than half of customers will pay more for a fashion product when the transaction makes them feel that the manufacturer/retailer has added something special. Here's where packaging design comes into play.

In the ideal sales experience, the packaging designer does the important work of not only maintaining consistency across a brand's image, but also of designing an attention-grabber that influences shoppers toward final—and sometimes future—purchase decisions. Therefore, to be consistent with fashion trends, packaging designers in the fashion industry must think and design like fashion designers.

What Constitutes Packaging Design for the Fashion Market?

Technically, anything used for protection or display purposes is a must-have item when considering fashion packaging, as well as any sales promotion material that helps to sell the product. Following are some packaging design items that apply to the fashion business:

Product & Development Items

1. Label/Imprint: Brand labels are the most important marketing tools. Presentation methods can be very diverse, but labels on clothes are usually sewn on the back, neck, or distal areas. Recently, imprints applied directly on fabric have been introduced to resolve sensitive-skin issues.

2. Wrapper: Some wrinkle-proof items like socks and underwear can be easily folded into the smallest size for best shipping results. Wrapper materials might be stickers, paper or ribbon, or even a simple plastic bag or shrink wrapper.

3. Box: Containers and fragile or oddly shaped merchandise require simpler and easier storable packaging. Boxes not only provide protection, but can also illustrate what's inside them for the benefit of shoppers. Merchandise display boxes usually require full-color and well-designed packaging to get a shopper's attention.

4. Shipping Box: Shipping boxes are usually a behind-the-scene item. Only factory workers involved with stocking have the chance to see, open, and throw away these boxes, before their contents are delivered directly from the factories to stores. Since they aren't seen by consumers, manufacturers are usually uninterested in these internal pieces and produce them at their lowest cost, with a one-color print or even no design. Though shipping does not have important visual requirements, it does have durability and safety requirements to prevent loss of merchandise due to shipping damage. Shipping boxes can contain dozens of products. Engineers carefully calculate and estimate what quantity and dimensions are the most effective space savers for skid-container shipping. Shipping boxes usually pass the drop test of the International Safe Transit Association (ISTA[1]), an organization concerned with transport packaging, to avoid damage during shipping.

Sales & Marketing Items

1. Small-Item Display: Small items require a display panel hanger. A bigger display to hold small merchandise is a very common design, not only as a simple display that allows shoppers to compare items, but also to avoid theft in retail stores.

2. Tag: How is pricing shown on clothes? There is no way to stick prices directly onto fabric, so a tag with the barcode and price becomes necessary. But these tags are not only useful at the checkout: as clothing can't speak for itself, tags can also provide information about a product's features and benefits. They provide an opportunity for marketers to take things further, supplying additional product information, building brand awareness and creating an appealing style to encourage consumers to take garments into the fitting room. All of this additional information can be squeezed onto one price tag or multiple, extra-fancy tags.

3. Shopping Bag: Shopping bags are widely used in all retail businesses. They can be made from disposable materials like thin plastic and paper or reusable ones like thicker plastic, canvas, synthetic fibers, and woven fabrics. All other items above (labels, wrappers, boxes, shipping boxes, displays, and tags) are supplied by the manufacturer, but shopping bags are produced by the retailers.

Packaging Design Project Process

Figure 01 shows the steps of the design process to help packaging designers achieve the best results.

Figure 01

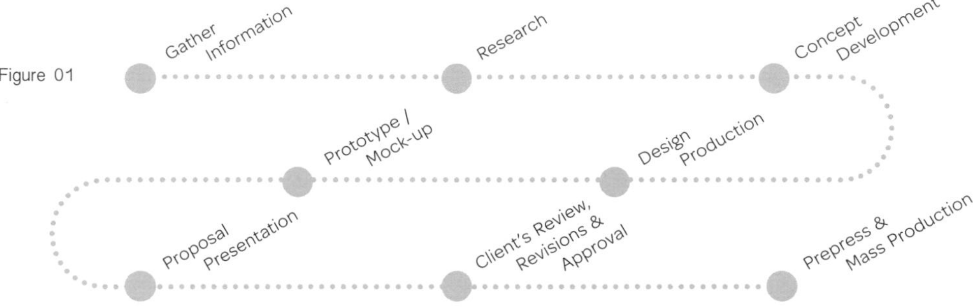

List of Market Segments for the Retail Clothing Market[2]

- Gender-Related Segments
- Age-Related Segments
- Geographic Segments
- Behavior-Related Segments
- Lifestyle Segments

1. Gather Information from the Client

Before starting any packaging design project, designers need to understand the scope of the work, ascertain the client's needs and preferences, and then gather information.

✓ Who is the target audience? Who are the competitors? (Who?)
✓ What is the project goal? (Why?)
✓ When is the deadline? (When?)
✓ What are the specifications of the project? (What?)
✓ What is the budget? (How much?)
✓ How should the design be presented? (How?)

- Match corporate branding? Any branding guidelines?
- What is the required message?
- What did the client have previously?
- What does the client have in mind?

No one can read the client's mind. Clients, usually the executives of the sales or marketing department, are more familiar with their own business than anyone else is—they know their niche in the fashion industry, their market segments, and their competitors. The fastest way to study a project is to learn directly from clients' experience and expertise. Some clients may provide particular direction or tell you what they like. Asking the right questions helps designers to win the case at the beginning and gives them a starting point.

2. Research the Field

Research! Research! Research! But how to research? Using appropriate keywords on Google and Pinterest is always a great way to start—all information is at the researcher's fingertips. Online research is not only a great way to find out about the client and their project, but also provides creative inspiration. Following are five common research directions for all design projects:

2.1 Brand Research

Designers need to find out all they can about the brand, as they are responsible for giving a brand its visual personality. As a book can't always be judged by its cover—the brand logo—it is important to research beyond this. What is the brand's position in the fashion industry? What is its history, mission, philosophy, and brand identity standard? By checking out the brand's past and present designs, designers can quickly learn what has already been done and plan the next moves. Unless marketers have already carefully evaluated the brand and determined that it is moving in a new and innovative direction, designs should be consistent with the existing brand personality across all projects. Improving the design doesn't mean making it totally different from what the brand stands for.

2.2 Competitor Research

Most markets have competition. Marketers do competitive research, as do designers. Designers should first have an understanding of what product and value positions they are up against, then further develop design strategies to stand out from all competitors.

2.3 Media Research

When doing brand and competitor research, designers should check all of the client's and the competitors' project media. When it comes to media research, the scope of the research need only extend to the same project type. If the project is a shopping bag, then all shopping bag designs should be researched, but not just in the fashion industry: the research should extend to other industries too.

2.4 Brainstorming Research

"Mind maps" are a great way for designers to come up with something different, something that will stand out, for their client. These visual thinking tools are excellent when brainstorming—providing a way to represent different wild-card ideas graphically using keywords—and work well combined with concepts from other media. Clever designers can apply a successful concept or theme from any design project to a packaging design project. This brainstorming process can sometimes result in unexpected surprises that stand out from more mundane packaging.

2.5 Site Research

It is important for designers to walk through both the client's and competitors' stores, and research to see where and how the product will actually be displayed in the store. Will it sit on shelves or hang on the walls? How will customers see the merchandise?

"Think outside the box" is an oft-heard expression, so it is important for designers to establish what "the box" is before they do anything else—instead of working on designs immediately, they should begin with the basics. Doing the research suggested above defines what the box is. Without knowing this, designers can't know whether their creative idea is inside or outside the box. Research is the key to gaining successful results.

Unfortunately, some young designers skip this part altogether or don't do enough research. Thorough research gives designers confidence during the design presentation. They will have a wider vision and excellent knowledge of what's been done before; what seems to have worked and what hasn't; what's been overdone, and so on. Providing clients with a clear explanation of why things have been done a certain way is a powerful persuasion tool!

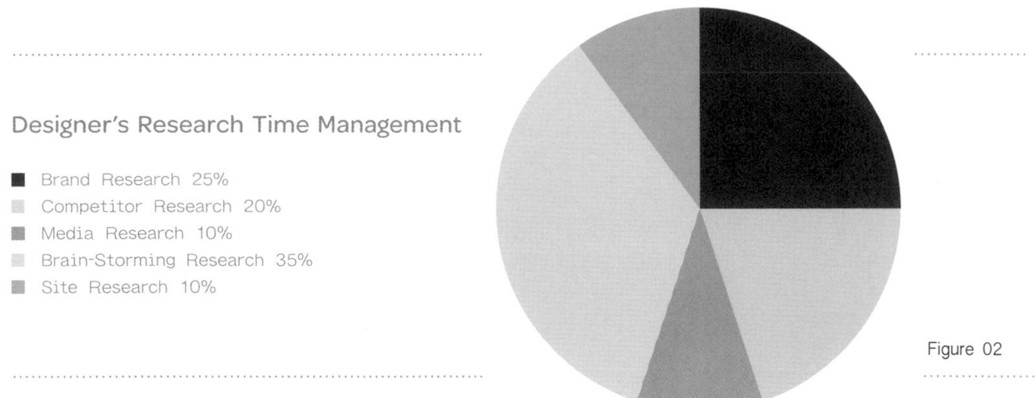

Figure 02

3. Concept Development

It's important that designers don't jump straight into graphic software to try to create their designs before a solid plan is formed. Instead they should grab pencils and paper and sketch their design ideas, and brainstorm, mind map, and communicate with an internal team. Including a copywriter at this stage is a great way to help work out a winning strategy. For some special, costly proposals, the client's approval may be required at this planning stage; if this is the case, ensure sketches are of a good, professional standard, not rough.

4. Design Production

For most single-page projects like packaging design, the designer needs excellent skills in and knowledge of Adobe Illustrator. Based on the sketches, designers will use computer graphics to present the concept and theme. The designer should decide upon any templates associated with the structure, such as dielines, sizes, and shapes before adding the graphics.

5. Prototype / Mock-up

Packaging design is a three-dimensional project. Never ask clients to "imagine" what it will look like—designers must present what it will look like. Most clients prefer to see the actual size and materials. Some manufacturing vendors will provide a prototype service. For low-budget or oversized projects, designers can use digital mock-ups instead of real products. Digital mock-ups can be done in Photoshop by retouching existing images or in 3D modeling applications. If mock-ups are provided at this stage, the designer should provide the real prototype after getting the client's approval and before mass production.

6. Proposal Presentation

With prototype or mock-up in hand, designers can put together a nice show-and-tell presentation to provide a compelling reason for why the client should use their designs, along with information about the way that their designs can help the client to be successful. Especially when explaining some special functions or showing how the packaging fits into the store environment, the designer should demonstrate visually. As a wrap-up, the designer should recap the entire design's evaluation.

7. Client's Review, Revisions & Approval

If the client loves the design with no revisions, this process could move straight to the client's final approval. But in most cases, clients will have revisions and will review several times before approving for mass production.

8. Prepress & Mass Production

Usually, designers coordinate with print vendors on the prepress process to ensure proper results. Designers send digital files to the print vendors when the vendors request them. Print vendors will send PDF files for digital proofing if it's a quick and very simple project. It's always better to request a color proof from print vendors since this is the last chance to make any changes. To avoid unnecessary argument later, most print vendors will request that designers sign off on going forward with process printing. So designers are well advised to carefully proof and adjust the colors at this stage—after all, they cannot judge the colors from the desktop screen or the printouts from low-resolution printers. This color proof is the closest approximation to the actual prints. For three-dimensional projects, it's a good idea to review the actual mock-up.

Designer's Time Management for Packaging Design Production

- Research & Concept Development 40%
- Design Production 40%
- Prototype/Mock-up 10%
- Proposal Presentation 5%
- Prepress & Mass Production 5%

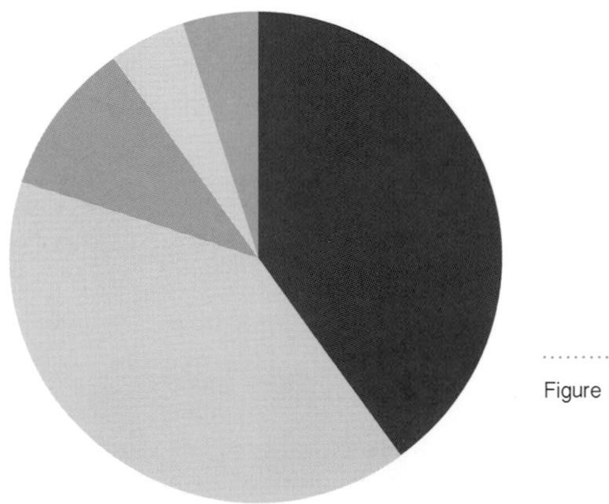

Figure 03

Some packaging designers put most of their time and effort into design production and prototypes. But the pre-design process is of equal or more importance. Without the right concept and strategy, the project will be less likely to achieve optimum results.

Design Elements of Packaging Design for Fashion

After going through all the research and conceptual development, the actual design execution begins. The graphic designer's role is to grow the design from a trifling, invisible, abstract idea into a concrete design that becomes well-known and develops explosive popularity. As with any other merchandise, there are some visual design elements and principles that are specific to designing packages for fashion.

1. Physical Structure or Shape

How should the merchandise be packaged? Should it be hidden inside a container or box or made visible? If the packaging is a container, what should the size and shape be? Should it be a conventional box or something unique? Should the designer create a structure dieline before starting all visual designs? Dielines are used when designing uneven, folded projects that will go from flat to dimensional, such as a pocket folder, an envelope, and most common packaging. It's a placeholder to help designers properly layout a document to identify what the live area is, the diecut, and the fold.

Though the dieline is not an actual design element, it is a required structural guideline for the outline shape, similar to the choice a painter makes on the size, shape and material on which to paint. Sometimes the structure of unique shapes plays an important conceptual role. However, a successful packaging design doesn't have to be overly crafty or use weird shapes; the project objective should always be put first. Any extra-fancy folds or a design that wastes materials could lead to much higher costs. Single packages can be designed both to stand alone or with a modular concept that can be turned into different, interesting shapes when put together, as in Figure 04, packaging for The Wonderful Socks (page 146).

Figure 04

Source: courtesy [ZUP Design]

Figure 05

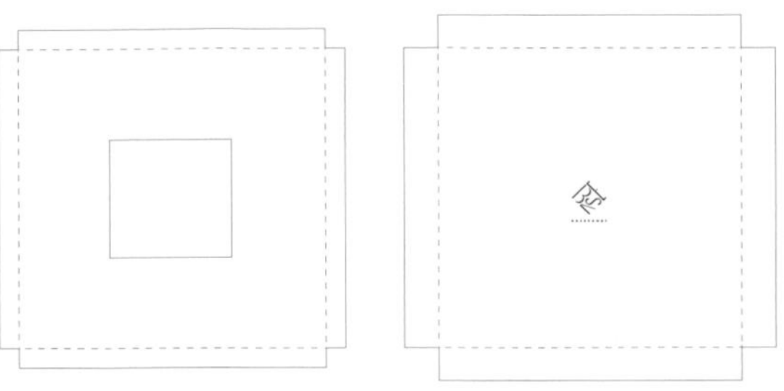

Source: courtesy [Michael Thorsby]

Dash lines are usually fold lines, while different colored solid lines are diecut lines. Dieline documents can be provided by the packaging engineer from the manufacturer or by packaging designers. When designing a three-dimensional object, designers should consider every side as an individual design canvas that always requires margins for better design results.

Dieline documents are usually placed as a separate layer in graphic applications like Adobe Illustrator. Designers can easily turn on the dieline layer to see the guideline; print factories can turn it on/off for final printings.

2. Brand Logo

Having a memorable brand logo is a must, especially for luxury brands. In fact, some luxury brands are so proud of their brand logos, they use nothing else because their brand means everything. Some big brands have many different product lines and each product line has its own logo and market position. Packaging designers should identify the hierarchy among brand logos. Some umbrella parent companies successfully position all subsidiary brands.

Product position and brand personality should be synced with the logo and the overall visual presentation. In the retail clothing business, market segments are roughly divided by gender, age, and style. For whom is the product intended? Females, males or either? Children, teenagers, young or old? What style is it addressing? Men's formal wear, ladies' lingerie or a casual outfit? This market positioning should be directly reflected in the logo and the look and feel of the entire package. The cute yellow logo of Mini 2 Mini (Figure 06; page 164) is clearly for a baby clothing line. The overall brand personality and color scheme are extended to the packaging.

Figure 06

Source: courtesy [Sara Petersson]

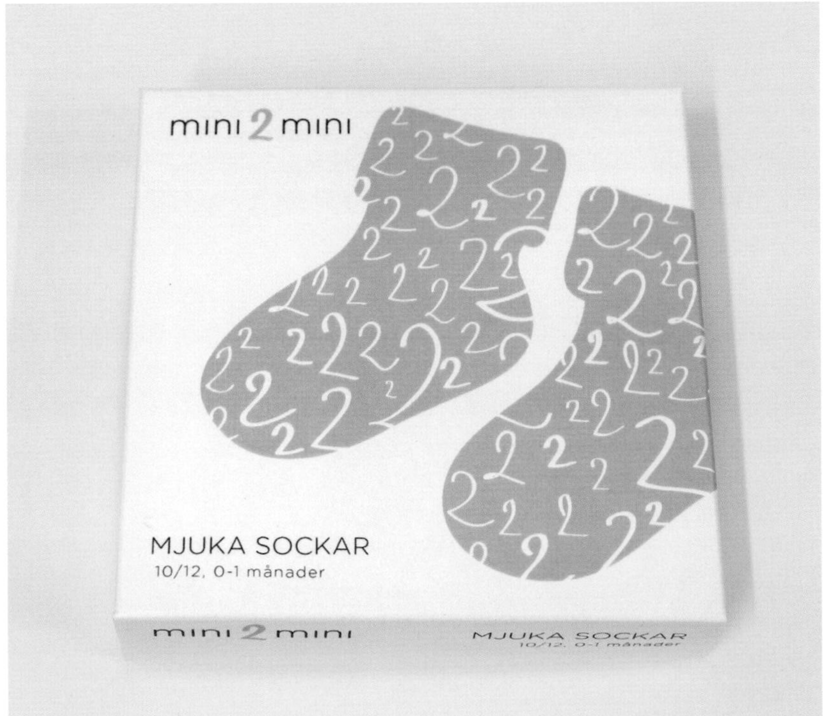

Brand Logos on Fashion Packaging

On most shopping bags of top luxury brands—Louis Vuitton, Gucci, Prada, Rolex, Chanel, Cartier, Burberry, Fendi, and Coach—logos are always the only element because the logo means everything.

Figure 07

Source: courtesy [Hey Studio]

3. Colors

Color is the key attention-grabber, as well as the most important part of a brand's identity. "Tiffany blue," for example, has been registered as a trademark color by Tiffany & Company since 1845, when Pantone created the custom color especially for Tiffany. It is such a part of the company's image that customers would likely be upset if it disappeared from the brand.

Similarly, the premier American lingerie retailer Victoria's Secret is known for its signature pink-striped shopping bags. In 2002, the company launched PINK, a new product line to cater to younger women. PINK's shopping bags retain the distinctive pink color, but instead of featuring the parent brand's stripes, the bags feature dots. This design retains a link to the parent brand while indicating that PINK also offers something different.

Barcelona-based footwear maker Arrels' brand (Figure 07; page 94) is inspired by Mediterranean culture, rhythm, and especially colors. The company applies those primary colors to its footwear products as well as the shoe-box packages.

4. Text

Like all other editing and packaging design projects, text is a fundamental part of communication in graphic design for fashion. According to the Federal Trade Commission (FTC), clothing covered by the textile and wool provision must be properly labeled with the types of fabric, fabric counts, the manufacturer, and the country of origin to avoid violation of the laws. Usually, the designer chooses simple and easy-to-read fonts for regulation copy of this kind, though the typeface may be as small as 4 or 5 point.

5. Images

Human beings process visual elements 60,000 times faster than they read words.[3] We live in a very visual world, and the adage "a picture is worth a thousand words" is often true. With the images of gloves produced by Gloves Verri (page 208) in Figure 08, shoppers can easily tell what is inside the packaging. The celebrity soccer player tells a story about the jersey in Figure 09; this packaging was created to unveil the Australian Socceroos national away team jersey (page 68) for the 2014 FIFA World Cup.

The opportunities to use photos or artwork on packaging are almost limitless, but the designer should choose images carefully so that they correspond with the brand personality. Some images can even become brand themes. Altar'd State sells feminine womenswear with boho-chic style. Its stores showcase soft tulle, antique lace, crochet, and flowing layers in subdued colors. Shopping-bag handles are made of cotton, the tag design features Indian henna images, and the ogee arch diecut adds to the mix that provides an exotic tone in keeping with the style of the merchandise.

6. Space

Also known as "negative space" or "background," when properly used, space gives more impact to what is included in a design. This technique is most often used in packaging luxury brands when the logo is a stand-alone one.

Some designers may not be comfortable with too much negative space because it seems "so simple that anyone can do it." So, how does one place a single object or a logo on a blank

Figure 08 Source: courtesy [Didier Roberti]

Figure 09

Source: courtesy [Marilyn & Sons]

Figure 10

Source: courtesy [Futura]

background with a designer's touch? A center position is too simplistic. But clever designers use a pleasing "golden ratio" proportion and unevenly organic positioning to achieve an effect when working with huge negative space. In the luxury-brand shopping-bag examples, the logo is often positioned in the center or closer to the bottom, not closer to the top. This is a common page layout technique that most viewers like: steady images that are heavier on the bottom and free at the top, rather than vice versa. This looks more balanced to most viewers.

Some designers may not use lots of negative space on publication designs that are handheld at a closer distance. This allows the reader to see many more details. However, when working on a fashion packaging project destined for print, designers should keep it simple to differentiate the product from the wide variety of other available merchandise. Simple is more likely to be noticed in a crowded field. Putting the simple typography logo of Hikeshi (Figure 10; page 40), a high-quality Japanese clothing line, in the middle of a big negative space matches very well with the brand's sophisticated, minimalist, and timeless fashion-brand image.

7. Materials

When choosing packaging materials these days, the sky's the limit. Paper and cardboard still have their place, but fabric with textures and designs, wood, glass, metal, ribbon, and plastic with the right pedigree are all turning up in innovative fashion packaging.

Choosing material is like choosing images. The right material gives a design a plus, but an inappropriate one could ruin it. In feminine fashion stores, ribbon and lace tend to replace traditional cotton for use as shopping bag handles, and they are also used to make decorative bows. Conversely, in an outdoor-apparel store, natural organic cottons will likely be chosen over ribbon. Using the right materials for the right product and even in the right position makes packaging very interesting and eye-catching. For example, the packaging of Figure 11 makes clever use of shoelaces as a handle.

Figure 11

Source: courtesy [Yandi, Alistair Marshall]

8. Texture

An extremely simple design using negative space is often seen on many luxury fashion brands. But these empty backgrounds are not necessarily blank, whether or not they contain color. Designers often fill the space with textures, but they are careful to avoid making the background too overpowering in relation to the main object and logo. There are three ways to create textural effects:

a. **Directly imprint on textured paper.** Designers should communicate with their paper suppliers to determine limitations and acquire samples. Some paper is not suitable to be printed with ink.

b. **Print textures on plain paper.** Add textured images to the graphic application and output it as a visual-only texture background.

c. **Add special effects to plain paper using an additional printing process.** These effects can be embossed or spot-glossed to turn them into a "touch-me" textured background. Textured images and special effects can even be mixed together to get dual visual and tactile results.

Design Tips for Fashion Packaging Designers

1. Clarify Marketing Objectives

What objectives should be accomplished through a particular packaging project? Is it a seasonal promotion or a new-product launch? How can the specific goal be achieved? What is the strategy? How can it be executed and evaluated? What is the timeframe? Designers should begin with the most important factor—project objectives—and then answer the above questions.

Project objectives should be kept in mind with every design step. For example, what images and colors are suitable for a Christmas holiday promotional project for a children's clothing brand? Since the objective is "holiday," the designer should use holiday-relevant images and colors and, of course, a cute theme that attracts a young age group. Without clarifying the objectives, designers cannot make the right design decisions. Figure 12 shows a sunglasses case—created for Chilli Beans' Cazuza collection—that can be folded completely flat. If the design objective for this project was for the case to occupy less space after the user has taken the glasses out, then it would have successfully reached that goal.

Figure 12

Source: courtesy [Chilli Beans, Leticia Ramos]

2. Define Brand Image & Brand Personality

"This is so X's type of clothes" is a commonly heard phrase. Shoppers have their own favorites and usually shop and wear certain brands simply because the brand's personality fits them. How do packaging designers deliver the message of "brand personality" to consumers? They need to work in conjunction with everyone else contributing to the final purchasing decision: fashion designers who design the actual merchandise; graphic designers who take care of the front-end advertising; and website creators who attract shoppers into the store or online. The three designers in particular—fashion designer, graphic designer and packaging designer—work together as a team to promote the brand. The key concepts at the forefront of these three designers' minds are the same: brand image and brand personality.

Figure 13

Source: courtesy [Spread Studio]

Examples of Brand Positions between Parent Brands & Subsidiaries

Abercrombie & Fitch makes modern yuppie clothing whose prices occupy the higher end of the youth retail market.

Subsidiaries:

- Abercrombie—children's clothing
- Hollister Co.—more affordable clothing marketed to teens
- Gilly Hicks—the women's sector of Abercrombie & Fitch, which markets lingerie and women's lounge wear

Gap[4] is known for its assortment of simple clothes such as T-shirts and denim; its target audience is young professionals. It has launched other stores for children and babies.

Subsidiaries:

- Banana Republic—luxury and business-friendly clothes for young professionals
- Old Navy—affordable, hip, and fun clothing for families and young customers; frequent discounts
- Intermix—a multibrand fashion line
- Athleta—a women's athletic-wear line

Figure 14

Source: courtesy [Galya Akhmetzyanova, Pavla Chuykina]

This theoretical impression of brand image and personality can be clearly expressed visually. The catalog and advertising models for a fashion brand are the most powerful purveyors of the message delivered to consumers, which is: "You can be just like her/him." This is the fashion industry's consistent trick; it's a no-brainer and is so direct, so ordinary, but it always works.

For example, the classical and elegant, poetic style of Underwearables (Figure 13; page 158) attracts consumers with similar values to the brand. In contrast, the vibrant color and funky design for the Oops underwear range (Figure 14; page 156) aims to attract younger, fun-loving women.

Victoria's Secret caters to young, hip customers who shop for fancy, frilly, and often sexy undergarments. Its well-known "angel" models and fashion shows attract millions of visitors via broadcasts, the company's website, and Super Bowl advertisements. Women want to be like the Victoria's Secret angels because men love them. This sexual brand image and personality is not only reflected in Victoria's Secret's products and advertisements, but also in its packaging. Compared to Victoria's Secret, Soma's undergarments are more utilitarian and conservative. Soma offers the same women's lingerie products, but the brand image and personality is totally different, and is represented by both the product styles and packaging designs. Clothing without an appropriate model to showcase the look won't sell, especially online. The same is true with packaging design: products and brands have to have the right packaging design to be attractive to consumers.

3. Design to Stand Out from Competitors

Competitor research is always an important part of marketing strategy development. Designers should develop a strategy to differentiate the product from its competitors through some unique or clever designs. Package design for fashion is an eye-candy effect, like a pretty red cherry on top of a sundae.

Individual fashion stores' marketing battles are brand-against-brand, but department stores wage closed battles that come down to designs of style and packaging that stand out among the many brands they carry. Designer Shoe Warehouse (DSW) represents many brands; the visual presentation to customers is not only the shoe designs, but also the shoe-box packaging. When displaying both premier and cheap brands together, style—rather than brand—makes the first impression that may lead to purchase. Find the right size and open the shoe box, then try the shoes on. The closed competitive comparison that happens between opening shoe boxes and experiencing how the shoes are packaged happens in a very short time and side-by-side. Designers must develop a quick-response design strategy to make their product stand out from the crowd.

To achieve this, the designer could do something as simple as using different or eye-catching box shapes, visual designs, and materials. Among all the same rectangular-shaped shoe boxes made from traditional materials and plain, subtle colors, a container with a nonrectangular shape that is made with nontraditional materials and colorful design will pop. To come up with a successful design like this, the designer first needs to research the competitors. Armed with the relevant information, they can then start to think about how to make the packaging different from the competitors.

Whether packaging designers use shape, material, or visual design as their design strategy, these elements all need to be cohesive with the brand image, brand personality, design concept, and theme. After doing the competitor research, they may find that no one uses round shapes, soft materials, and urban-style designs. This doesn't mean, however, that they should automatically create their design with round shapes, soft materials, and urban-style designs; they need to consider why these things haven't already been done by the competitors. It might be a concealed rule for a certain industry or simply inappropriate. For example, designers don't use red color tones when working on financial reports, even for a client whose brand color is red. To be consistent with the brand, designers should use red, but why don't they? Because in the financial world, red ink is used to represent monetary loss, and even the use of the color might be a reminder of that.

Designers use many different methods and techniques to make their designs stand out from the crowd, but what they use must be appropriate. Abercrombie & Fitch[5], a high-end, casual, clothing and lifestyle brand for the youth market, always sprays its cologne brand through the stores and on clothing as a unique marketing strategy. Black-and-white images of muscle men are used in the catalog, in advertising, and on packaging.

Urban Outfitters is an innovative specialty brand that is considered hip, stylish, kitschy, irreverent, bohemian, and retro; in keeping with its somewhat offbeat image, it sometimes carries unusual merchandise. Urban Outfitters' packaging design aims to be a reflection of the spirit of its brand personality and clothing style. Designers must keep this in mind when considering color, illustration, images, other graphics, and even type treatment.

4. Make Effective Use of Attention Grabbers

Most sales and marketing project objectives are about increasing sales. How can a packaging designer help increase sales? First of all, by helping shoppers find their client's product! If consumers can't see it, how can they buy it? The overall package design must say "Look at me!" when shoppers glance at all merchandise, including the competitors', from a distance. After shoppers pick up a product, hold it in their hands and read all the details, the design must say "Buy me!". If the designer hasn't first influenced the shopper to pay attention to their client's product, there will be no further likelihood of a purchase.

Attention grabbers make a design stand out from competitors. The shape, material, and design style mentioned earlier can all attract attention, but of all these factors, design style is the most challenging one. Unlike general print graphic designers who work with two-dimensional, paper-based projects, packaging designers have to use various materials besides paper, and their bag of tricks can include three-dimensional shapes. But when it comes to design style, packaging designers do work like graphic designers in terms of adherence to basic design principles, which include balance among contrast, harmony, and utility. Individual shapes, materials, and design styles should all work together.

5. Present a Clear Hierarchy

Shoppers seldom take the time to carefully read labels or advertisements: instead, they scan. With this in mind, designers need to clarify a product's information hierarchy and then create a design to reflect this. What information should be the high priority on packaging projects? Usually, it is product brand, product name, and important information about the product itself. Some packages have nice product images, because images are best at communicating what's inside. But in fashion, the field where looks mean everything, shoppers care very much about actually seeing the merchandise, so it's always better to make at least part of it visible. If the goods are in a container or a box, there could be a cut-out window to allow shoppers to peek at the colors and textures. For products that are covered, the product name is the highest priority, but in retail fashion, the brand name comes first. This can be routinely seen with luxury-brand products, such as watches, jewelry, cosmetics, gift sets, and similar merchandise.

To figure out a product's information hierarchy, a designer should prepare a list of all the information and other elements that will be involved in the packaging, and then arrange it in order of importance. Prioritizing is key. When designing anything, not just packaging projects, designers should ask themselves what needs to go first, second, third, and so on, then plan to make everything visually fit this order. After finishing the layouts, they should double-check that everything is in the right order.

In terms of design, what elements should be used to demonstrate importance? Size and contrast do it best. Viewers won't miss the largest image and text or the color object with the most contrast. Work with type and image sizes: large, medium, and small to reflect, respectively, the first, second, and third items in the hierarchy. Color is not as simple as size; it involves hue, tone, and opacity, so designers must consider all three factors when working with color. Also, in most cases, one color should harmonize with another so that the image or text will be visually pleasing, and all elements will work together to make one unified, and beautiful, package design.

6. Storytelling

People usually think of storytelling as something only found in books, but it can be a powerful design tool. Storytelling helps designers and marketers develop unique design concepts and themes, and, most importantly, get a shopper's attention. It can take the form of a small, extra element, an interesting page layout, or a special material that makes viewers smile and think "What a clever idea!".

Designers need to consider the "story" behind their design, that is, why they did what they did. The aim of the storytelling concept is to close the gap between designer and audience so the two become much closer. The message is clearly delivered to the audience via simple design elements or materials, and the design theme must follow this storytelling concept to completion. For example, if the story (concept) is about "Little Red Riding Hood," the design theme will have a red riding hood, not a green jacket.

Storytelling is sometimes a clever idea, but designers should be careful to avoid appearing too crafty. Also, if the storytelling involves extra material and a more-involved production process, the designer should be aware that these things usually cost more. Being creative doesn't necessarily require paying more: as the advertising adage goes, "It's not creative unless it sells." The most persuasive proposal is not just creative: it's cost-effective creativity that works. Figure 15 illustrates a nonprofit breast-cancer-awareness promotional project for the Keep a Breast Foundation (page 167). The 360-degree, cute and sexy bikini display covers both top and bottom by using one simple shape, and fits both sides so well. That is the creative story behind this design.

Figure 15

Source: courtesy [Jessie Michelle Smith-Walters]

7. Use Imagination & Innovation

Designers shouldn't be afraid to do something completely different from what they've seen before in packaging. When brainstorming and researching, it's a good idea to study other industries to see what can be applied from one industry to another. Innovation is not only about being different: it can also be an improvement on pricing, function, and value.

8. Design with All Possible Factors in Mind

Designers should create with the store display and what the customer will see in mind, trying to look at the design from the customer's perspective. Packaging expense is part of the merchandise cost, so they should always keep the cost in mind, too.

Atelier Noir, a division of Rudsak, is a leather accessories brand made especially for Costco stores throughout the United States. Atelier Noir sells shoes, but unlike the practice in regular shoe stores, the shoe boxes don't wind up in fancy shopping bags. Packaging designers combined the shoe box and shopping bag by simply adding handles to the boxes. This improvement not only resolves the no-shopping-bag issue, it also reduces costs and makes the product easy to pull from the shelves. This clever solution illustrates that considering all possible factors when designing—store environment, method of store display and customers' shopping behavior—makes it easier to achieve the project goals. In Figures 16 and 17, designs for Boom Bap (page 114) and Startas (page 106) shoes respectively, shoe boxes have a carrier function added so that they effectively double as shopping bags, as in the Atelier Noir example.

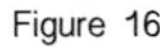

What's "in"?—Design Trends

Consumers often pursue rarity. However, visual design and fashion are both fickle. When one design becomes more common, there is always another corresponding design that becomes more valuable because it is rare and stands out from the same crowd. The word "organic" is used all over, not only to describe what people eat, but also to describe what

Figure 16 Source: courtesy [Pedro Sousa]

Figure 17 Source: courtesy [Leo Vinkovic]

they see. In the graphic world, organic often refers to a free style and originality. The two main organic trends at the moment include handwritten typefaces and unique illustrations, each discussed following, along with other current design trends.

1. Handwriting Typeface

Most people don't bother to open printed junk mail, but they will open mail that's been handwritten and carefully sealed like a special invitation. Why? Because the handwriting shows that the senders made the effort to write their message out longhand instead of using computer-generated copy and bulk-mail printing. But for the many commercial mailers who send millions of printed pieces, handwritten copy is an impossibility. But there is a solution that approximates real handwriting: the handwriting font for the computer. Font designers have been busy creating fonts that mimic all sorts of handwriting styles. As handwriting fonts become more popular for commercial projects, the use of a personal writing style gains importance to continue the "personal" theme and set a piece apart from the competition.

What makes a signature so personal? Everyone has their own unique handwriting style. Handwriting, whether script, cursive, or print style, always provides interesting strokes that no existing font can duplicate. Every letter "a" of a computer font is identical to every other letter "a" of the same font, no matter how many times it is printed. But when a person writes by hand, the same isn't true. People aren't machines, but the quirkiness of real handwriting makes it fun to read, and it's dynamic. Calligraphy is widely used when writing Asian characters. Its brushstrokes can be thick, thin, straight, curved, neat, or grungy. Roman alphabet hand lettering tends to be suave or swirly, and it can have fancy flourishes.

To make designs unique, designers can think about the "trend rule" mentioned earlier. When one design gets too popular, a new one is rare and therefore more valuable. While computer handwriting fonts are widely used, a handmade personal handwriting style takes design further and stands out even more because it is so special, original, and unique. Of course, it takes more effort to produce: the designer must hand-draw, scan, digitize, and then finally edit it as an image. But it is so original that no one can duplicate it, just like the font design for La Stantería Clothing Co. (page 58) in Figure 18.

Figure 18 Source: courtesy [La División Brand Firm]

2. Unique Illustration

Royalty-free stock photos tend to be pretty cookie-cutter. After years of using such photos for convenience and cost effectiveness, designers and their clients have begun to find original and organic graphics more appealing. Audiences are increasingly appreciative of a unique design that tells viewers "You are so special" and "Only for you." Unique styles of illustration are spectacular, and they often become the brand icons that extend to all of the company's product lines. However, when these illustrations are used throughout all product lines, designers must be cautious about consistency. Figure 19 shows a children's clothing brand (page 170) that effectively uses different, simple outline illustrations across its various product lines, corresponding with the theme of being an astronaut, a firefighter, and so on.

The trend toward nostalgia doesn't end with old-fashioned handwriting and unique illustrations. When everyone else is trying to figure out how to draw digitally on a computer, innovative designers think in the opposite direction and revert to traditional media: paper and brush. Natural paper effects can never be replaced, but they can be reproduced for today's digital world. Traditional media artwork can be transferred to digital and become a part of the editing process. Combining design with handwriting and illustrations, the ice-cream-shaped packaging for Los Playeros (Figure 20; page 46) has a relaxing summer theme. Instead of using fancy model photos, unique characters were created to illustrate fun summer activities.

Influenced by the freehand lettering style trend, designers introduced wiggly illustrations that became original design elements. Unique illustration trends include both avant-garde and old-fashioned styles. Using an old-fashioned style doesn't mean choosing one that is outdated or unpopular; it usually means harking back to a particular period when busy, ornate elements were popular. Their use in a contemporary setting can give viewers a nice visual surprise.

Figure 19 Source: courtesy [Alen Zdorova]

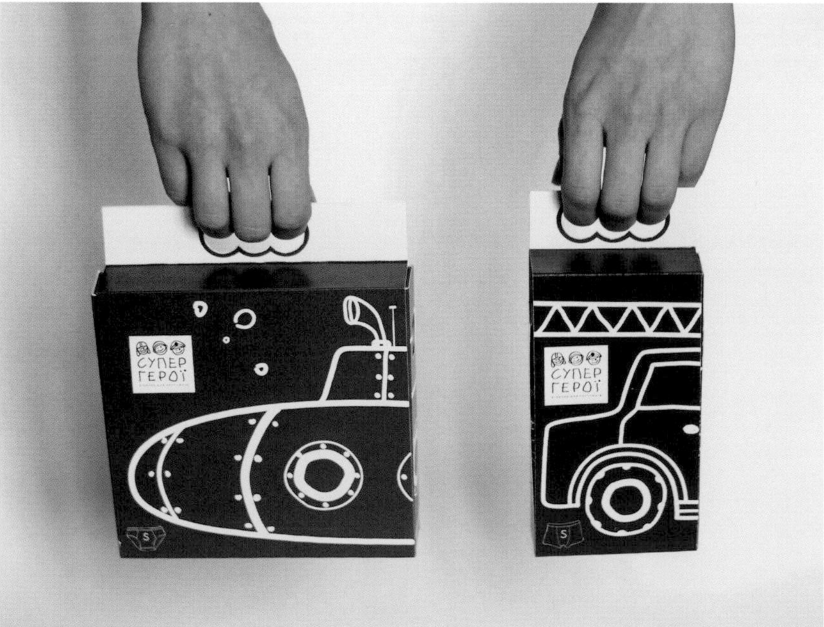

Figure 20 Source: courtesy [Paola Coiduras, Eric Novo]

3. Simplicity

In this informational internet world, when pixel advertising costs more than a giant highway billboard, and shoppers can view all merchandise on one small cell-phone screen, all visuals have become ASAP, that is, "as simple as possible" and also "as soon as possible" (in terms of how long something takes to download). The easiest data to process is small in file size. To keep it small, designers should use simple colors and shapes. Today, the desire for simplicity influences everything from the corporate website to the company identity to almost everything else, including packaging design.

The Dieline Packaging Design Award predicts that the trend in packaging design will be essentialism.[6] When "less is better" it affects both shapes and colors. The shapes will be simple and geometric and the colors will be flat. Unlike traditional glasses holders, the ANVE Sunglasses Case (Figure 21; page 204) uses a simple round shape folded in half to protect the glasses and make them easy to hold.

4. Eco-Awareness—Reduce, Reuse, Recycle

According to the Environmental Protection Agency (EPA), in the past 10 years in the United States, packaging waste declined from 36 percent of total waste to 30 percent.[7] This was due to the use of fewer materials, which resulted in a reduced environmental impact. Other contributors to the reduction were recycling and the use of energy recoverable source materials.

People everywhere are becoming more concerned about the environment, so the new mandate for fashion packaging is to be eco-friendly, making packaging from sustainable and recyclable materials, including paper and cardboard. The use of soy-based ink for print materials is appreciated, too. Something that both clients and shoppers don't want is unnecessary packaging, which adds more to costs and increases waste.

Figure 21 Source: courtesy [ANVE]

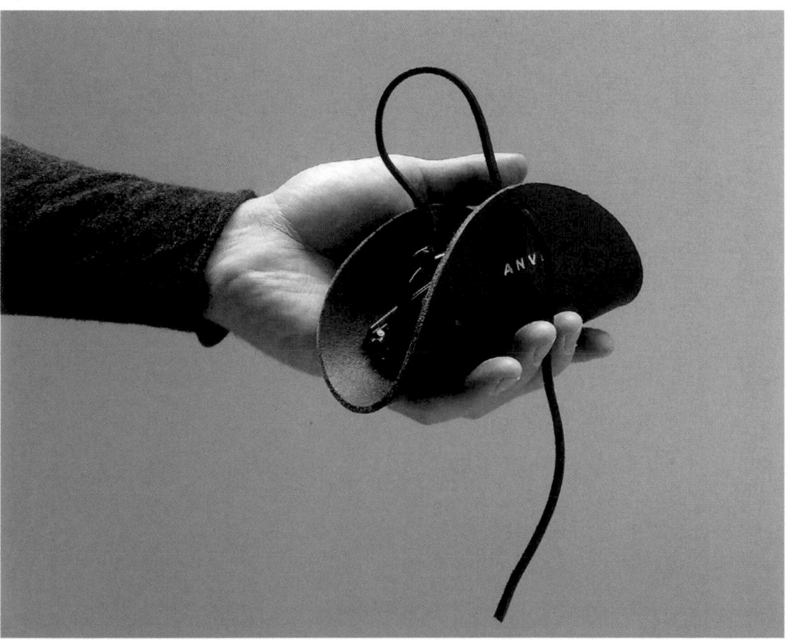

Figure 22 Source: courtesy [Hey Studio]

Making packaging materials simple, in line with the "less is better" trend, will be eco-friendly. Not only are fewer materials good for the environment, projects could also cost less. Puma's new shoe-box design combines the shoe box and the bag. The box itself is so easy to flatten that shoppers can easily recycle it. The topless shoe box not only saves on materials usage, but it also allows shoppers to easily peek at the shoes and then try them on.

A real coup for packaging designers is to create packaging that can be reused. This feature scores on two counts: shoppers get something extra that is useful, and it's also a walking advertisement for the brand wherever the shopper takes it. For example, Lululemon Athletica packages its workout clothing in an attractive tote bag that customers frequently take to their yoga classes. That's free placement marketing for Lululemon Athletica. The reusable bag for Arrels (Figure 22; page 94) can be widely used everywhere the target buyers are.

Reusable bag materials can be canvas, woven synthetic fibers, or thick plastics that are more durable than disposable plastic or paper bags. (Disposable plastic bags have already been banned in many places, a phenomenon likely to continue, which adds to the need for more durable designer bags.) Regular reusable shopping bags are often used in grocery stores, but some shoppers collect high-quality or luxury-brand shopping bags to carry for the look or the brand, even though the bags are not made from very durable materials.

In many countries, including some states in the United States, grocery stores no longer provide plastic bags, so shoppers must bring their own reusable grocery bags. To make these bags even more convenient, they can be designed to be foldable and compact, so that they'll easily fit into a purse. Small, reusable bags are becoming a shopping-bag trend, as shoppers save them for future use at stores that no longer provide bags. Whether designing packaging to reduce materials or to utilize recycled or recyclable source materials, designers are all contributing to a decreased environmental impact, an extremely important issue.

5. Color Trend

The trend in colors changes yearly. Since 2000, the Pantone Color Institute has been selecting a Color of the Year. As the fashion industry's arbiter of color, Pantone chose "Marsala" for the 2015 Color of the Year, and in 2016, the selected colors were "Rose Quartz" and "Serenity"[8] (see Figure 23).

The latest color trends influence not only the fashion industry, but also other color-trend-conscious industries, such as electronics and appliance manufacturing. Cell-phone manufacturers like Apple are always quick to jump on a trendy bandwagon. Some recent color trends can be seen by looking at past versions of Apple's iPhone: the phone was first black, then white was added, then both silver and gold, and now there's also rose quartz.

6. E-Commerce: What's Next?

More and more, consumers are enjoying online shopping, where they can make purchases in seconds from the convenience of their homes. Online store revenues are increasing annually. Some fashion brands are even sold only online instead of in physical stores. Online retailers' 2015 holiday sales increased between 15 percent and 16 percent over 2014 sales in the United States.[9]

With online shopping, merchandise comes directly to consumers' doors. While some shoppers visit retail stores to see or try on the merchandise, many never see the displays on retail store shelves. As a consequence, some retail stores are opting for smaller physical spaces and increasing their online presence. This virtual-store trend could have serious implications for the fashion industry. Customers' shopping behaviors have changed, so packaging designers should pursue creative methods to take advantage of this trend.

With online shopping, consumers no longer see how the merchandise is packaged before making their purchasing decision. There are no clothing tags or shopping bags to look at. Shoppers receive unadorned brown cardboard shipping boxes delivered by Federal Express, UPS, USPS, or another carrier. This new selling process will have an influence on the design of packaging. People may assume their packages come from the retail e-store, but they are really "drop shipped" directly from the manufacturer or a giant fulfillment warehouse like Amazon.com's. Now there's a whole new package that can be redesigned: the shipping container. Instead of a plain brown cardboard box, could it be something else? This is a wonderful opportunity for innovative fashion packaging designers to step in with creative ideas.

Drop Shipping

Drop shipping is a common e-commerce supply-chain management that changes the sequence of shipping. Retailers deliver a product to a customer without having seen, packed, or shipped the item. Retailers do not stock goods in their warehouses but instead transfer customer order and shipment details to their suppliers, either the manufacturer, another retailer, or a wholesaler. The supplier will ship the goods directly to the customers. To hide this fact from their customers, retailers ask suppliers to ship merchandise without a return address, or they customize a packing slip to include retailers' contact information. Drop shipping eliminates the possibility of losing money on overstocked items and the costs of shipping and packing.[10]

Figure 23

Source: courtesy [Pantone]

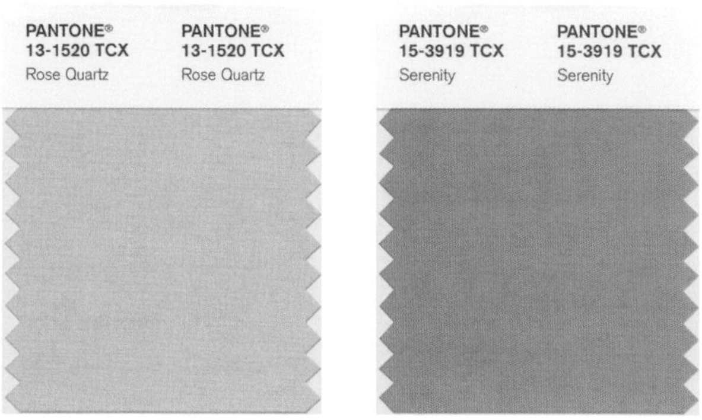

PANTONE® 13-1520 TCX Rose Quartz

PANTONE® 13-1520 TCX Rose Quartz

PANTONE® 15-3919 TCX Serenity

PANTONE® 15-3919 TCX Serenity

Designers are no longer just inside their own graphic world; they must learn the new business language. Business has changed to e-commerce and virtual stores, so designers should adjust their designs to fit the requirements of the top parcel carriers, such as USPS, UPS, and FedEx—for example, leaving a blank area in the design for the carriers' standard labeling—as well as clients' warehouse labeling capabilities.

Summary

Change comes at a bewilderingly rapid rate in the fashion business as well as everywhere else. Will more and more shoppers buy clothing online? Probably. To encourage online clothing shopping, many e-commerce sites provide very detailed size charts and free return or store pick-up services. But there will always be people who want to see a piece of clothing, feel it, and try it on before buying, the ones who say: "I'd never shop online for clothing. I have to try it on." So brick-and-mortar retail stores may become smaller and fewer, but they're not likely to go away.

In addition to the fact that online shopping has changed consumers' shopping behavior, environmental awareness has become another lifestyle-changing factor. Sustainable

References

packaging has become a part of everyday life. The packaging designer must think how shoppers think and do what they do to maximize brand exposure.[11] What kind of reusable bag would consumers want to use? And what are the target consumer markets? Packaging designers could design a backpack-style, reusable shopping bag for a sports clothing brand that could be later used for a sporting activity. Or for a family style clothing brand, the emphasis for reusable bags could be on durability, so the bags could be reused for heavy grocery shopping. Designers not only need to think the way shoppers think, they also need to think the way marketers and clients think.

The principles of design detailed here don't change. Good design will always be good design. But business environments change swiftly, and designers need to quickly adjust their capabilities and conceptual thinking to keep up to date with business needs. Especially in the fast-changing fashion marketplace, packaging designers should be acutely aware of fashion trends so they can develop appropriate packaging designs. Change may be frightening to some general packaging designers, but for fashion packaging designers, change means opportunity, and that creativity will always be in demand. The design tips, skills, techniques, and trends included here will serve fashion packaging designers well.

1. *ISTA* (2016), Retrieved from "Our Story," www.ista.org
2. Suttle, R (2016), "List of Market Segments for the Retail Clothing Market," Retrieved from Small Business, http://smallbusiness.chron.com/list-market-segments-retail-clothing-market-32446.html
3. Gutierrez, K (July 8, 2014), "Studies Confirm the Power of Visuals in eLearning," Retrieved from Shift's eLearning Blog, http://info.shiftelearning.com/blog/bid/350326/Studies-Confirm-the-Power-of-Visuals-in-eLearning
4. Shpanya, A (March 31, 2015), "Three Brands That Prove the Relationship between Pricing and Positioning," Retrieved from Econsultancy, https://econsultancy.com/blog/66249-three-brands-that-prove-the-relationship-between-pricing-and-positioning/
5. Stampler, L (May 30, 2014), "This Is the Reason Going Into Abercrombie & Fitch Gives You Anxiety," Retrieved from TIME, http://time.com/2799621/abercrombie-fitch-cologne-anxiety-study/
6. Wenzlau, G (January 14, 2016), "4 Emerging Packaging Design Trends of 2016: Essentialism," Retrieved from The Dieline, http://www.thedieline.com/blog/2016/1/13/emerging-packaging-design-trends-of-2016-essentialism
7. Lilienfeld, B (April 22, 2015), "From Crisis to Myth: The Packaging Waste Problem (Op-Ed)," Retrieved from Live Science, http://www.livescience.com/50581-packaging-no-longer-the-nightmare-some-claim.html
8. Pantone (2016), "Introducing Rose Quartz & Serenity," Retrieved from Pantone, http://www.pantone.com/color-of-the-year-2016
9. Guy, S (December 1, 2015), "Online Sales Surge While In-Stores Sales Drop to Start the Holidays," Retrieved from Internet Retailer, https://www.internetretailer.com/2015/12/01/online-sales-surge-as-stores-sales-drop-start-holiday
10. Wikipedia (2015), "Drop Shipping," Retrieved from Wikipedia, https://en.wikipedia.org/wiki/Drop_shipping
11. Davis, D (2016), "Creative Strategy & the Business of Design," Retrieved from HOW's website, http://www.howdesign.com/resources-education/graphic-design-trends-2016

Clothes Packaging

Hard Lunch T-Shirt Packaging

This T-shirt packaging is part of the new identity of Russian streetwear brand Hard Lunch. The concept adapts fast-food packaging to suit streetwear products, and includes roll boxes for tees and pizza boxes for hoodies and sweatshirts. The sleek design has an emphasis on typography and incorporates textured surfaces and a perforated tear strip in the middle of the T-shirt boxes to provide customers with an unexpected user experience. Fully consistent with the aesthetics of the brand, this creative approach toward packaging results in a holistic, complete, and unique image for the Hard Lunch brand. Enjoy the meal!

Client
Hard Lunch Clothing

Size
200mm x 84mm x 52mm

Designer
Vladimir Strunnikov

Completion
2014

Material
Paperboard

HARD
ALWAYS HUNGRY COMMUNITY
CLOTHING

ART OF LIFE
SATISFY HUNGER SAVING
APPETITE
RUSSIAN STREETWEAR BAKERY
HARDLUNCH
CLOTHING
ALWAYS HUNGRY COMMUNITY
HARD LUNCH CLOTHING

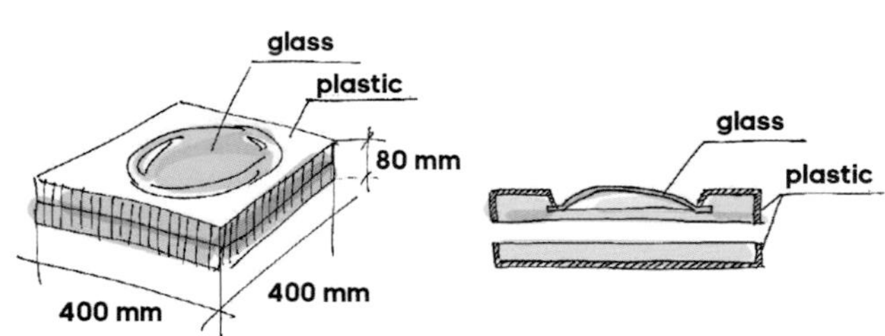

adidas Press Kit

To celebrate the 2014 FIFA World Cup, adidas designed a new away kit for the Russian national football team. Inspired by Russia's great achievements in space exploration, adidas' designers incorporated elements relating to the cosmos into the shirts. For the away-kit launch event, advertising agency TBWA\Moscow created a special press package that reflected the philosophy of the kit's new design. Made from plastic and glass, the package was reminiscent of a spaceship with a view of earth. Each journalist attending the launch received a press kit, which included the new official shirt. The kits' minimalist and ergonomic design contributed to them being well received among media professionals.

Client
adidas

Design Agency
TBWA\Moscow

Designer
Andrey Bochkov

Material
Plastic, glass

Size
400mm x 400mm x 80mm

Completion
2014

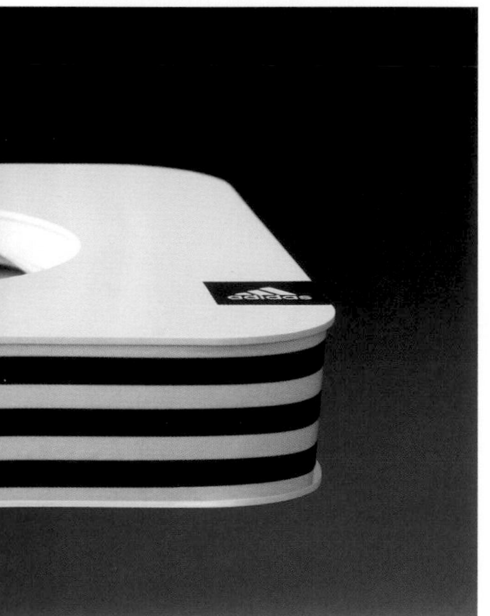

adidas

TechnoFold

"Creative Packaging" is a competition that is held at the design forum at Vienna's Museums Quartier. Entrants are required to create environmentally friendly packaging designs that help reduce waste. Answering this brief, TechnoFold is an innovative design concept for T-shirt packaging. It's reusable packaging that cleverly assists in folding T-shirts quickly and effortlessly. Also with the environmental focus in mind, the designer chose material that is simultaneously recyclable and durable, allowing TechnoFold to be functional as a folding device.

The name "TechnoFold" relates to the packaging's mechanism and overall functional qualities; it's also a title that is relevant and engaging to younger generations. A minimalist design approach was adopted to reduce the amount of ink used during production, and the graphics optimize the available surface area. Each package is able to hold three folded T-shirts at a time.

Designer	Size
Bastian Müller	450mm x 250mm
Material	**Completion**
400gsm recycled paper	2012

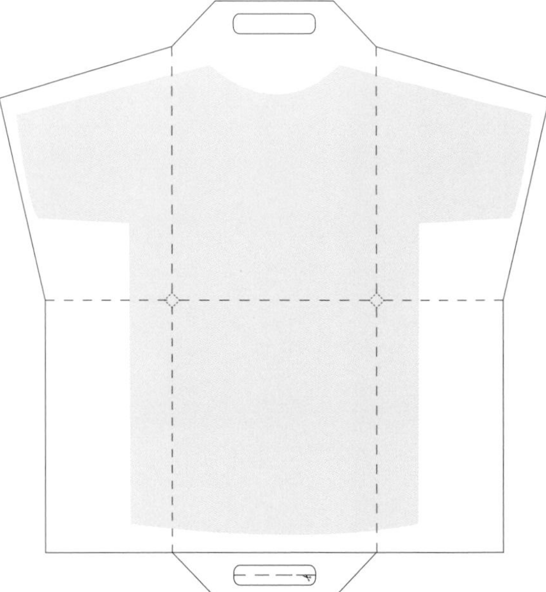

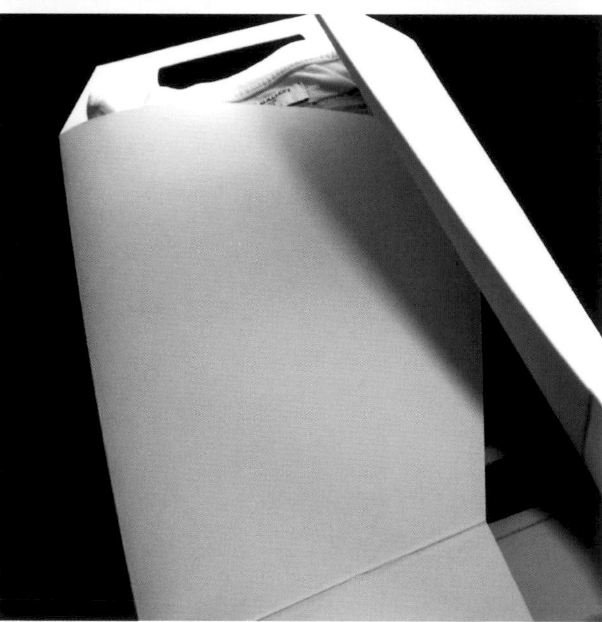

Gift Box

The creative challenge for this project was to construct a memorable and user-friendly gift box—combining fashion with packaging—for Tiny People, a children's clothing brand. Oval tabs on the sides of the packaging allow the clothing to be placed inside the gap that forms in the middle section. A strong brand presence is evident on both sides of the packaging, incorporating address and other store information, but the focal point is a very cute bear with a ribbon, bound to make customers feel happy. Boxes come in two predominant colors—shiny pink and a sober blue, commonly used for girls and boys respectively—and are made of fine cardboard reinforced with tabs in the bottom of the box to prevent things falling out. A lovely final touch is a long lace that allows the package to be carried over the shoulder like a bag.

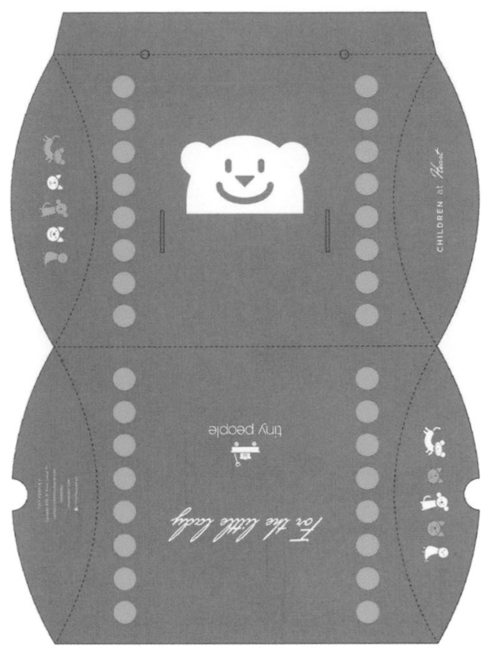

Client
Tiny People

Design Agency
Analog Agency

Designer
Misael Ávalos

Material
Cardboard, ribbons

Size
280mm x 360mm x 80mm

Completion
2014

For the little lady
tiny people

CHILDREN at Heart

O!Shirt

It's the camera obscura! This project was developed in conjunction with the Copernicus Science Centre in Warsaw, and the aim was to create an educational product inspired by the sun. Definitely not your usual packaging, a T-shirt is placed in the cardboard box and the spot where a graphic would normally go is covered with a photosensitive substance. The box is then sealed so no light can get in. You then take the box to somewhere/something you'd like to capture on film, place the box in front of the thing to be photographed, and uncover the hole on the front of the box. After about 15 to 20 minutes, a picture will appear on the T-shirt!

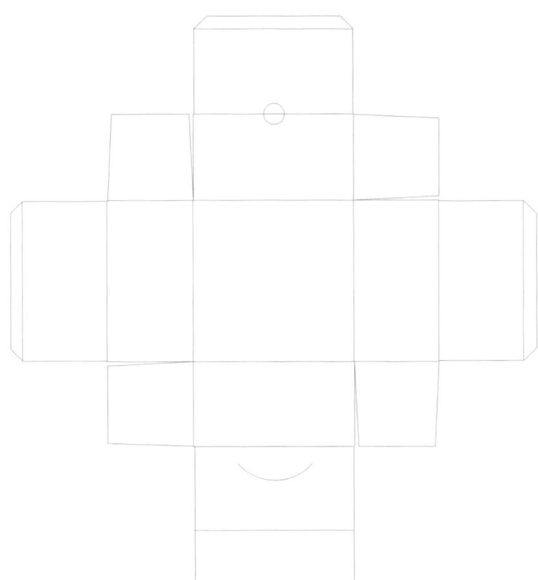

Client
Copernicus Science Centre

Design Agency
NOTO Studio

Designers
Anna Wręga, Kaja Nosal

Material
Cardboard, photosensitive substance

Size
190mm x 190mm x 100mm

Completion
2013

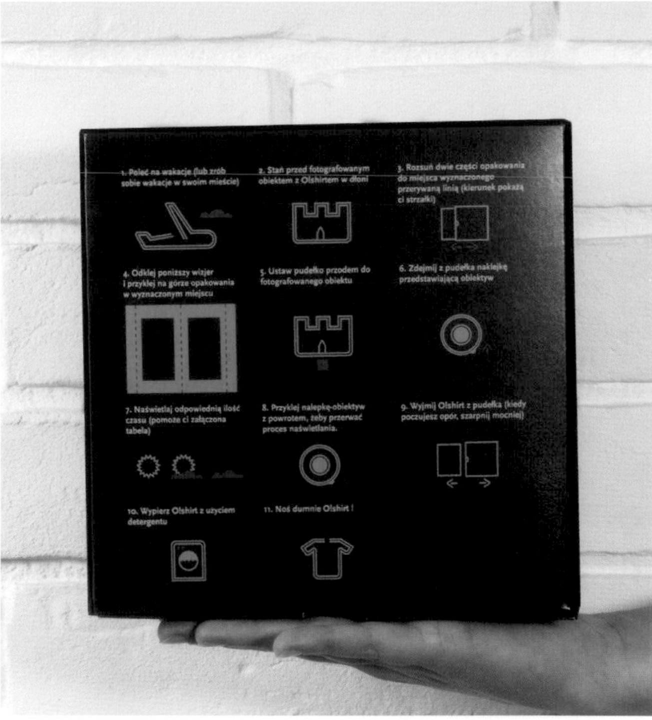
1. Poleć na wakacje (lub zrob sobie wakacje w swoim mieście)
2. Stań przed fotografowanym obiektem z Olshirtem w dłoni
3. Rozsuń dwie części opakowania do miejsca wyznaczonego przerywaną linią (kierunek pokażą ci strzałki)
4. Odklej poniższy wizjer i przyklej na gorze opakowania w wyznaczonym miejscu
5. Ustaw pudełko przodem do fotografowanego obiektu
6. Zdejmij z pudełka naklejkę przedstawiającą obiektyw
7. Naświetlaj odpowiednią ilość czasu (pomoże ci załączona tabela)
8. Przyklej nalepkę-obiektyw z powrotem, żeby przerwać proces naświetlania.
9. Wyjmij Olshirt z pudełka (kiedy poczujesz opór, szarpnij mocniej)
10. Wypierz Olshirt z użyciem detergentu
11. Noś dumnie Olshirt !

O!

Hikeshi

Hikeshi is a high-quality clothing line that belongs to the Japanese brand Resquad. The general concept for this packaging was inspired by the firefighters of the 18th century, during the "Edo" period (now Tokyo). They were considered to have as high a status as samurais. The typographic selection and color palette turn the brand into something modern, but the materials, composition, and combination of elements make Hikeshi a timeless brand.

Client
Toshihiro Sato

Design Agency
Futura

Material
Manta

Size
220mm x 390mm x 140mm

Completion
2015

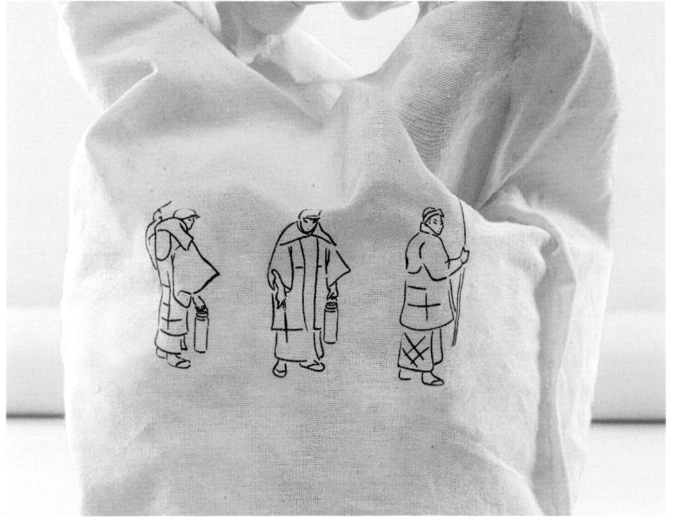

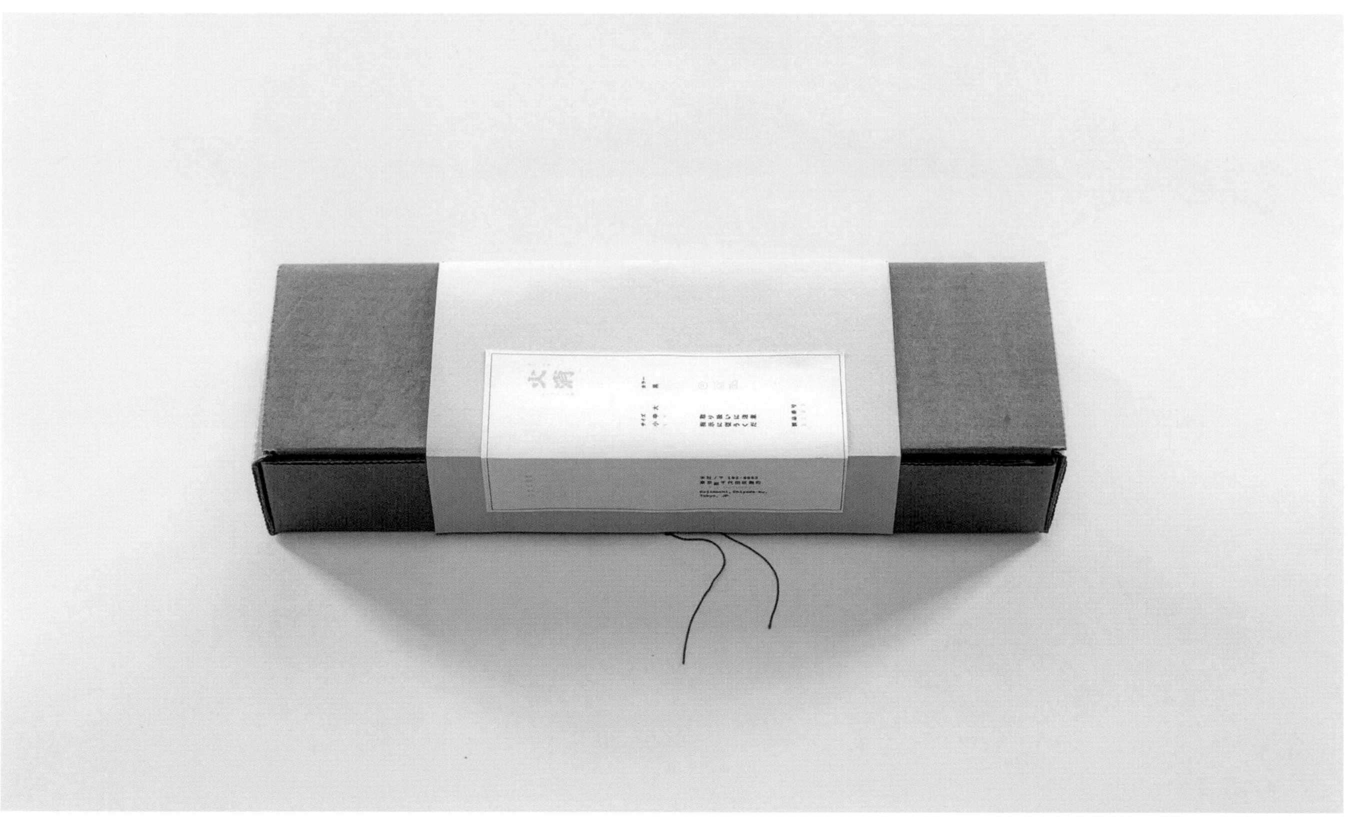

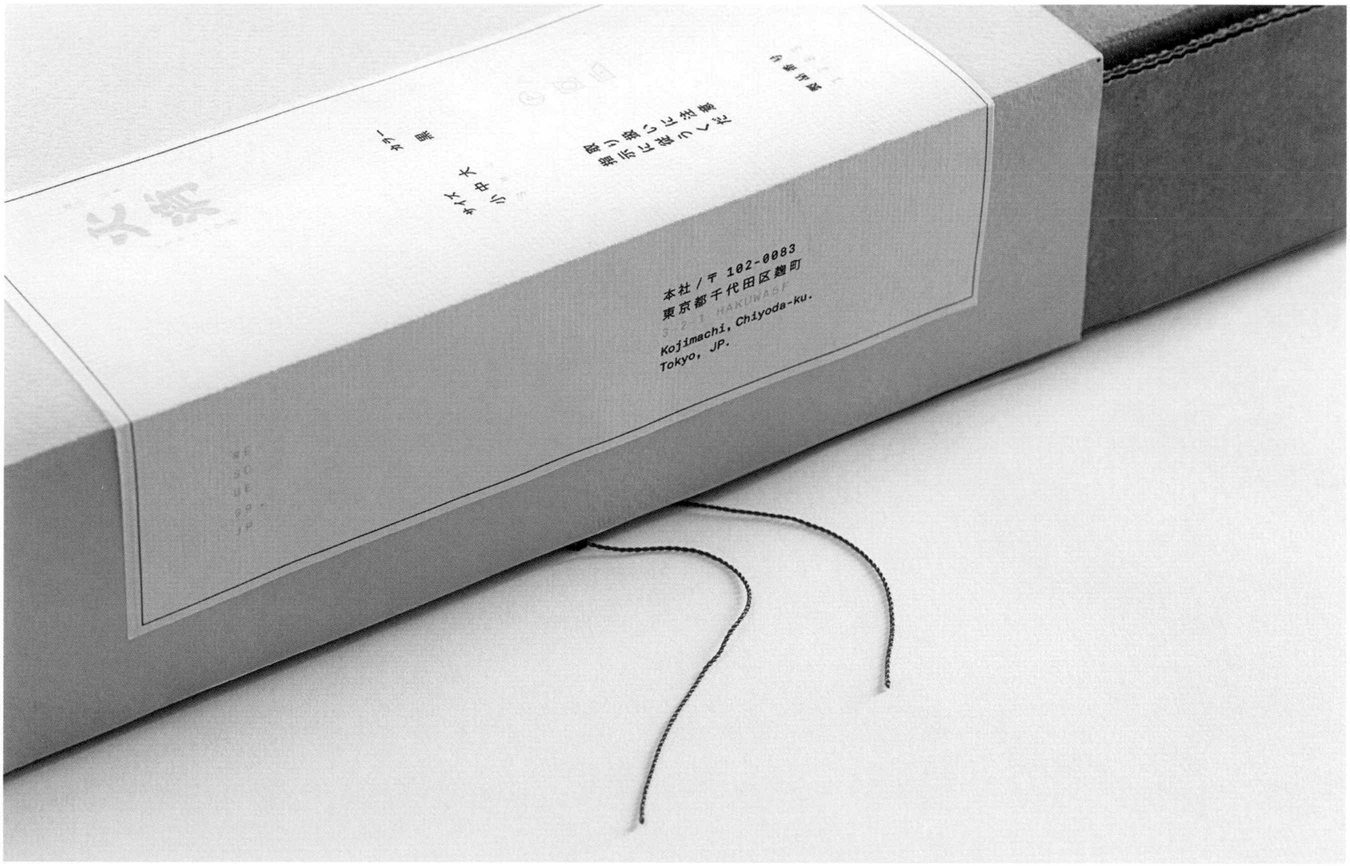

本社 / 〒 102-0083
東京都千代田区麹町
Kojimachi, Chiyoda-ku.
Tokyo, JP.

Mustang—The Inside Out Mailing

This packaging created for Mustang jeans was limited-edition, and was only available online on Workers' Day (1 May). It's essentially 'inside-out' packaging, whereby the box contains the delivery slip and the bill, and the actual jeans being shipped are the wrapping for the box, creating a three-dimensional parcel. Enhancing the theme of "Workers' Day," the designer used hemp rope to secure the parcel, giving it a heavy and "tough" look. Every detail, including the color and stonewashed effect of the jeans, contributes to the sense of Mustang jeans being true workers' gear.

Client
Mustang

Design Agency
KOREFE. Kolle Rebbe Form Und Entwicklung

Collaborators
Christian Doering (Creative Director), Katharina Ullrich (Designer), Tom Schuster (Stylist)

Material
Paperboard, hemp rope

Size
240mm x 340mm x 80mm

Completion
2014

MADE TO LAST
2013
WORKER'S DAY
LIMITED EDITION

MADE TO LAST
2013
WORKER'S DAY
LIMITED EDITION
MUSTANG

Guangyuan Ramie Textile —Shirt Packaging

Designer Wen Li was inspired by a childhood memory when working on this project for the Guangyuan Ramie Textile Company. When she was a child, her mother sewed a shirt for her, first drawing the pattern on the cloth with a piece of chalk, then tailoring and sewing it, magically transforming the piece of square material into a shirt. Following this warm memory, the designer created the structure of the Chinese character for "ramie" (麻), a type of material, by cutting out pieces of ramie material then reassembling them to form a graphic representation of the Chinese character. This symbol was then used as part of the design for the shirt packaging.

Client
Guangyuan Ramie

Design Agency
ONE & ONE DESIGN

Designer
Wen Li

Material
Specialty paper

Size
355mm x 265mm x 60mm

Completion
2013

www.gyramie.com
天地之源
縱橫之美
廣源麻品

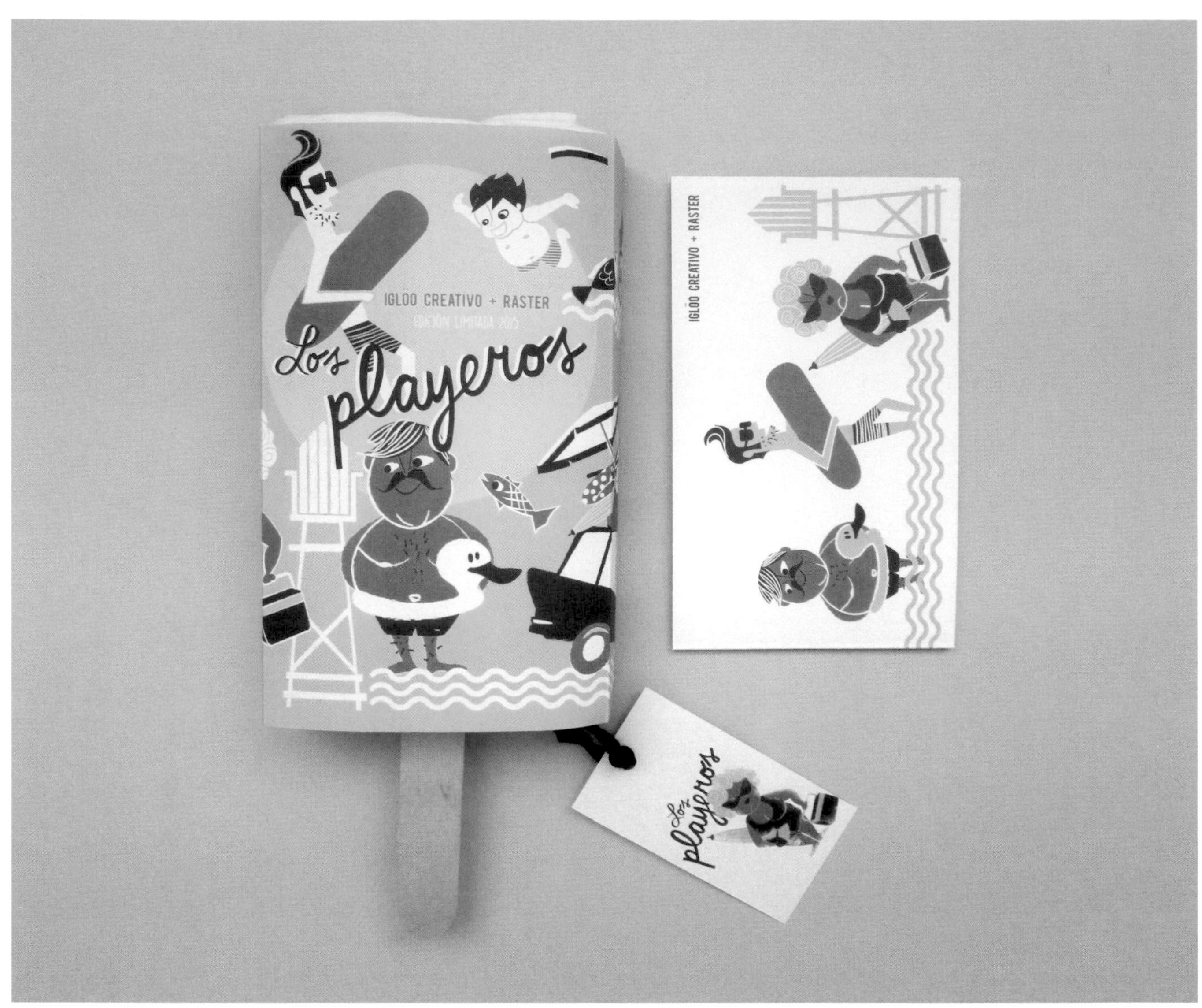

Los Playeros

"Los Playeros" is a self-promotion project by Iglöo Creativo and Raster Digital that was made in the summer of 2015 to welcome in that season and as a way for the company to thank its clients for their loyalty. The designers got creative with this project, coming up with a series of illustrated characters and using them on innovative T-shirt packaging, as well as on the limited-edition T-shirts themselves. The idea was to deliver something related to summer so the packaging is designed like an ice-cream wrapper, which encloses the T-shirt. This immediately attracted the attention of clients, especially as they were not expecting to find a T-shirt on the inside of the packaging.

The illustrations used in the design were typical characters you might see on a Spanish beach in summer (including the leading character, called "Pedalete"): an old man with a mustache, a woman with her umbrella and icebox, young surfers, and so on. A chromatic range of fresh and summery colors was used in the design, combining cold hues with a warmer orange.

Client
Iglöo Creativo, Raster Digital

Designers
Paola Coiduras, Eric Novo

Material
Carton, wood, paper

Size
100mm x 35mm x 235mm

Completion
2015

Los playeros
Los playeros
60/100

Los playeros
Los playeros

Promotional Packaging

The mandate for this project was to make some promotional packaging for clothing. Designer Jessica decided to create packaging for the Artoo and Threepio leggings from Black Milk's "Star Wars" collection. Inspired by the universe of *Star Wars*, she came up with the idea of making the packaging reusable as an intergalactic lamp. The cylindrical form is aesthetic, easy to carry, and also reminiscent of light sabers. The cover is made of paper, on which the name of the product, the size, Black Milk's logo, and a picture of a far, far away galaxy are printed. To allow customers to see the leggings through the packaging, and also to let more light out when the lamp is on, the designer cut out the letters from the *Star Wars* name, using the original *Star Wars* typography. The package contains an awesome pair of leggings, a bulb, a piece of electric wire, and humorous printed instructions.

Designer	Size
Jessica Ledoux	365mm x 77mm
Material	**Completion**
Plastic cylinder, paper	2014

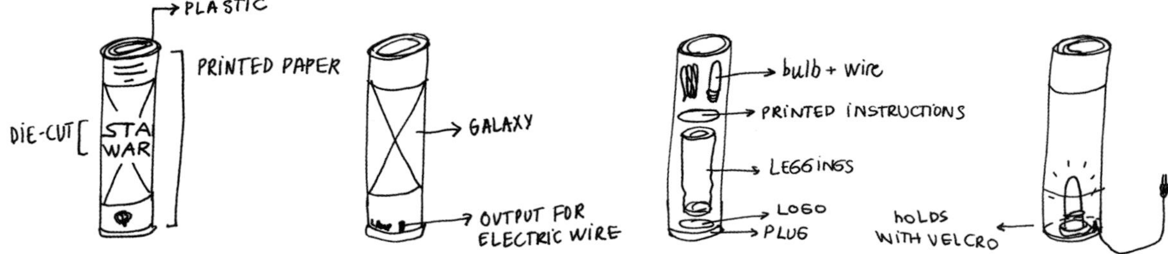

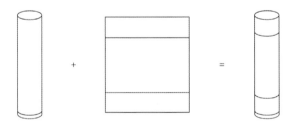

Revolution T-shirts Packages

REV Streetwear commissioned design agency Romaxaweb to create a packaging design for its T-shirts with a revolutionary theme. Taking into consideration the gravity of the theme, it became clear to designer Roma Hymon that the packaging should be very impressive. The idea to design T-shirt packaging in the shape of a Molotov cocktail leaped into his mind immediately, but the process of making the design a reality was quite complicated. After trying many options, the designer created the perfect packaging for the T-shirts by rolling them up but leaving the sleeves hanging out one end—the rolled-up part of the T-shirt, secured with string, looked like a bottle and the sleeves created the effect of fire, thus emulating a Molotov cocktail. In order to keep the T-shirts clean and free from external damage, they were also wrapped in craft paper.

Client
REV Streetwear

Design Agency
Romaxaweb

Designer
Roma Hymon

Material
Craft paper, twine

Size
225mm x 130mm x 20mm; 225mm x 60mm x 50mm

Completion
2014

НОСИ
НА ГРУДЯХ
ВІРШІ
ШЕВЧЕНКА
СЛАВА УКРАЇНІ!
REV.COM.UA

НОСИ
НА ГРУДЯХ
ВІРШІ
ШЕВЧЕНКА
СЛАВА УКРАЇНІ!

Puma Arsenal 2015–16 Home Kit PR Packaging

Name & Name was commissioned by Puma in Germany to design the launch packaging for Arsenal's 2015–16 season football shirt. The design features Arsenal's red and white colors and large writing that says "Powered by Fans." To match the writing, the box unfolds like an explosion; when opened, it shows a large image of red electrical energy and triggers a cracking electricity sound effect. The red shirt is carefully folded inside. There are two boxes: a VIP version and a regular version. The VIP version features gold-foil-embossed letters and special, premium-weight, sparkling paper inside. The packaging is used for marketing and PR mailings of the new kit to bloggers and reviewers around the world.

Client
Puma Germany

Design Agency
Name & Name

Designers
Ian Perkins, Aja Lee, Christine Tseng, Tasha Chen

Material
Cardboard

Size
450mm x 350mm x 100mm

Completion
2015

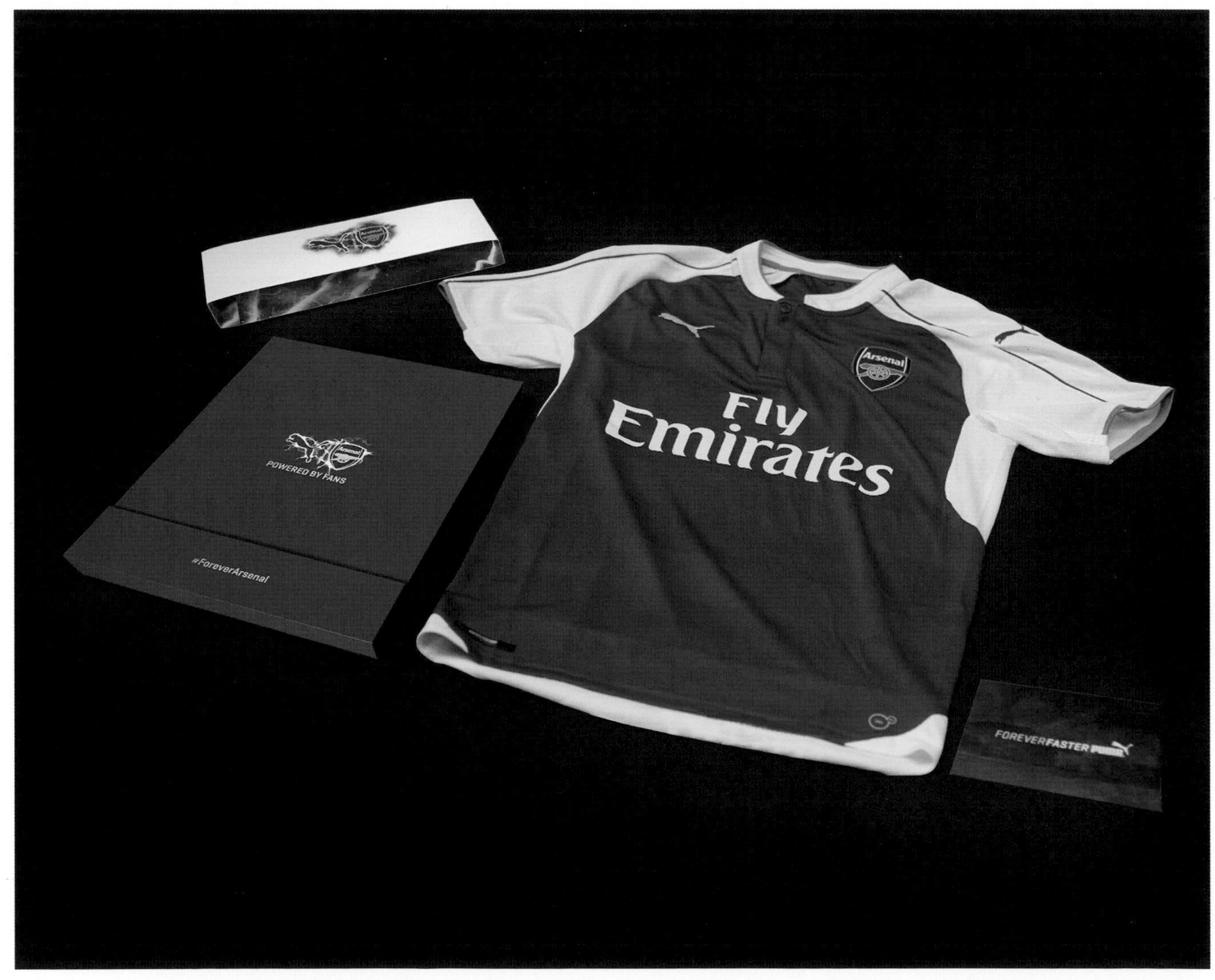

#ForeverArsenal
POWERED BY FANS
POWERED BY FANS

ERA ORA STUDIO

When the designers of ERA ORA STUDIO moved to North Carolina from Italy a few years ago, they brought simplicity, elegance, and craftsmanship with them. Their T-shirts are certified by WRAP (Worldwide Responsible Accredited Production) and are printed in the designers' new hometown of Winston-Salem using water-based ink, which gives the artwork an extremely soft touch. Packaging is very important to these designers; they like to consider it as being like a present to be unwrapped so that the purchase of their product is a pleasant experience for customers.

They use a simple brown paper bag to package their T-shirts, adding a bold black sticker on the side and a white sticker in the center. This makes for a very urban look, speaking to a young (in age and at heart) consumer inclined to streetwear. Each product is carefully wrapped in tissue paper before being placed in the bag, and a thank-you card is included as a sign of gratitude to the purchaser.

Design Agency
ERA ORA STUDIO

Designers
Alberto Larizza, Kristal Trotter

Material
Brown paper bag, tissue paper, stickers

Size
260mm x 180mm x 30mm

Completion
2015

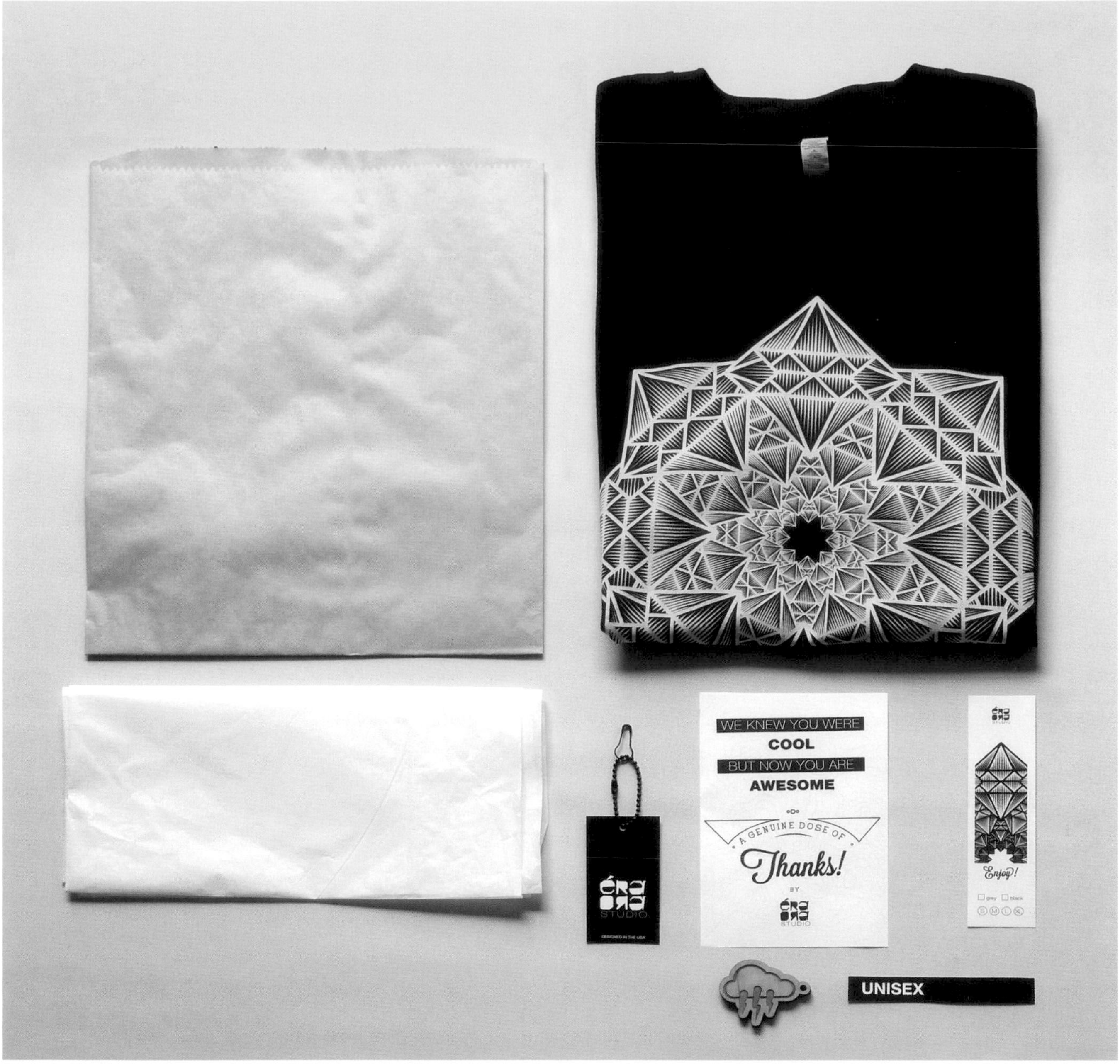

WE KNEW YOU WERE
COOL
BUT NOW YOU ARE
AWESOME
A GENUINE DOSE OF
Thanks!
BY
STUDIO
Enjoy!
UNISEX

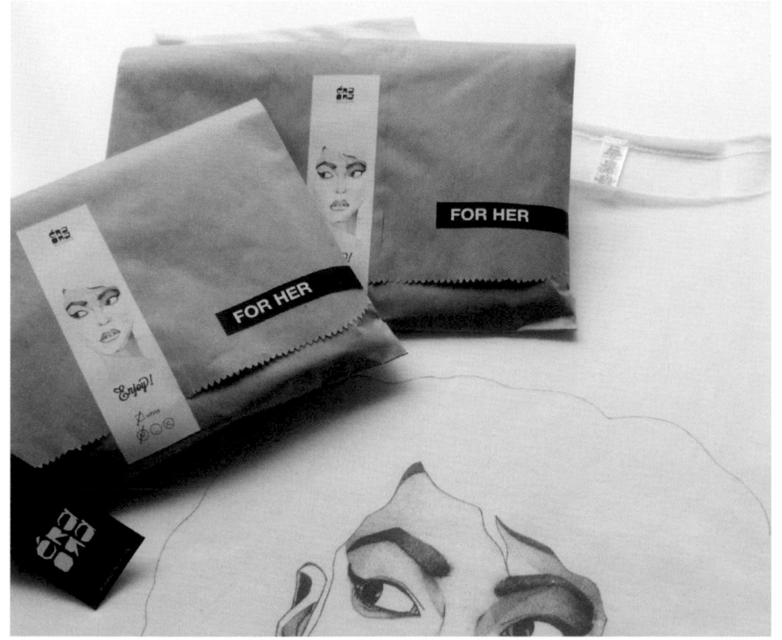
FOR HER
FOR HER
Enjoy!

Enjoy!

Socceroos National Team Kit

This packaging design was all about unveiling the new jersey that the Australian Socceroos would be wearing at the 2014 FIFA World Cup. The jersey featured brand-new laser-cut technology that helps aid performance in the heat. The designers wanted to replicate this in their design of the packaging by incorporating the same laser-cut patterns into the lid of the box that the jerseys would be displayed in. They then continued with the laser theme by etching the national crest and Nike logo into the sides of the wooden box and engraving the recipient's name onto the lid to personalize each one. When the jersey was removed, the base of the box revealed a story about the Socceroos' spirit and fighting mentality from past World Cup appearances, providing motivation for the players in the lead-up to the tournament.

Client
Nike

Design Agency
Marilyn & Sons

Material
Acrylic lid, pine wood box

Size
380mm x 310mm x 60mm

Completion
2014

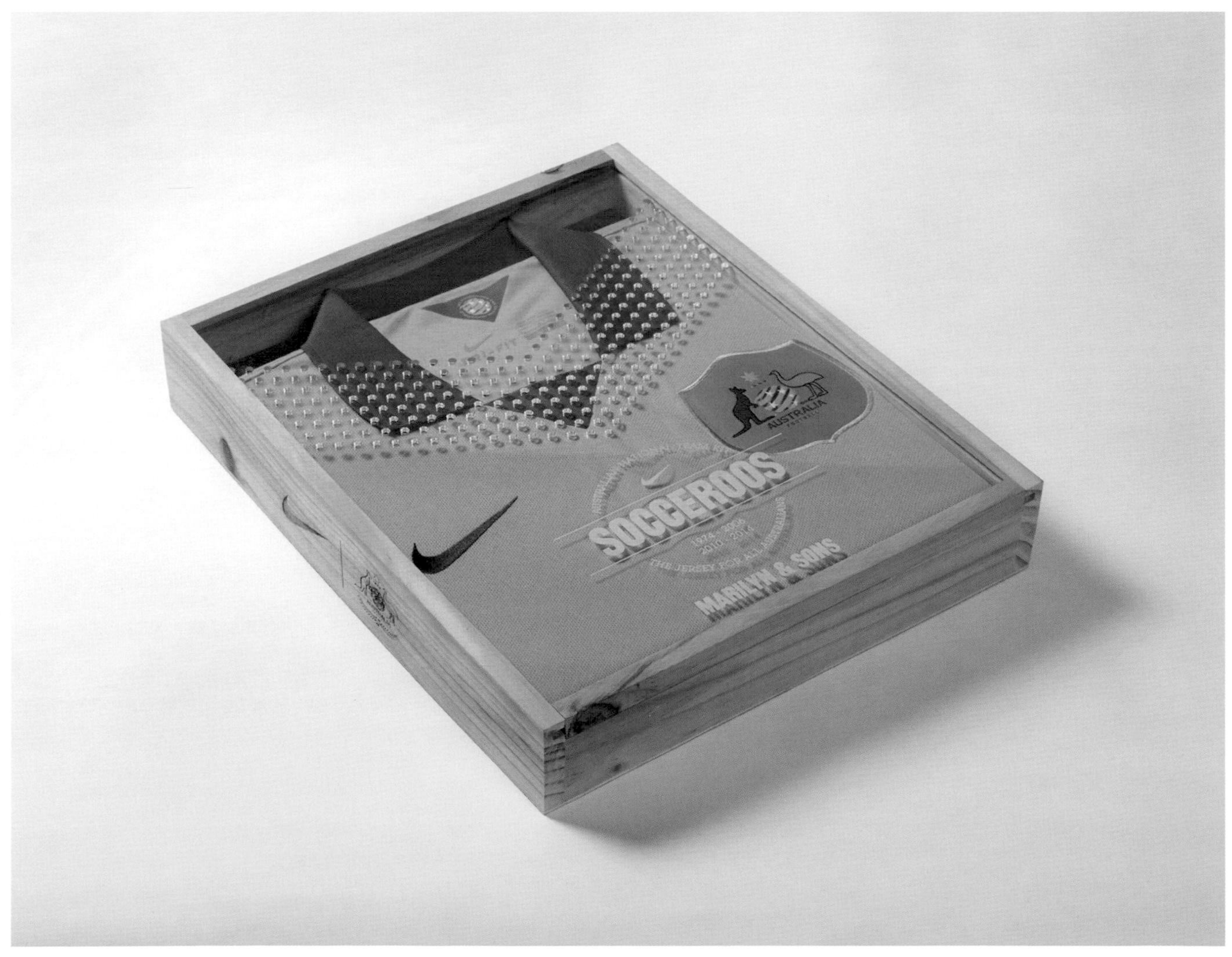

AUSTRALIA
SOCCEROOS CAN
Socceroos Captain
WEAR IT WITH PRIDE.
#GOSOCCEROOS.

AUSTRALIA

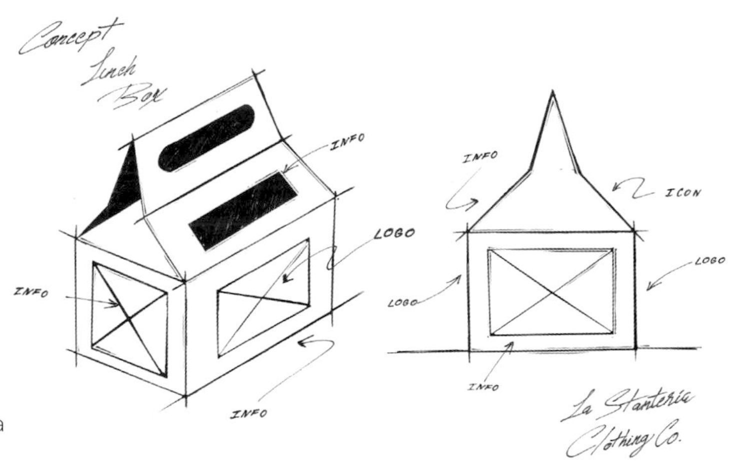

La Stantería Clothing Package

This interesting project to design packaging for La Stantería Clothing Co.'s hand-printed T-shirts was born of Mexican creativity to see things from another perspective. The designers wanted to turn an everyday object into something else, thus giving it a new meaning, so the packaging they created looks like a lunch box but is actually a functional clothing package capable of carrying up to three T-shirts. The main objective was to communicate the essence of the brand, creating a fresh, modern, aesthetic identity, and making it attractive to young people. Black on a white background was used in order to create contrast and give greater visual impact. After trying several materials, the solid bleached sulfate was thought to be a practical material for the packaging, as it is easy to assemble and handle, and can also protect the product during transportation from the store to the purchaser's home.

Client
La Stantería Clothing Co.

Size
195mm x 115mm x 195mm

Design Agency
La División Brand Firm

Completion
2015

Material
Solid bleached sulfate

HANDLE WITH CARE
La Stantería
MTY
MEX
CLOTHING CO.
2015
ORIGINAL T-SHIRTS

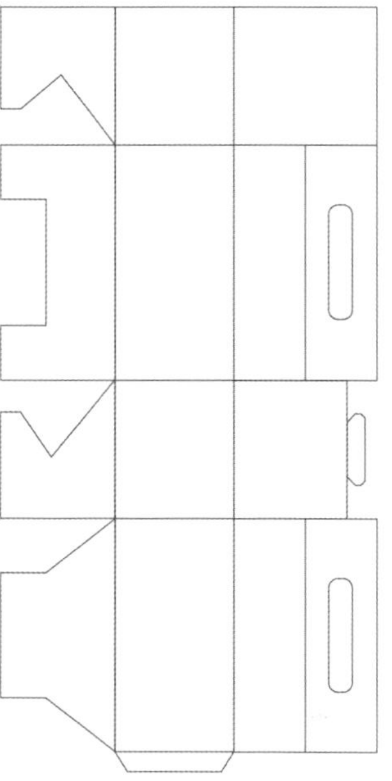

The Standard Dress Shirt

Most dress shirt packaging is a wasteful combination of plastic, cardboard, tissue paper, and hidden pins. Dress shirts are difficult to unpack, restock in stores, and disassemble at home. In contrast, this packaging for the Standard Shirt Co. is in an upright form that makes it easy for sales clerks to create a tidy display. When the customer decides to try on a shirt, the package can be unfolded easily and neatly. If they decide against purchasing, a simple guide inside the package assists in refolding the shirt, leaving the package looking just as polished as before. Once purchased, the customer can reuse the package to fold shirts when packing a suitcase, or refold the package and pop out the perforated hook to create a structural shirt hanger. Extra collar stays are perforated into the packaging. A minimal color palette and bold, informative icons help customers navigate the style and fit options easily.

Designers
Elizabeth Kelly, Jille Natalino, Rob Hurst, Erin Bishop, Joanna Milewski, Mary Durant

Material
Recycled paperboard

Size
241mm x 216mm x 95mm

Completion
2013

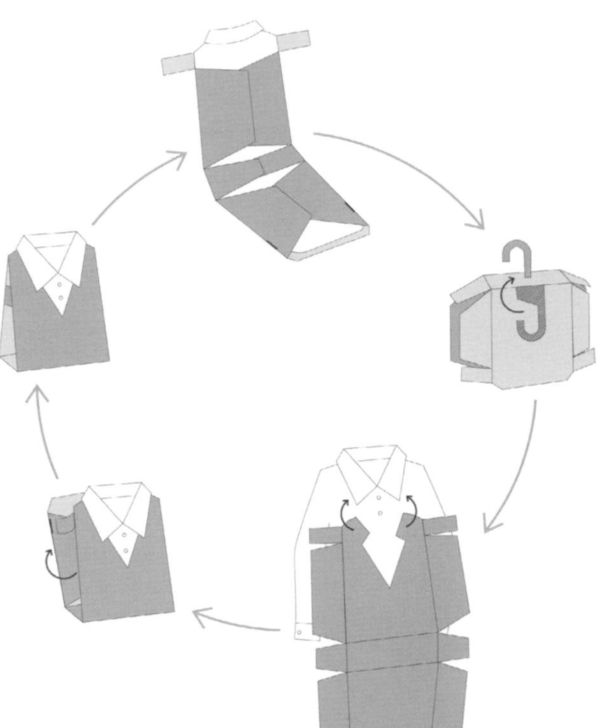

STANDARD
STANDARD
SHIRT CO.

STANDARD
SHIRT CO.
fold
2
fold
7
collar
1
collar
1
Insert
6

FC Barcelona 2013–14 Jersey Packaging

For this limited-edition packaging of FC Barcelona's 2013–14 home jersey, elegance and sobriety were key to the overall design. These qualities were achieved by combining textured paper with typography stamped in brilliant black and gold. A booklike container is housed within a box to add an element of literature to the design, and also to highlight the limited-edition feeling. For the final presentation of the packaging, the designers also created an exhibition space within the official Camp Nou megastore in Barcelona. They installed black modular shelving with golden lining into the space, lining the boxes up like books on the shelves to create a library aesthetic.

Client
America Nike

Design Agency
Oxigen

Designers
Sònia Rodríguez Grau, Astrid Ortiz

Material
Arjowiggins Curious Metallic Bronze paper, Fedrigoni Sirio black paper

Size
255mm x 255mm

Completion
2013

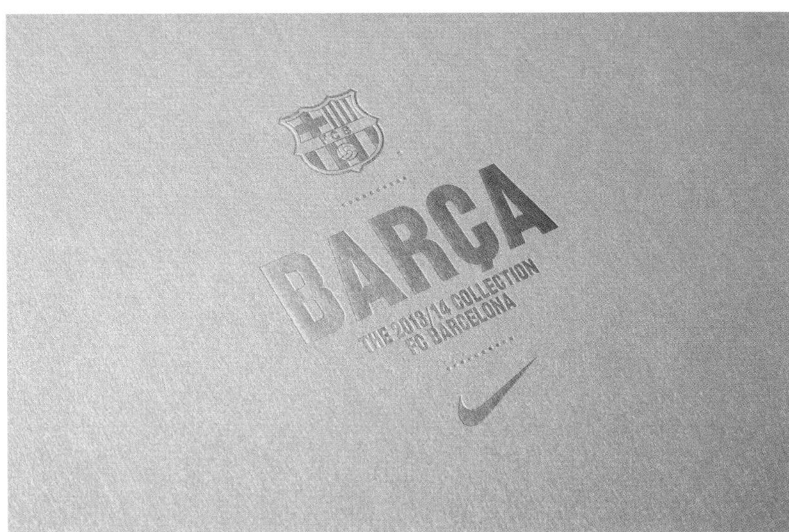

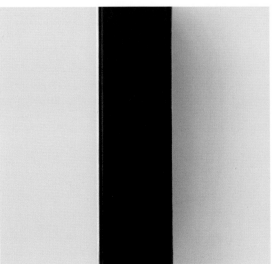

BARÇA

Luna—Premium Handmade Wear

Maria Linaris is a young fashion designer who creates knitted clothes and accessories under the Luna—Premium Handmade Wear label. Her creations have a modern approach and high aesthetic quality, and designer Adamantia Chatzivasileiou's logo captures these qualities, giving the brand a visual signature.

The packaging created by Chatzivasileiou allows customers to see and feel the texture and quality of the clothing contained inside the box, which is part of the Luna experience. Packaging consists of two boxes: a colored transparent one that allows the piece of clothing to be visible, and an outer hard-paper one, which the colored one fits into. The boxes have a special dieline, which was inspired by the logo, and the chosen colors are in light feminine tones.

Designer
Adamantia Chatzivasileiou

Material
Paperboard

Size
Clothing box /
300mm x 250mm x 57mm
Accessories box /
100mm x 82mm x 60mm
Bag /
450mm x 350mm x 120mm

Completion
2015

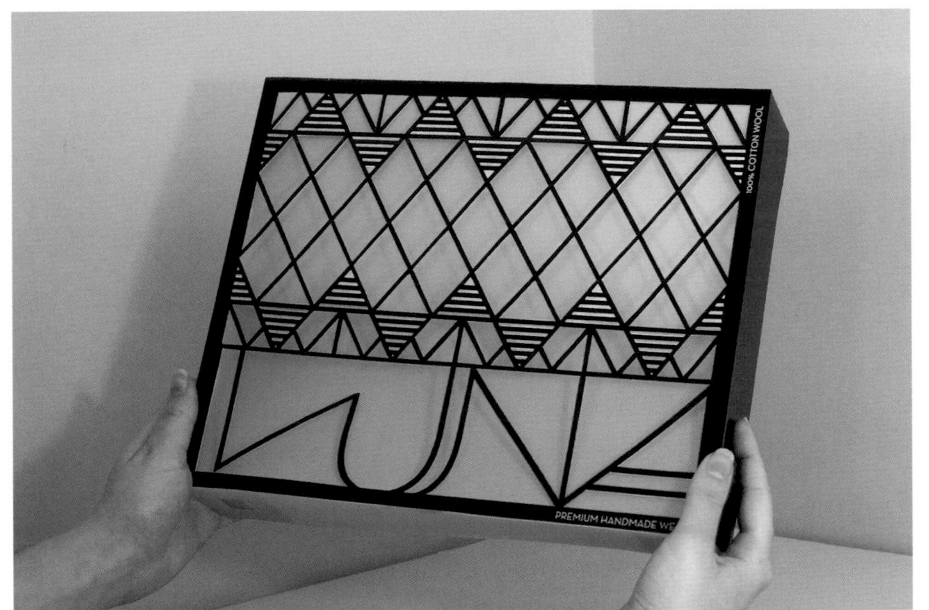

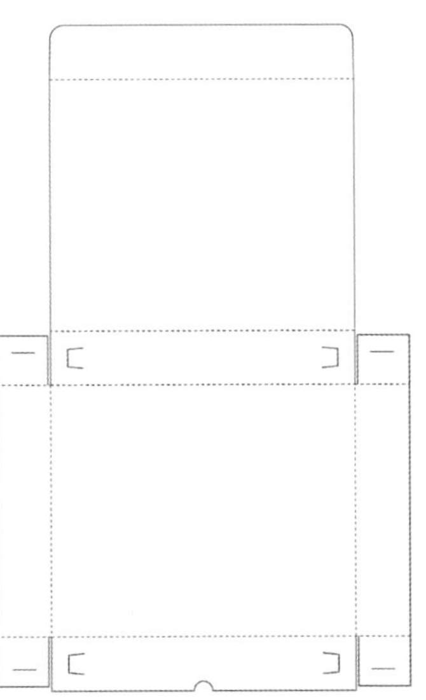

100%
COTTON
WOOL
PREMIUM HANDMADE WEAR

PREMIUM HANDMADE WEAR

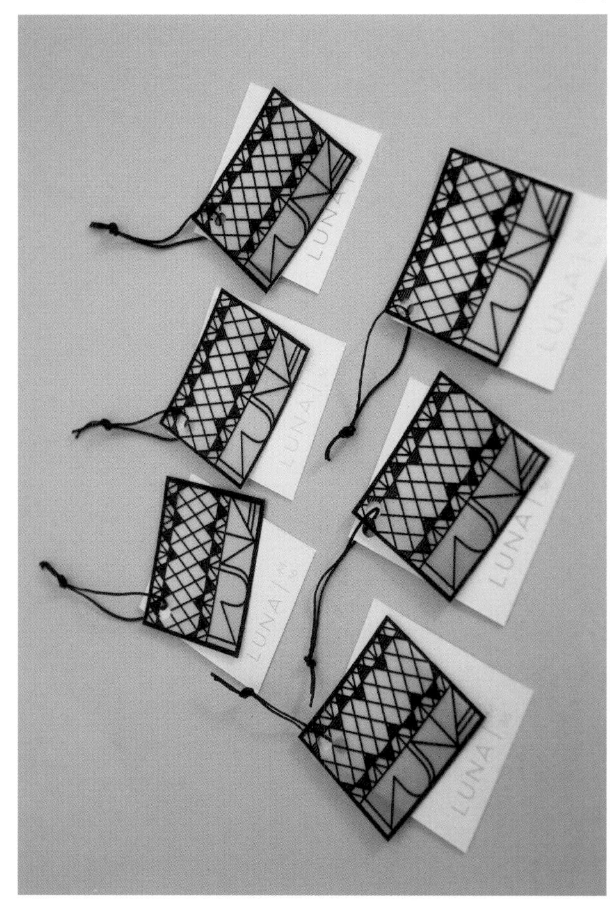
LUNA

Cono Poster & T-shirt Package

The challenge of this project was to make multipurpose packaging that could contain both posters and T-shirts—one package for two needs—for Cono, a division of graphic design firm Noblanco. A triangular shape was chosen for the packaging as it could accommodate both mediums when they were rolled up, was optimum in terms of space, and could be easily mailed. The packages can be regarded as puzzles that can be easily put together. Raw cardboard printed in one color provides the palette, and, for this first edition (the graphics are meant to change in the future), handmade lines were used to imitate wood grain. The result is versatility with some minor details able to communicate the values of the brand.

Client
Cono

Collaborators
Ovum (Structural Design), Noblanco (Graphic Design), Carlos J Roldán (Designer)

Material
328gsm uncoated chipboard

Size
90mm x 90mm x 270mm

Completion
2012

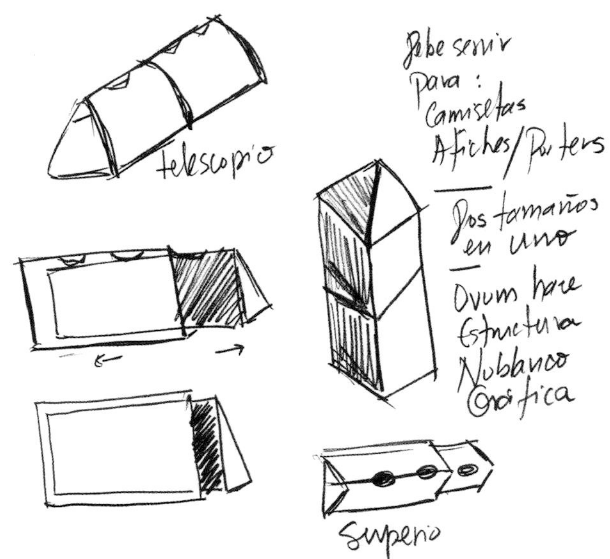

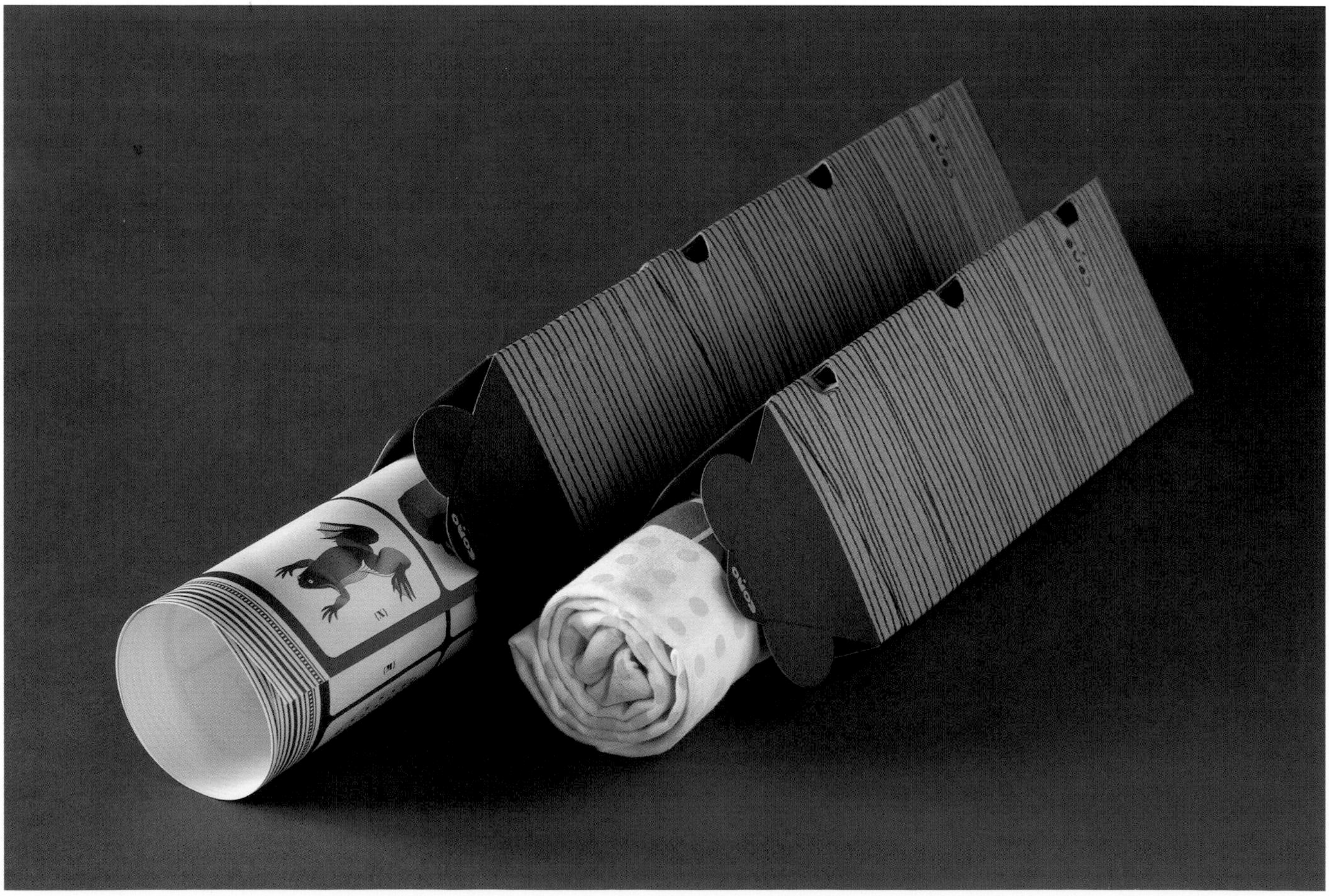

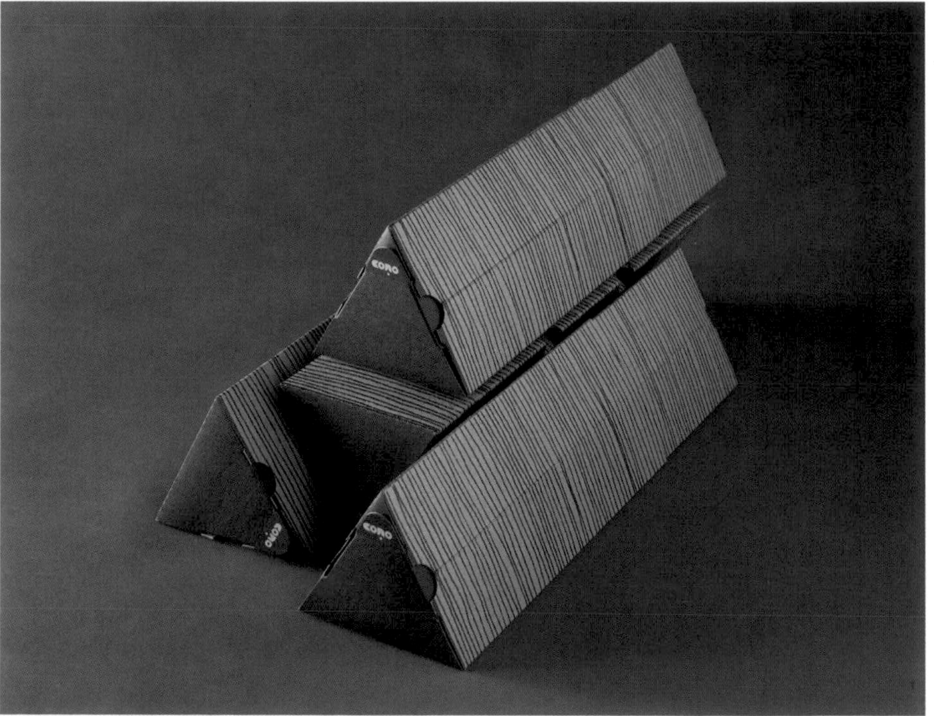

Socceroos National Away Team Kit

This packaging by Australian design agency Marilyn & Sons was created to unveil the Socceroos' new jersey for their 2014 FIFA World Cup away games. The branding behind Nike's campaign for the away-team jerseys was "Risk Everything," which took on a bad-guy, superhero-like persona. Marilyn & Sons reflected this in its designs by using a lo-fi finish on the box the jersey was enclosed in, with pops of energy, color and attitude screen-printed on top. The agency wanted the box to tell a story as it was opened, to provide an understanding about the attitude needed to take into away games.

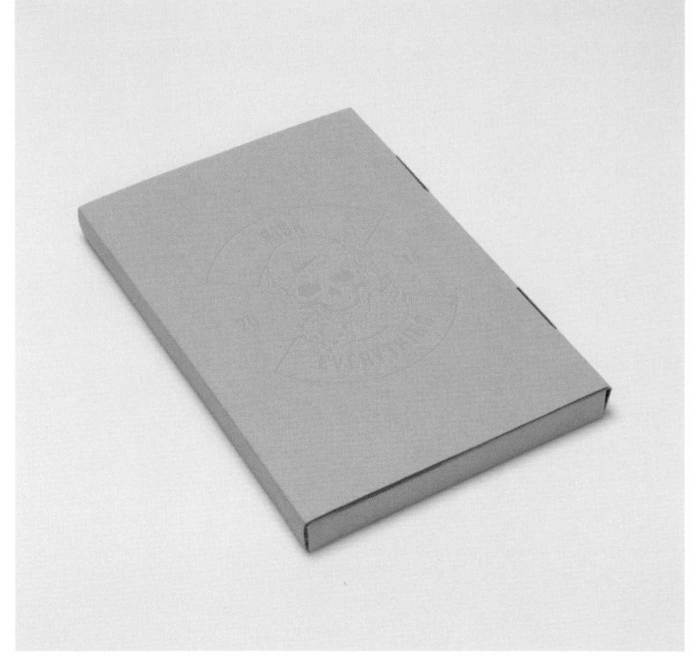

Client
Nike

Design Agency
Marilyn & Sons

Material
Cardboard

Size
430mm x 300mm x 40mm

Completion
2014

RISK
20
14
EVERYTHING

CALL IT GUTS. CALL IT ARROGANCE.
CALL IT WHAT YOU WILL.
FOOTBALL BELONGS TO THOSE WHO
ARE WILLING TO TAKE RISKS.
THOSE WHO BELIEVE THERE
IS NOTHING TO LOSE,
EVEN WHEN EVERYTHING IS AT STAKE.
THOSE WHO DEFY LOGIC,
TRADITION EVEN GRAVITY.
THEY ALWAYS TRY. THEY NEVER REGRET.
AND EVEN WHEN THEY SHOULDN'T,
ESPECIALLY THEN,
THEY RISK EVERYTHING.
SHARE YOUR JERSEY ON SOCIAL TO SUPPORT THE
SOCCEROOS AS THEY PREPARE TO RISK EVERYTHING IN BRAZIL
#GOSOCCEROOS

DRI-FIT
AUSTRALIA
CALL IT GUTS. CALL IT ARROGANCE.
CALL IT WHAT YOU WILL.
FOOTBALL BELONGS TO THOSE WHO
ARE WILLING TO TAKE RISKS.
THOSE WHO BELIEVE THERE
IS NOTHING TO LOSE,
EVEN WHEN EVERYTHING IS AT STAKE.
THOSE WHO DEFY LOGIC,
TRADITION EVEN GRAVITY.
THEY ALWAYS TRY. THEY NEVER REGRET.
AND EVEN WHEN THEY SHOULDN'T,
ESPECIALLY THEN,
THEY RISK EVERYTHING.
SHARE YOUR JERSEY ON SOCIAL TO SUPPORT THE
SOCCEROOS AS THEY PREPARE TO RISK EVERYTHING IN BRAZIL
#GOSOCCEROOS

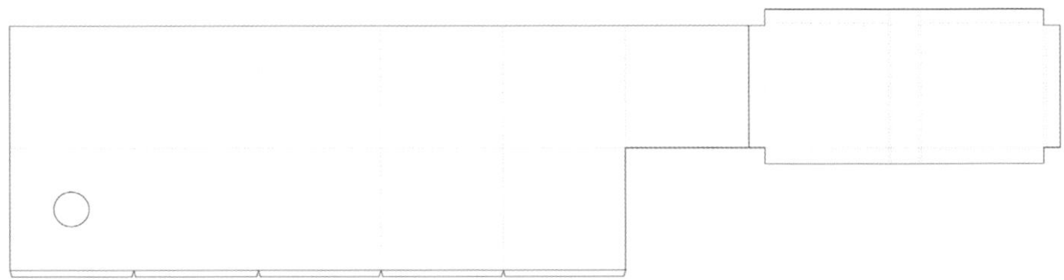

STASIS

STASIS is a 24-hour ambient music festival that takes place on a polar night in Reykjavík, Iceland. The branding of the entire festival and its corresponding assets was informed and inspired by location and sound. In contrast to other genres of music, ambient music tends to be droning and contemplative. As a result, the typography of the STASIS logo is similarly long and interweaved, stretching out six letters like the way ambient musicians can seemingly stretch out a phrase or loop ad infinitum.

The color palette is predominantly dark with bright gradients, drawing from the natural hues of the aurora borealis. Likewise, the textures that adorn the packaging were produced from scanned charcoal rubbings and reference the arctic Icelandic landscape.

Designer	Size
Kelvin Kottke	337mm x 337mm x 76mm
Material	**Completion**
Cardboard	2014

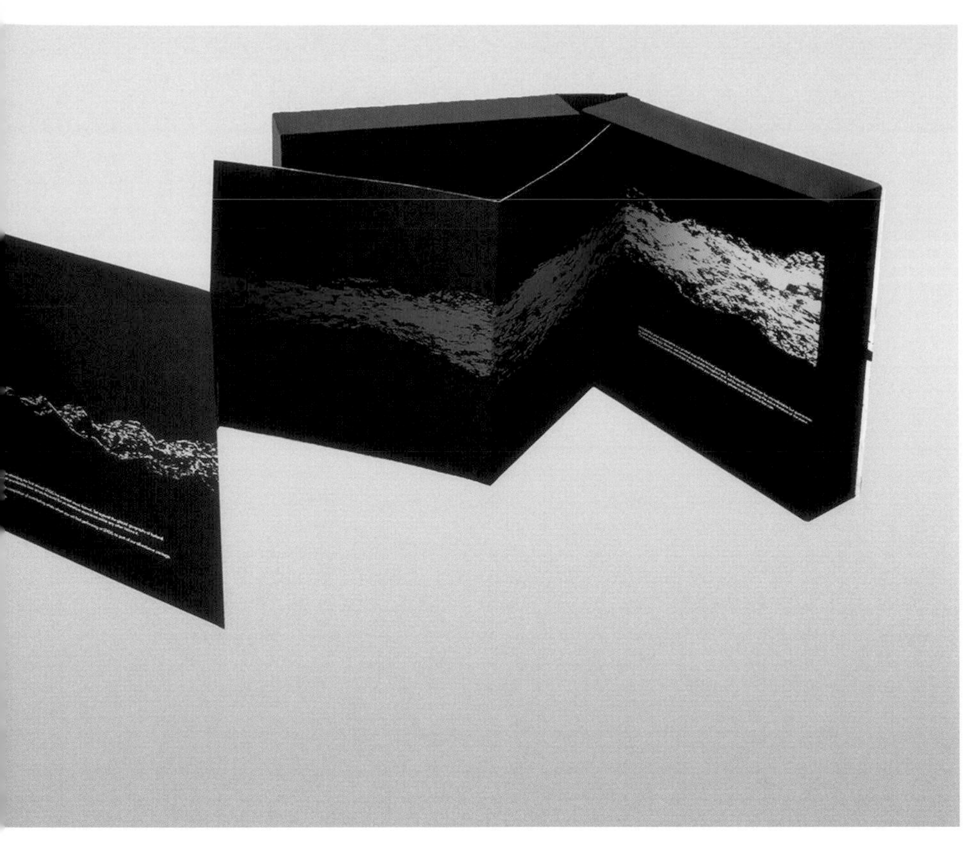

live ambient music festival

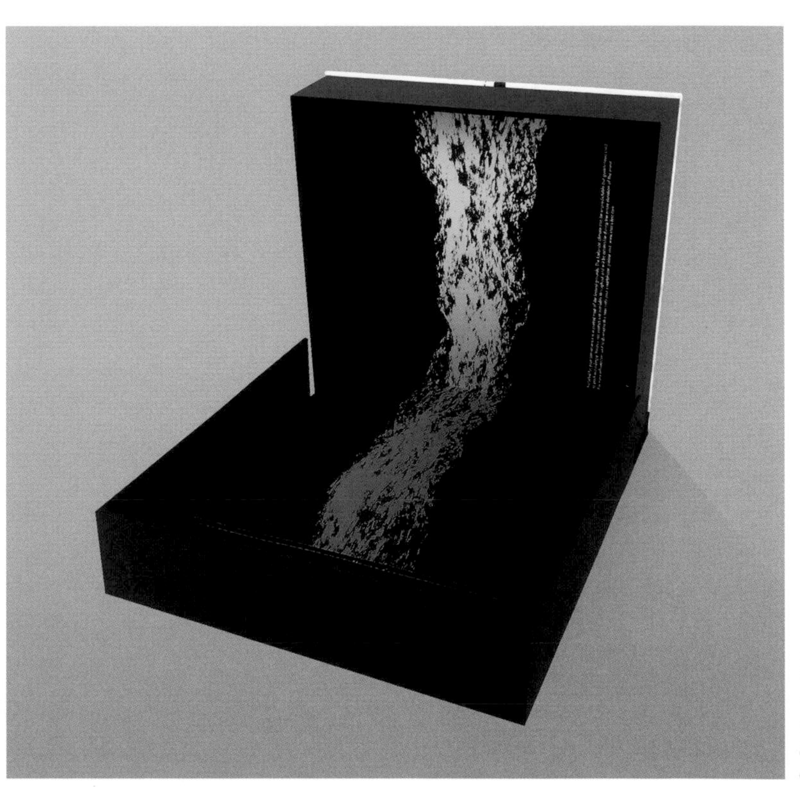

Nike Most Wanted Package

"Nike Most Wanted" is a global search for the best 16- to 21-year-old unsigned footballers. Winners spend a minimum of one month at the Nike Academy in St George's Park, England, receiving elite coaching that develops their game to a higher level. For this event in Moscow, a special box was developed, which was awarded to each participant.

For this packaging, designer Nikita Rebrikov decided to use bright contrasting colors to achieve a youthful look, since the event is for young footballers. For the typography, he used a bold and strong font that could stand on its own to complement the event logo, and to highlight how important this event would be to its participants. Rebrikov wanted to design something that would impress whoever opened the box, so he had the idea to make a football field in the box itself to send the message to the recipient of the box that they were holding possibility in their hands.

Client
Nike

Design Agency
FRprint Agency

Designer
Nikita Rebrikov

Material
Cardboard, artificial grass

Size
550mm x 350mm x 80mm

Completion
2015

NIKE.COM/FOOTBALL

MOST
2015
WANTED
ЗАЙМИ СВОЕ МЕСТО
СРЕДИ ЛУЧШИХ

NIKE
2015

Stroll with the Walrus

"Stroll with the Walrus" is a T-shirt brand designed by Thailand's Zlapdash Studio. The design studio wanted to design a box for packaging its T-shirt, but it didn't want just an ordinary box so it opted to create a triangular style of package. Easy and fun but also stylish describes the branding of the T-shirt, and the illustrated walrus and typography on the packaging reflect these qualities. Each box fits one soft and light cotton T-shirt, and customers can easily carry the packaged product.

Client
Stroll with the Walrus

Size
80mm x 100mm x 70mm

Design Agency
Zlapdash Studio

Completion
2015

Material
Cardboard

Athos Packaging

Athos' smart fitness apparel reveals real-time physiological data with surface EMG technology, helping wearers get more out of every workout, and every exercise. Uneka designed the Athos packaging using bespoke details, bold graphics, and carefully placed messaging that invites the user to "look within." The sleek, matte-black shipper lifts open for a two-part reveal: a compact, hinged gift box houses the "core," and the true brains of the operation. A soft-touch premium pouch holds the apparel. The core connects magnetically to its charger, which sits below to create a natural, functional securing mechanism in the packaging. Lifting the device housing reveals the smooth, matte-black pouch, foil stamped with the white Athos logo for elegantly branded impact. It's packaging as cutting edge as Athos apparel.

Client
Athos

Design Agency
Uneka

Designers
Steven Shainwald, Nathan Nickel

Material
Rigid box, EVA foam, folded paperboard, folded corrugate, polypropylene bag

Size
Garment bag /
360mm x 240mm
Shipping box /
450mm x 275mm x 65mm

Completion
2015

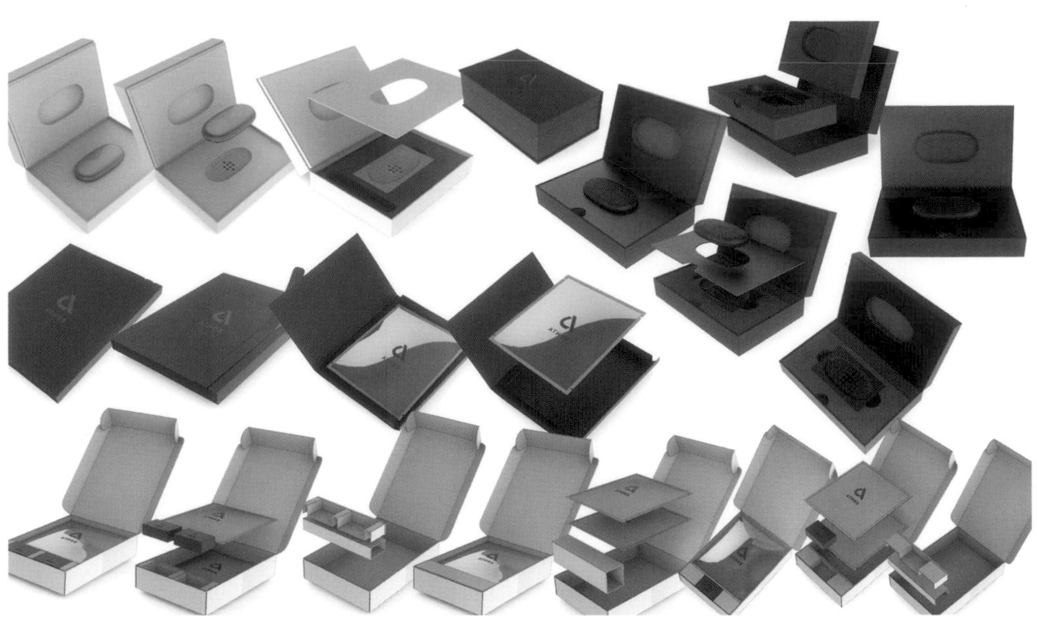

The Woven for ourCaste

This conceptual packaging rethinks the way ourCaste's woven shirts could be displayed in retail stores. The packaging pattern was designed to match the actual woven shirt located inside the tube, which ultimately captures the customer's attention, giving them an idea of the shirt design even though the shirt is secured by the packaging. Designed to be simple and contemporary, much like ourCaste's brand aesthetics, the packaging uses a cylindrical tube to keep the structure in place and the shirt nicely rolled up for traveling purposes.

Client	Size
ourCaste	330mm x 89mm
Designer	**Completion**
Sterling Foxcroft	2013
Material	
Balsa wood	

OURCASTE

Merrell T-shirt Package Design

This T-shirt case is a simple faceted structure that pops up into a sharp-looking geometric compartment that can be easily hooked into a carabiner, making it very useful when traveling. The package has topographic maps overlaid on each side, referencing the amazing diversity and unique sense of adventure that California offers at every turn, which Merrell embraces. Reinforcing the thrill of adventure, the package design keeps the original bright-orange color of the Merrell brand intact. The designer was able to engineer true product innovation that was backed by a multidimensional design strategy.

Client
Merrell

Size
248mm x 140mm

Designer
Shaily Shah

Completion
2014

Material
Textured paper

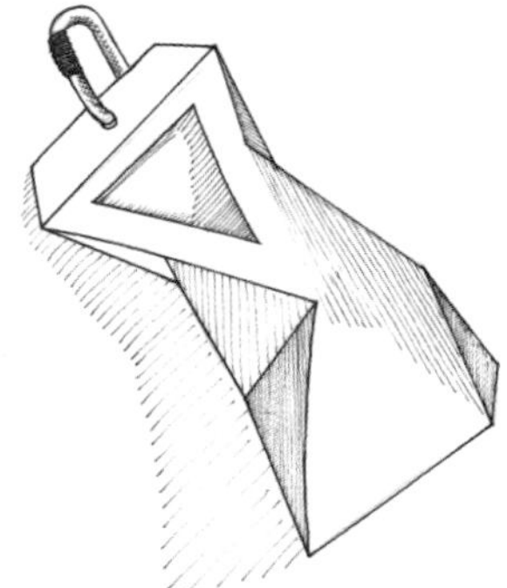

SURVIVE THE OUTDOORS!
MERRELL

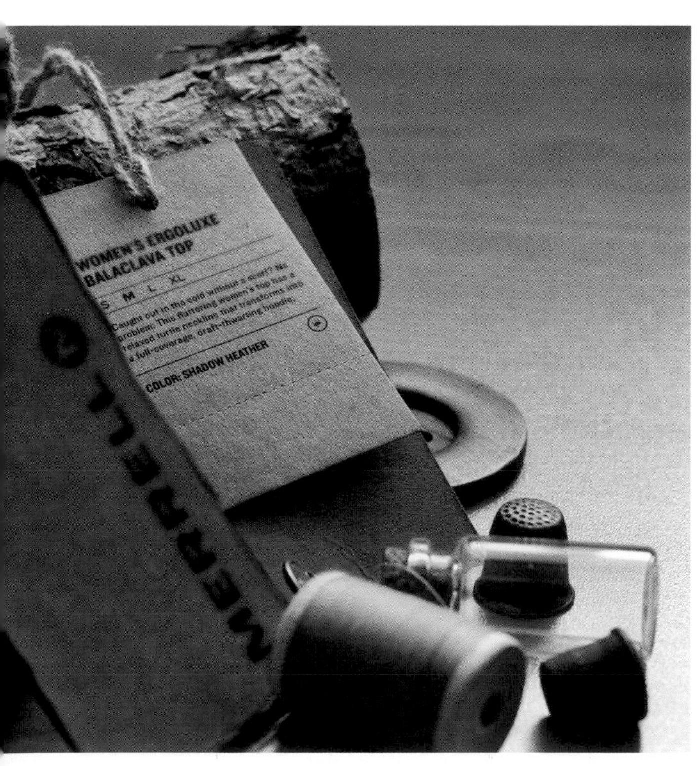
WOMEN'S ERGOLUXE
BALACLAVA TOP
S M L XL
Caught out in the cold without a scarf? No problem. This flattering women's top has a relaxed turtle neckline that transforms into a full-coverage, draft-thwarting hoodie.
COLOR: SHADOW HEATHER
MERRELL

Aromode

Aromode shirts are "aroma therapy wear," emitting scents such as lavender, rosemary and chamomile. In designing packaging for this project, designer Kim Ji-Hwan references herbs and swirling aromas in an effort to make the customer feel as though the product is connected to nature. A soft color palette is used, and wavy, organic lettering further enhances the nature connection, positioning this product as one that might help people de-stress. The functional side of the packaging enables the shirts to be neatly folded in the shape of a jacket, with the collar on the outside.

Designer	Size
Kim Ji-Hwan	255mm x 185mm x 90mm
Material	**Completion**
195gsm matte art paper	2015

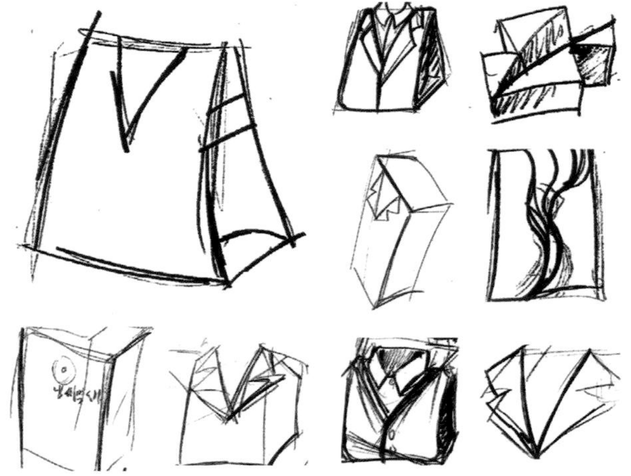

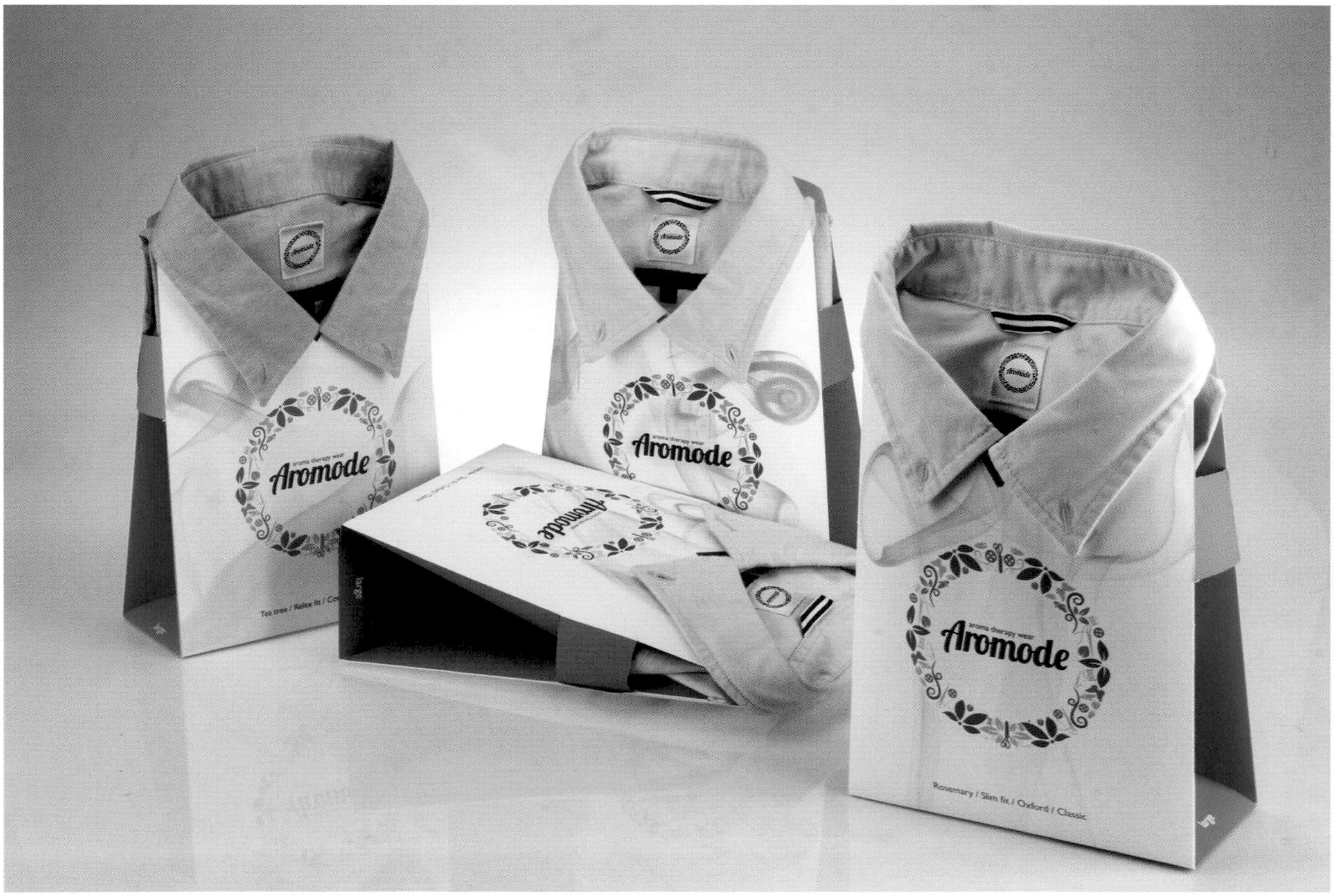

Aromode
aroma therapy wear
Aromode
Rosemary / Slim fit / Oxford / Classic

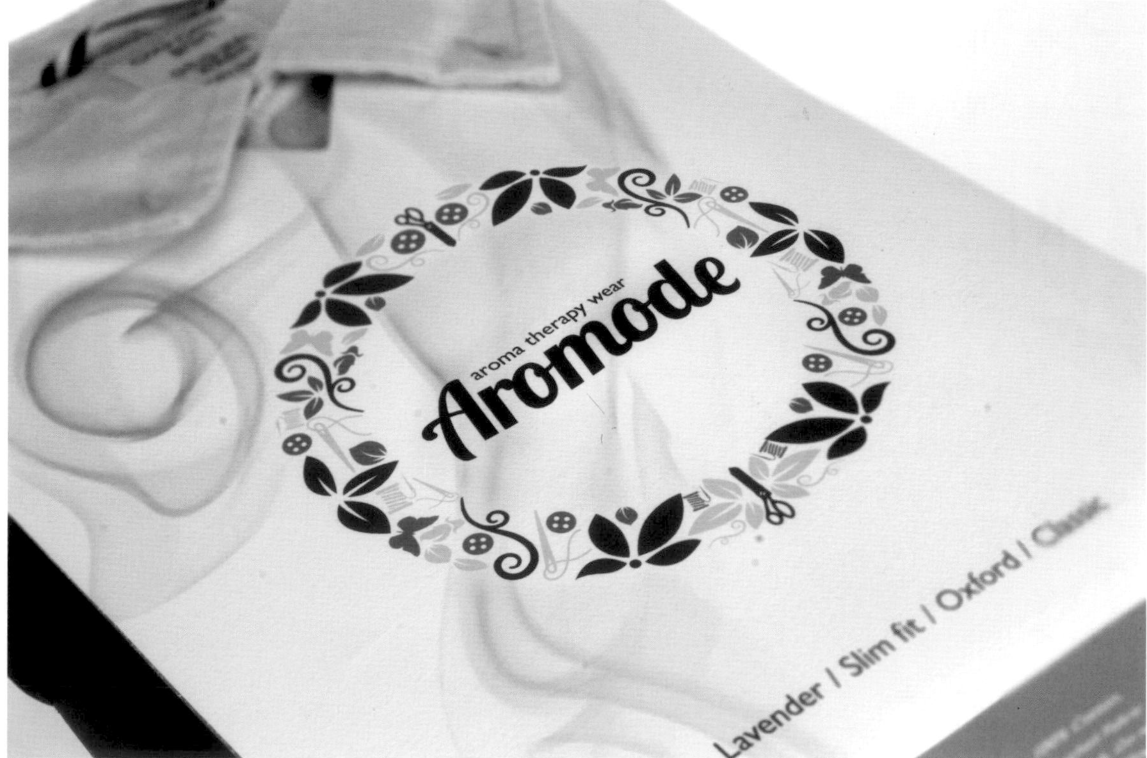
aroma therapy wear
Aromode
Lavender / Slim fit / Oxford / Classic

Packaging for Active T-shirt

The Active T-shirt brand is targeted to teenagers who like outdoor activities such as traveling, or just hanging out. Designer Harianto Chen uses a gray-and-yellow color palette for this T-shirt carton to evoke the happiness, activity and spirit of young people. A sans-serif typeface is used to create a modern and friendly impression, while the angled opening design adds dynamic and active elements to the overall packaging. Cloth is used for the outer packaging, which is environmentally friendly and reusable, and also makes the item easy to carry.

Client
Active

Designer
Harianto Chen

Material
210gsm art carton

Size
200mm x 70mm x 70mm

Completion
2013

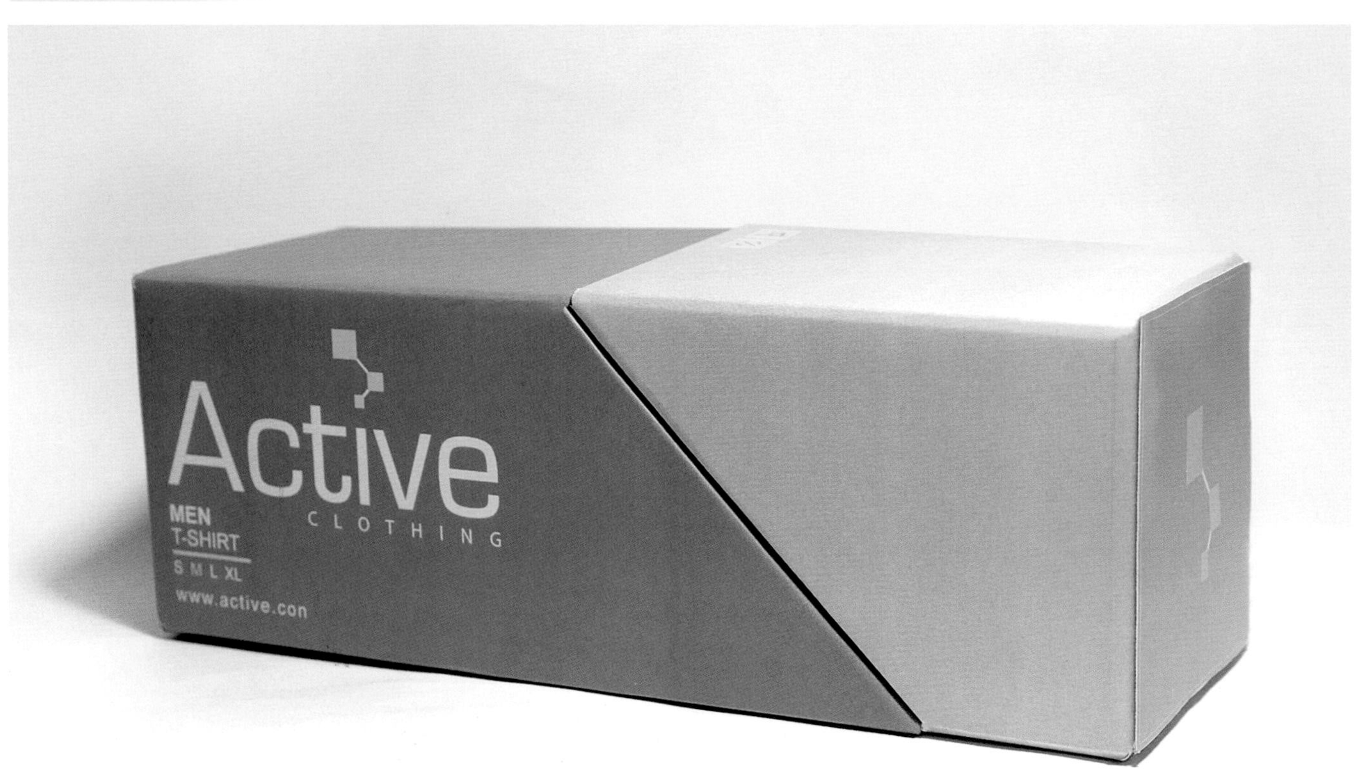

Active
CLOTHING
www.active.com
Active
CLOTHING

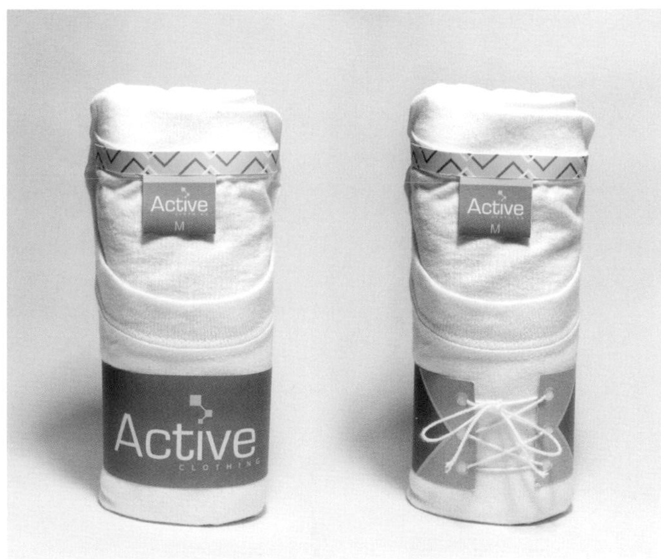
Active
M
Active
M
Active
CLOTHING

Active
CLOTHING
Made in Indonesia
www.active.con

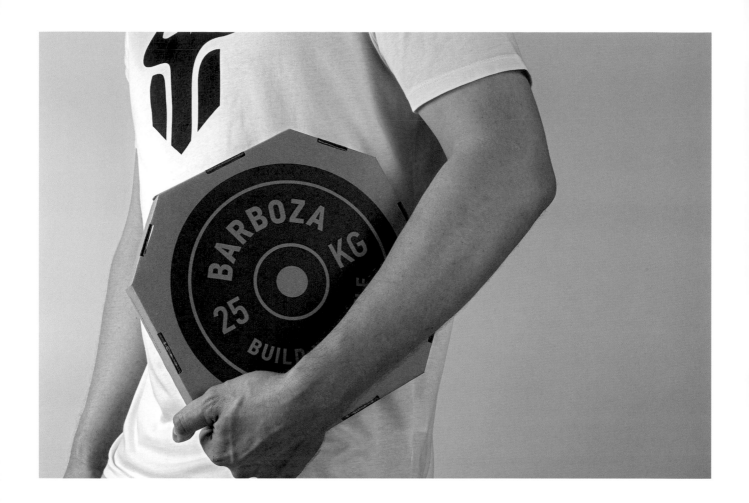

Barboza T-shirt Packaging

The pattern printed on this packaging looks like a barbell, and the slogan is "Build Yourself": together these design elements tell us that this is a T-shirt for athletes. The whole package looks simple and clean with minimal decorative elements, while the octagonal shape makes it unusual and elegant. Made from a combination of sustainable materials, this is completely recyclable packaging. The print is made with water-based paint and the adhesive is a glue based on potato starch, providing not only a health-friendly packaging alternative to PVC bags, but also ensuring sustainable environmental practices.

Client
Barboza

Designer
Maksim Arbuzov

Material
Sustainable cardboard

Size
550mm x 550mm

Completion
2015

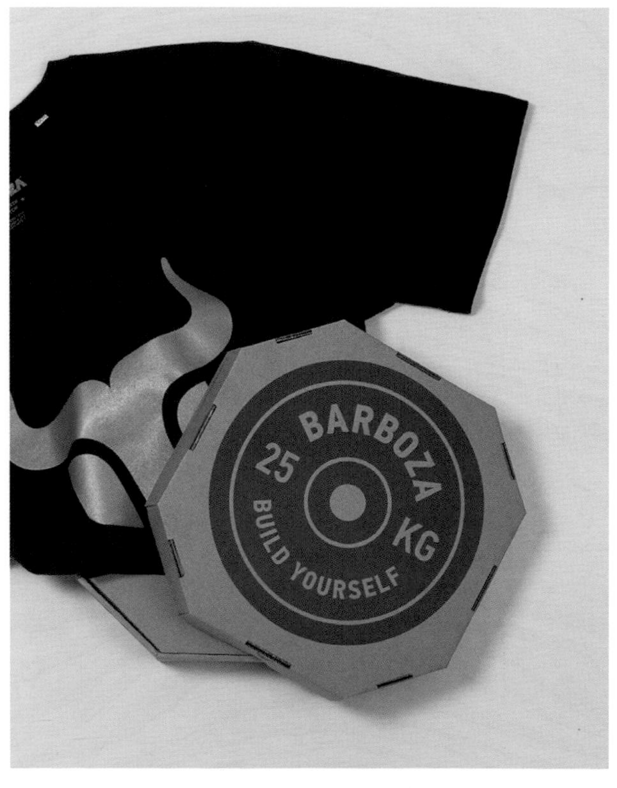

BAR
25
KG
BUILD YOURSELF
www.barbozasport.com

BARBOZA
Conquer Bc
Fitness Shirt
Black/White
L
Model
Conquer Bc
Type
Fitness Shirt
Color
Black/Gold
Size
XXL
Model
Conquer BC
Type
Fitness Shirt
Color
Black/Coral
Size
XL

#BuildYourself

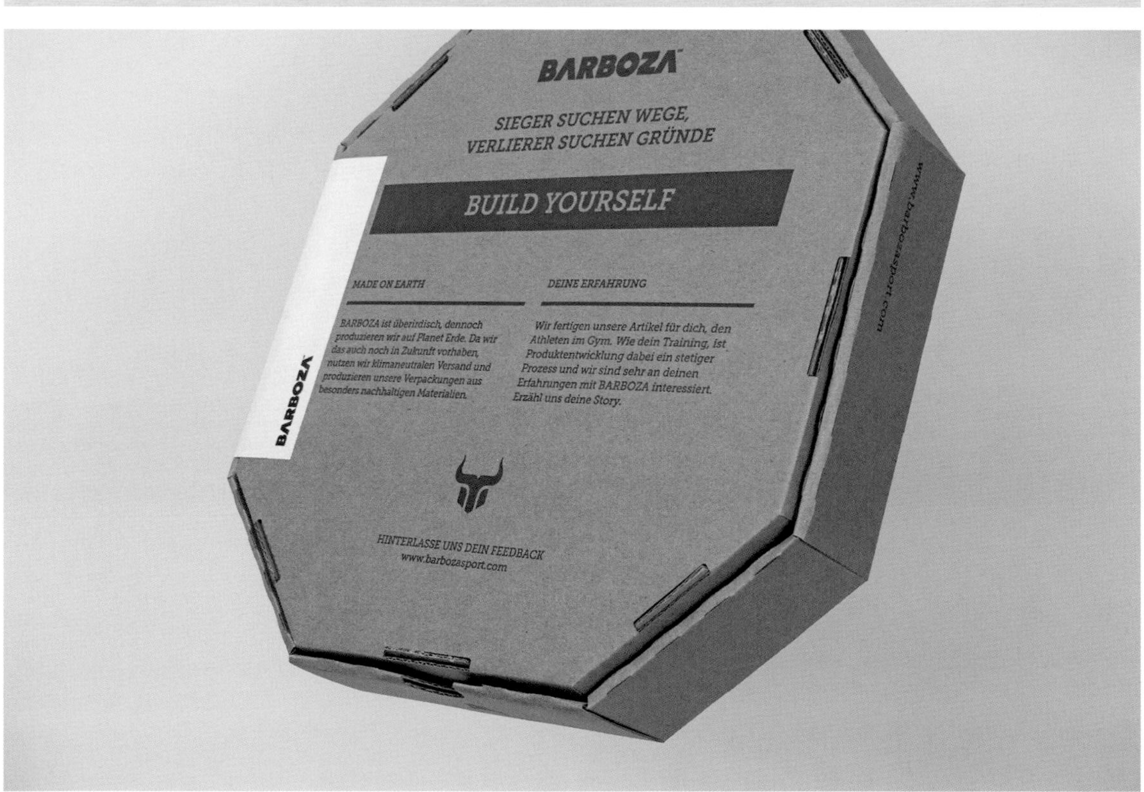

BARBOZA
SIEGER SUCHEN WEGE,
VERLIERER SUCHEN GRÜNDE
BUILD YOURSELF
MADE ON EARTH
BARBOZA ist überirdisch, dennoch produzieren wir auf Planet Erde. Da wir das auch noch in Zukunft vorhaben, nutzen wir klimaneutralen Versand und produzieren unsere Verpackungen aus besonders nachhaltigen Materialien.
DEINE ERFAHRUNG
Wir fertigen unsere Artikel für dich, den Athleten im Gym. Wie dein Training, ist Produktentwicklung dabei ein stetiger Prozess und wir sind sehr an deinen Erfahrungen mit BARBOZA interessiert. Erzähl uns deine Story.
HINTERLASSE UNS DEIN FEEDBACK
www.barbozasport.com
BARBOZA
www.barbozasport.com

FC Barcelona 2014–15 Jersey Packaging

The design concept for this limited-edition packaging of FC Barcelona's home jersey for the 2014–15 season involved conveying the elegance and values of the club. This was achieved through the consumer's interaction with the box that contains the jersey. "Made to Win," the club's slogan, was the design's main inspiration—the designers wanted to make consumers feel as if they had won by receiving this box, further enhancing its limited-edition feel. A combination of high-end papers with metallic blue ink (a main color of FC Barcelona) give the box a very desirable feel. After completion, the box went on sale in official stores in Spain, the United States, and Japan.

Client
America Nike

Design Agency
Oxigen

Designers
Sònia Rodríguez Grau, Carlos Pérez

Material
300gsm Folging, laminated polyester

Size
270mm x 310mm

Completion
2014

BARÇA
THE 2014/15
FC BARCELONA
HOME JERSEY

THE 2014/15
FC BARCELONA
HOME JERSEY

Footwear Packaging

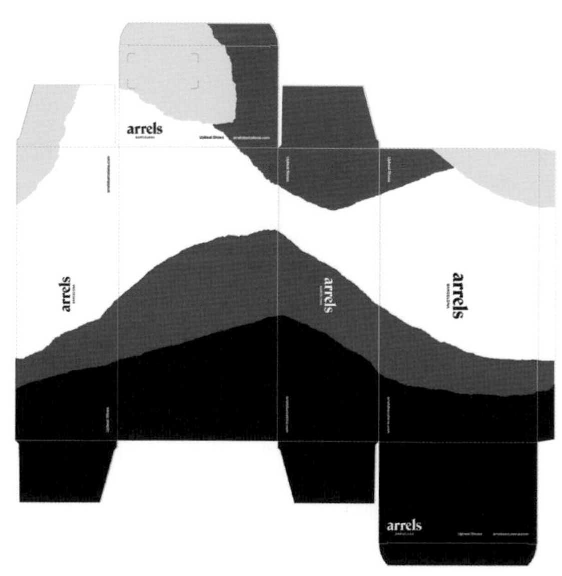

Arrels Packaging

Arrels, which means "roots" in English, is a Barcelona-based footwear brand making shoes for the urban market. Creating the packaging for this brand meant finding the right balance between its urban look and its rural roots and between being handmade and mass-produced. This duality is reflected in the two colors of the identity and in the pattern created for the boxes and the shoes—an idea that was carried over to the brochure. The design of the pattern plays with the idea that if you were to rip up all the layers of concrete that cover the urban landscape, you would find the original, natural surface of the earth underneath.

Client
Arrels Barcelona

Design Agency
Hey Studio

Material
Cardboard

Size
336mm x 183mm x 118mm

Completion
2015

arrels
BARCELONA
arrels
BARCELONA

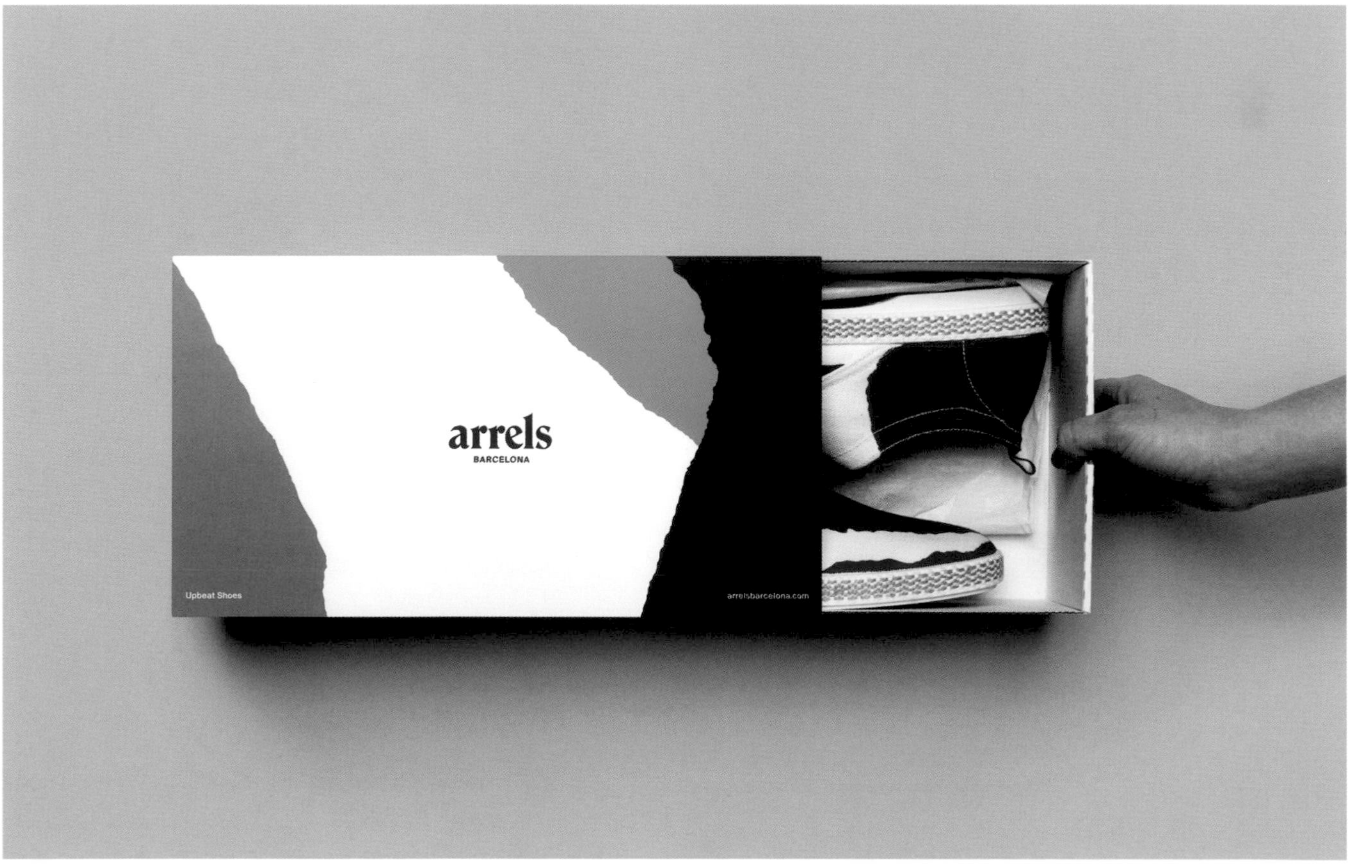
arrels
BARCELONA
Upbeat Shoes
arrelsbarcelona.com

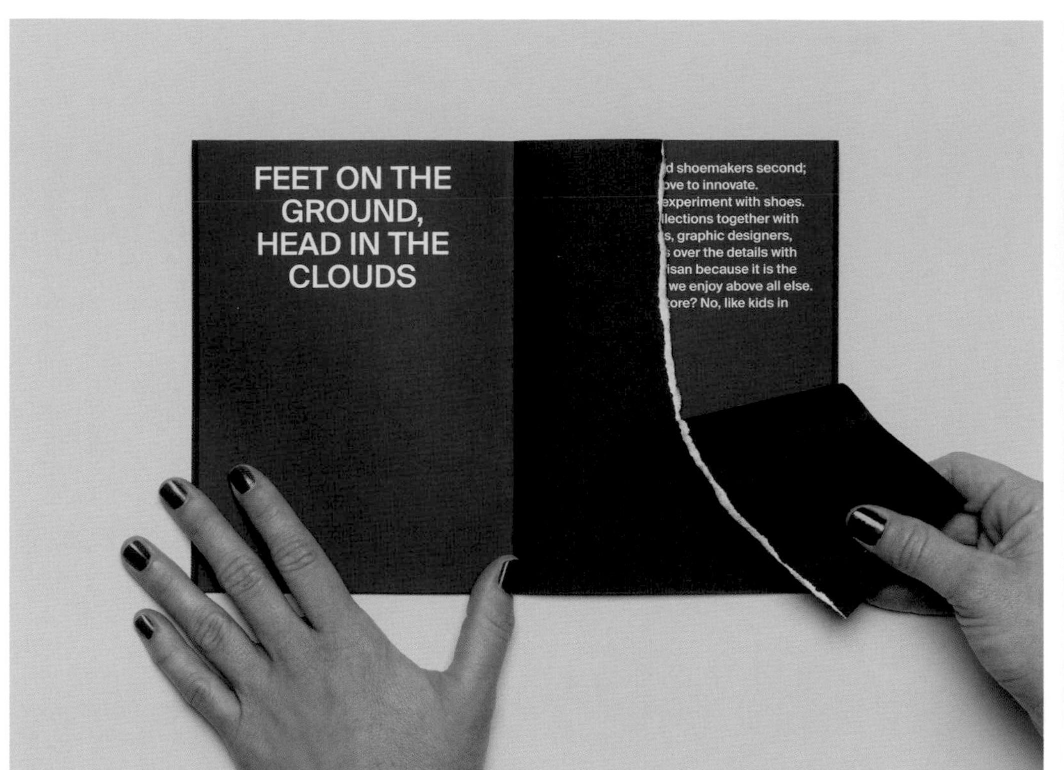
FEET ON THE GROUND, HEAD IN THE CLOUDS
d shoemakers second;
ove to innovate.
experiment with shoes.
llections together with
s, graphic designers,
s over the details with
isan because it is the
we enjoy above all else.
ore? No, like kids in

MADE OF BARCELONA
arrels
BARCELONA

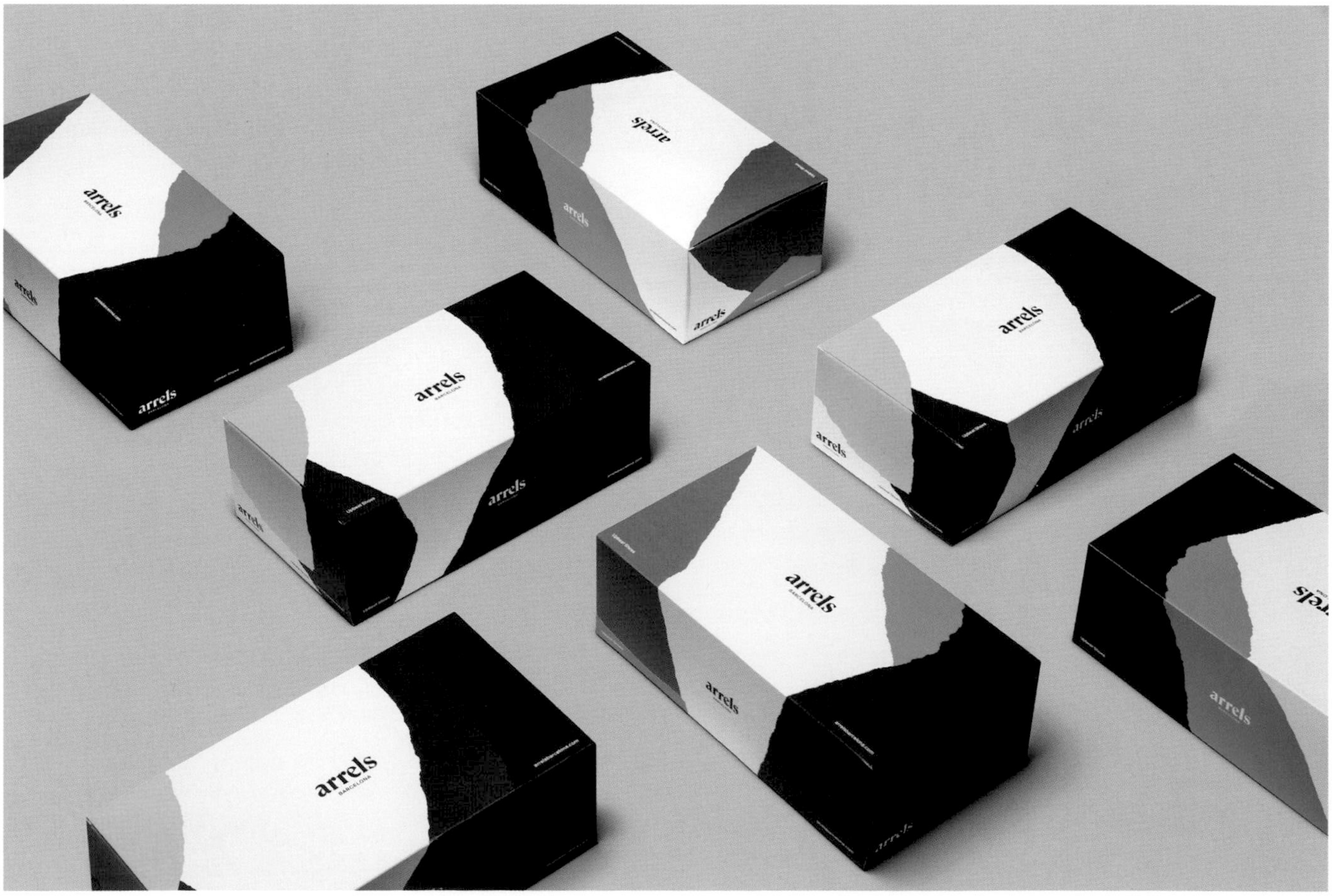

HUMAN
arrels
BARCELONA

arrels
BARCELONA

Packaging for Camelot Brand

The design concept of the packaging series for the Camelot footwear and clothing brand is based on the uniqueness of the niche occupied by these goods. The main mission of the series is to convey the informal brand spirit, its rebelliousness, and a sense of eternal youth and energy.

The packaging series presentation concept is founded on the idea of producing VIP-collection clothes and accessories that will be sold in a limited quantity at an event and after the event in some select stores. In this case the package consists of a large box, within which smaller components are contained: a Camelot boots package; a leather jacket package; three packages for accessories (a bracelet, a belt, and a pair of gloves), and a package for a bottle of rum. A 3-millimeter-thick cardboard was selected for the package manufacturing, as such cardboard seemed to be suitable for selling heavy clothing items.

Client
Camelot

Designer
Anastasia Akimova

Material
Wood, cardboard

Size
820mm x 470mm x 200mm

Completion
2014

ОСТАВЬ
СВОЙ
СЛЕД!

ОСТАВЬ
СВОЙ
СЛЕД!

ОСТАВЬ
СВОЙ
СЛЕД!

ОСТАБЬ

ОСТАБЬ
СВОЙ
СЛЕД!
camelot

ОСТАБЬ
СВОЙ
BACARDI
BLACK
ESTD 1862

ОСТАВЬ
СВОЙ
СЛЕД!
camelot

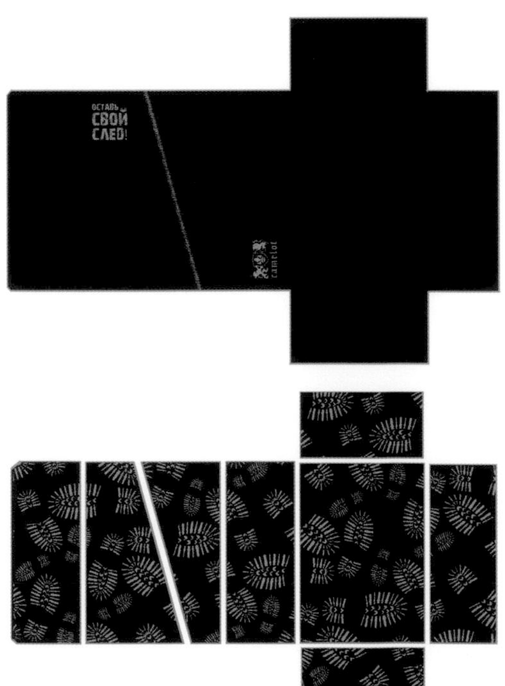
ОСТАВЬ
СВОЙ
СЛЕД!
camelot

FUTBOX

Regular shoe boxes usually come in different sizes because of the different size of shoes. FUTBOX solves this problem for packaging manufacturers because it's able to be adjusted by tightening or loosening the extra shoelaces outside the box. It also comes with different opening, carrying, and presentation styles. Its standing position best displays the product inside, while its horizontal position is best for storage inside a shop. The design also gives better access to the product with its front, top, and side openings.

Designers
Sencer Ozdemir, Busra Mehlike Kurt Caliskan

Material
Cardboard

Size
320mm x 220mm

Completion
2012

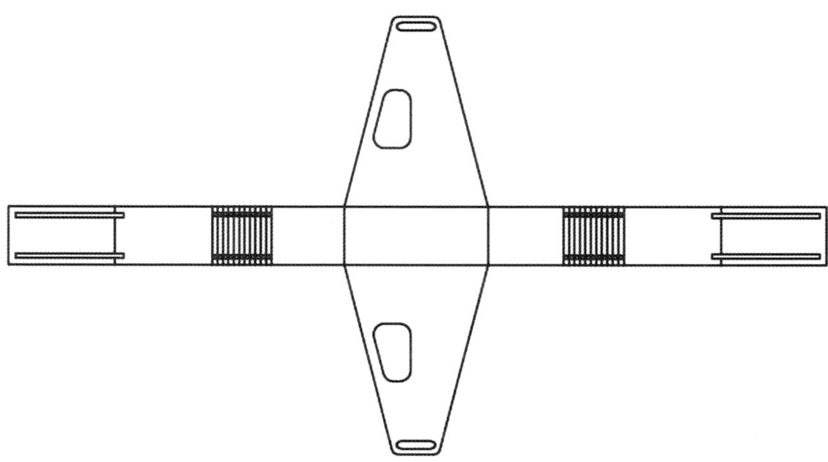

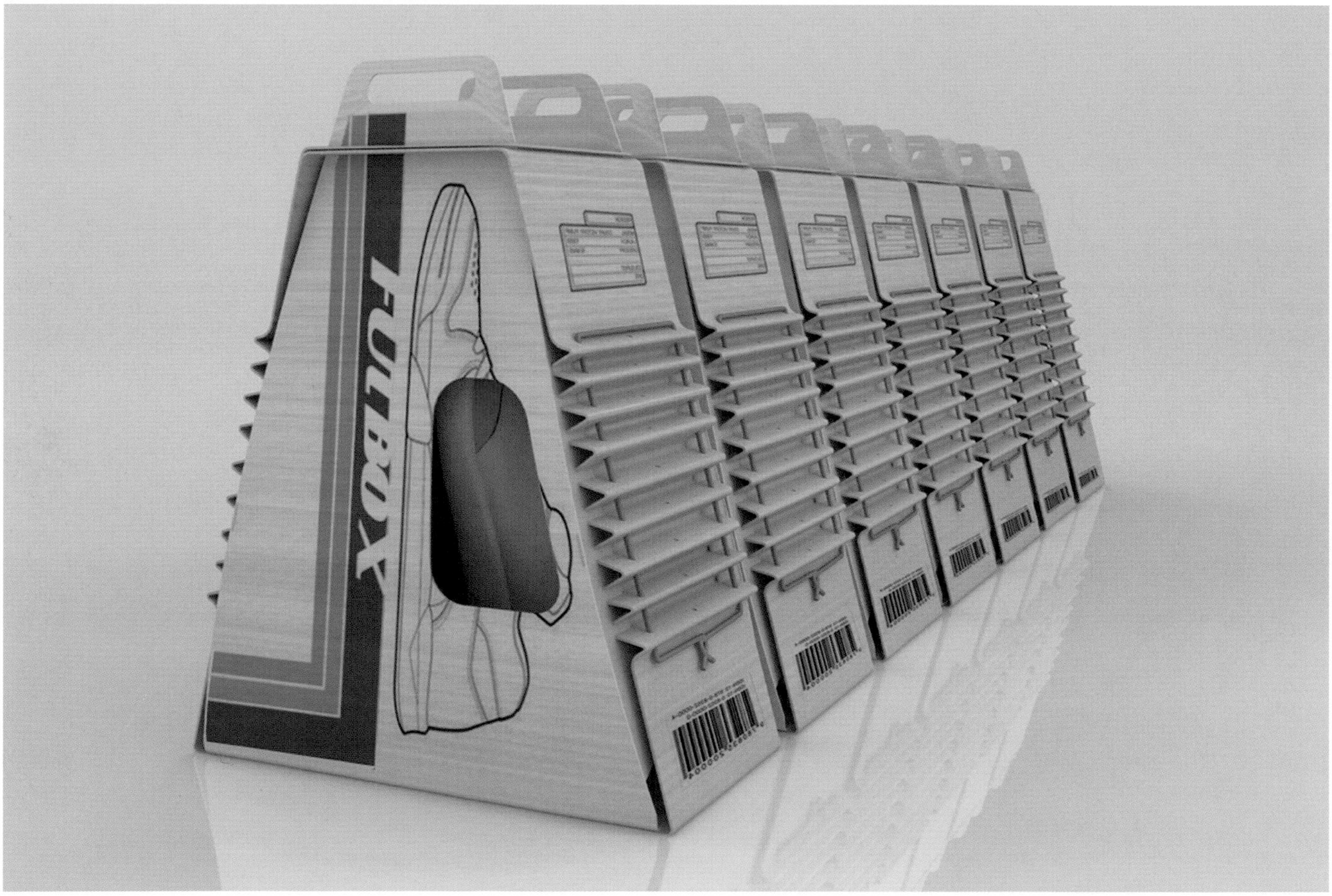

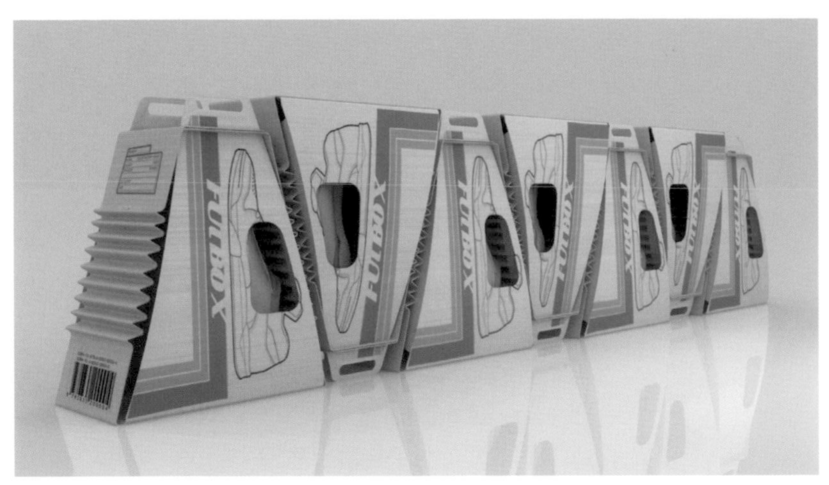
FULBOX

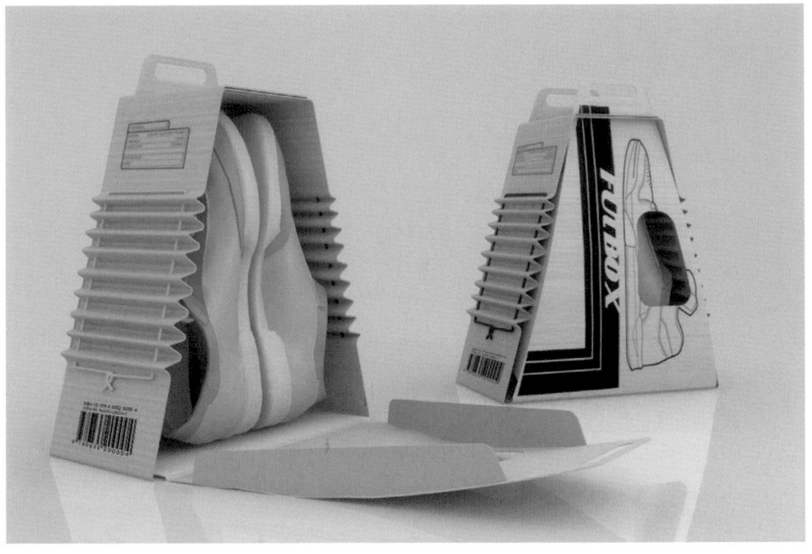
FULBOX

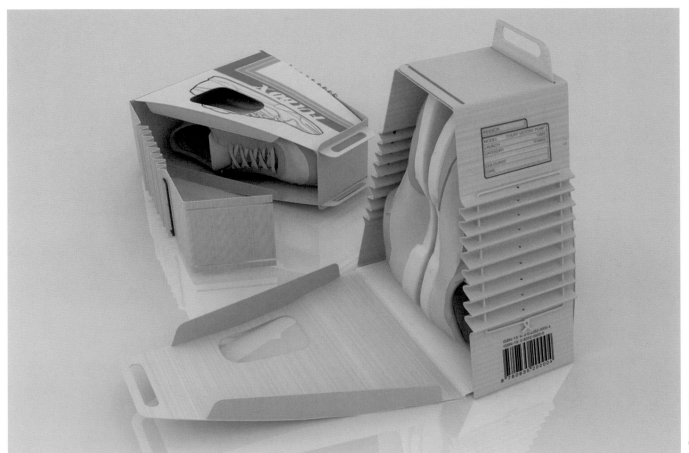

Nike iD Mercurial Packaging

Nike iD Mercurial is a football boot inspired by fast cars. A competition was run by Nike across eight countries for football-loving teenagers to win a pair of the desirable boots, and each of the eight boxes of boots was delivered to the winners by a professional footballer. Everton's Aaron Lennon presented the British winner with their own custom-made shoes.

The advertising campaign for the boots featured the boots in the bonnet of a sports car, and to reinforce the connection once the boots were in the consumers' hands, design agency AKQA and production company Nirvana developed a shoe box that resembled the contoured, sleek shape of a car bonnet, complete with a magnetic spring opening. The shoe box was made from Chemiwood, a resin-based board commonly used in commercial model making that has no grain and gives a smooth, flawless finish. Acrylic was laser-cut to create air vents and vacuum-formed to create the curved bonnet shape. Once complete, the boxes were sprayed in the custom colors chosen by the winners, using actual car paint from Ferrari and BMW.

Client
Nike Football

Design Agencies
AKQA, Nirvana cph

Collaborators
Andrew Tuffs (Creative Director), Alfons Valls (Designer)

Material
Chemiwood, acrylic

Size
225mm x 655mm x 455mm

Completion
2013

CX54 FVU

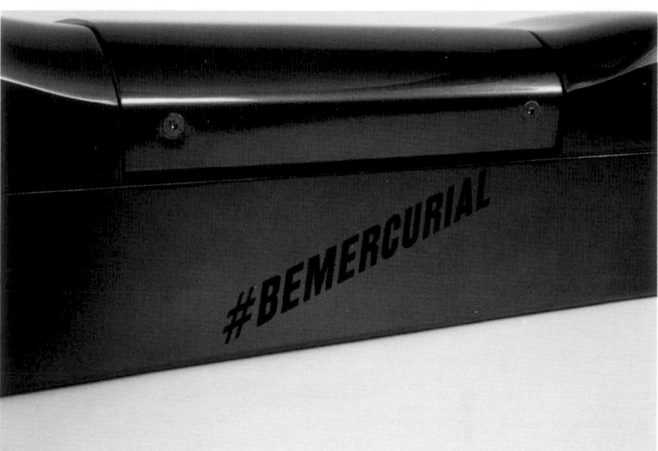
#BEMERCURIAL

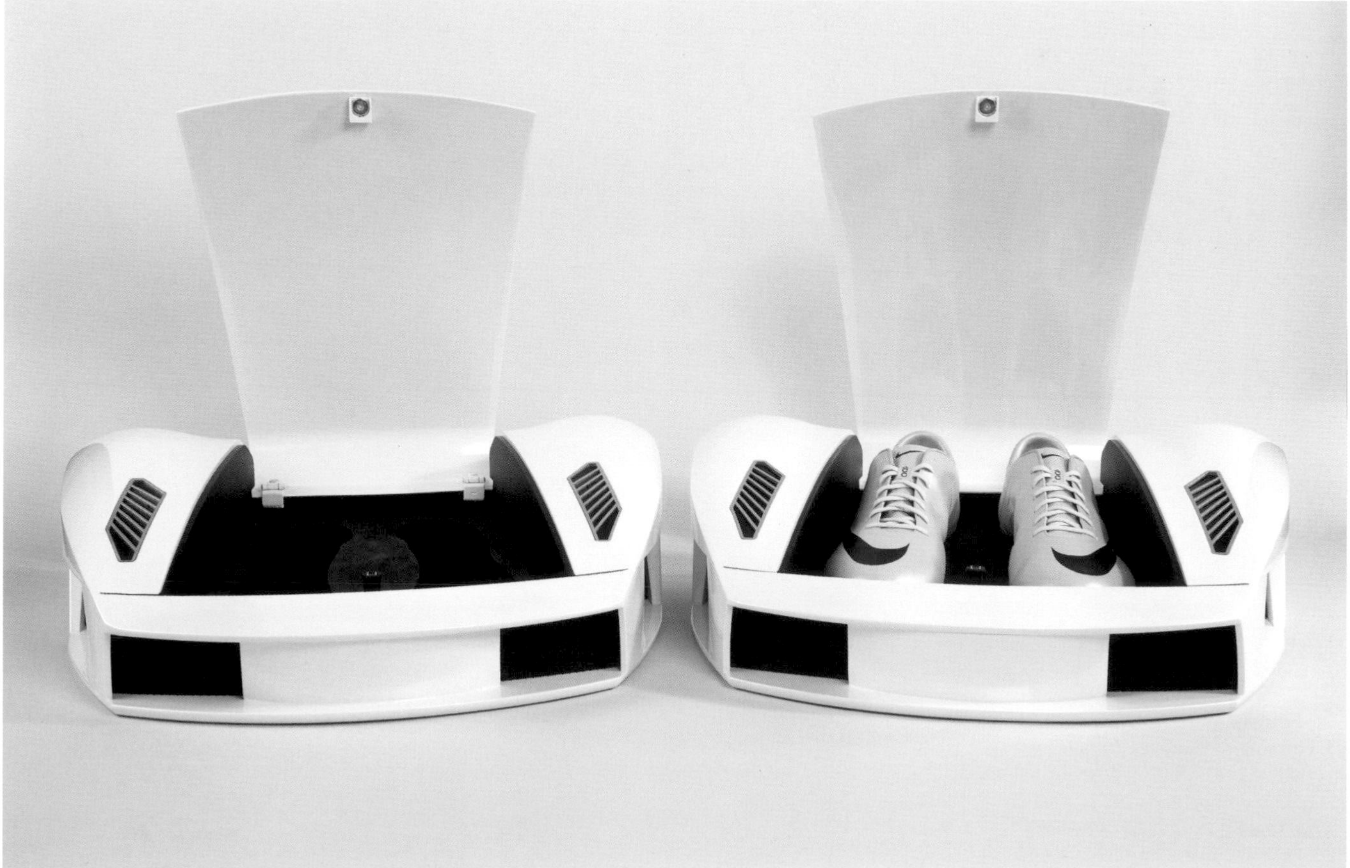

Startas Shoes Packaging

Startas are completely handmade shoes, produced since 1976 in the Borovo factory in Vukovar, Croatia. They symbolize the sports equipment and clothing style of the former Yugoslavia. The Borovo shoe factory does not use materials that are harmful to the environment in the production of Startas shoes, and leaves no large amounts of waste after production. The design goal of the new packaging is to emphasize the preservation of the environment and symbolize Startas as a nature-friendly brand. In line with this, the shoe box design incorporated a handle in the top so that the box could act as a kind of bag as well, eliminating the need for plastic bags to also be produced (and saving the company the additional expense). The packaging incorporates a new visual identity and the new Startas Basic collection aims to create better brand recognition, market positioning and communication with existing and potential customers.

Client
Borovo

Designer
Leo Vinkovic

Photography
Vedran Marjanovic

Material
Kraft paper

Size
300mm x 125mm x 100mm

Completion
2013

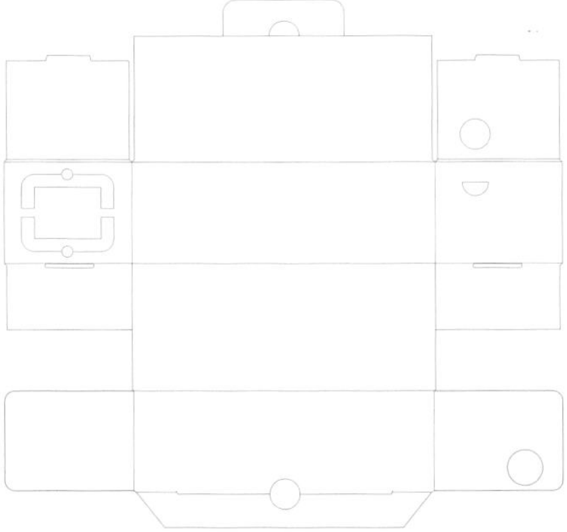

startas
TIRKIZ/LJUBIČASTO
43

startas

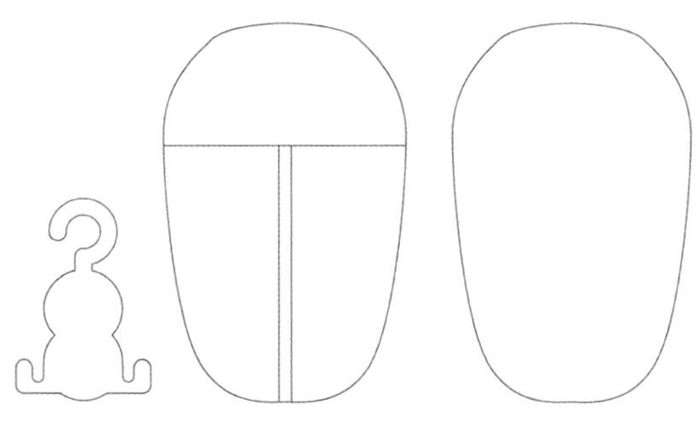

Goza Vintage Slipper

KARATE is an old and traditional factory that produces durable slippers (aka flip-flops, thongs) from recycled materials (mainly vehicles' tires). Its blue-and-white slippers (colors that are synonymous with the brand) are the basic footwear that every Southeast Asian person would have worn in the 1970s. These are not just slippers—they're reminders of times past.

KARATE wanted to celebrate its 40th anniversary by producing something different as a brand-refreshing campaign, so it produced the "Goza" vintage slipper brand and commissioned Low Yong Cheng to put a new spin on an old favorite. Inspired by another iconic daily product—the red, white, and blue nylon bag—the designer took this material further and turned it into a nicely crafted slipper package complete with wooden hanger, successfully bringing the KARATE slipper back on trend in the process.

Client
KARATE

Designer
Low Yong Cheng

Material
Nylon, wood

Size
400mm x 200mm

Completion
2014

Puma EvoSpeed Limited Edition Packaging

For the launch of the Puma EvoSpeed football boot, the designers were briefed to create an impactful piece of bespoke packaging to be sent out to influential bloggers and select press. With a challenging timeline, they needed to deliver an eye-catching solution that would showcase the boot and the technology. To reflect the high-speed capability of the boot, the box takes its inspiration from the angular faceted shape of a stealth bomber. A hinged aluminum outer skin folds back to reveal the boots housed in a laser-etched, glow-edged acrylic tray. The matte-black and fluorescent-green outer has contrasting gloss varnish graphics taken from the patterns on the boots running across all surfaces.

Client
Puma

Design Agency
Everyone Associates

Designers
Alan Watt, Jonathan Coleman

Material
Promolyte, neodymium magnet, Perspex

Size
350mm x 225mm x 130mm

Completion
2013

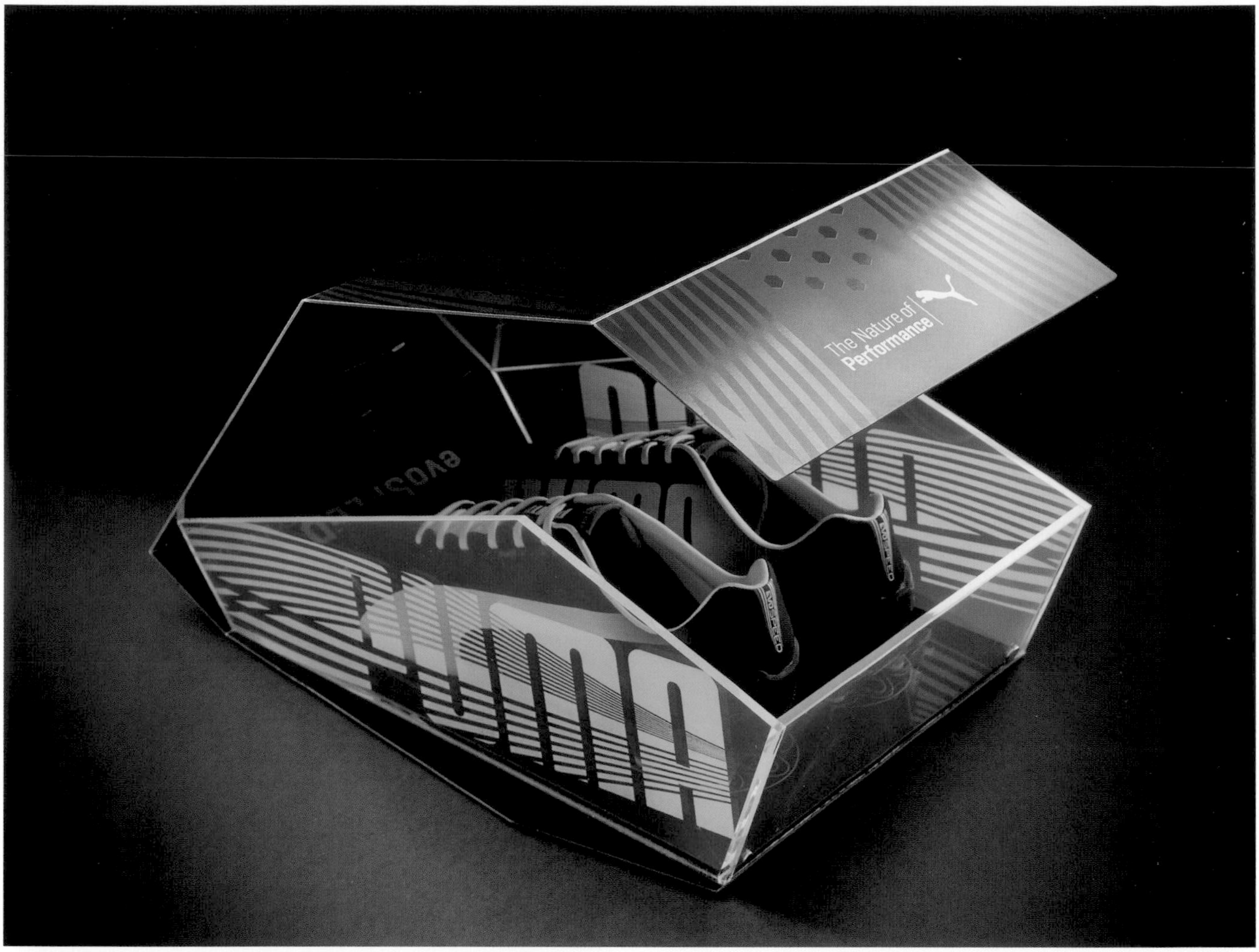

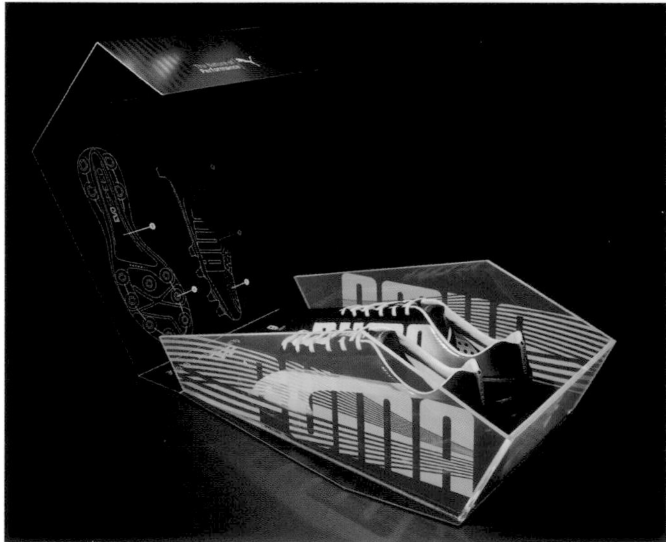

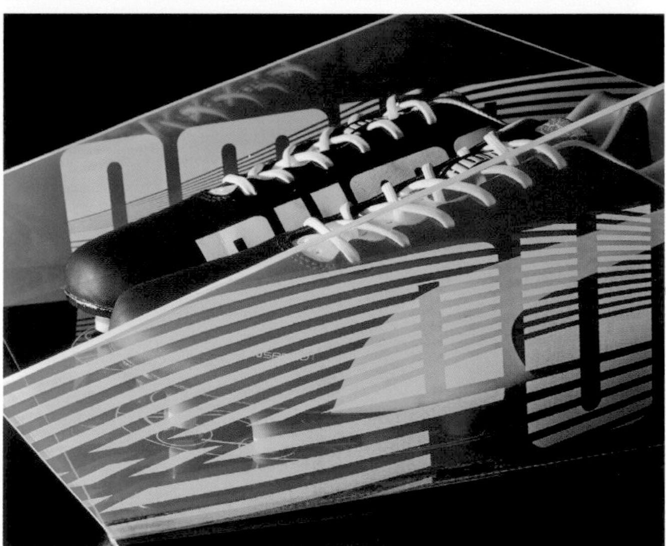

SPEED
evoSPEED 1.2

EVO SPEED

evoSPEED
BLINK AND THEY'LL BE GONE

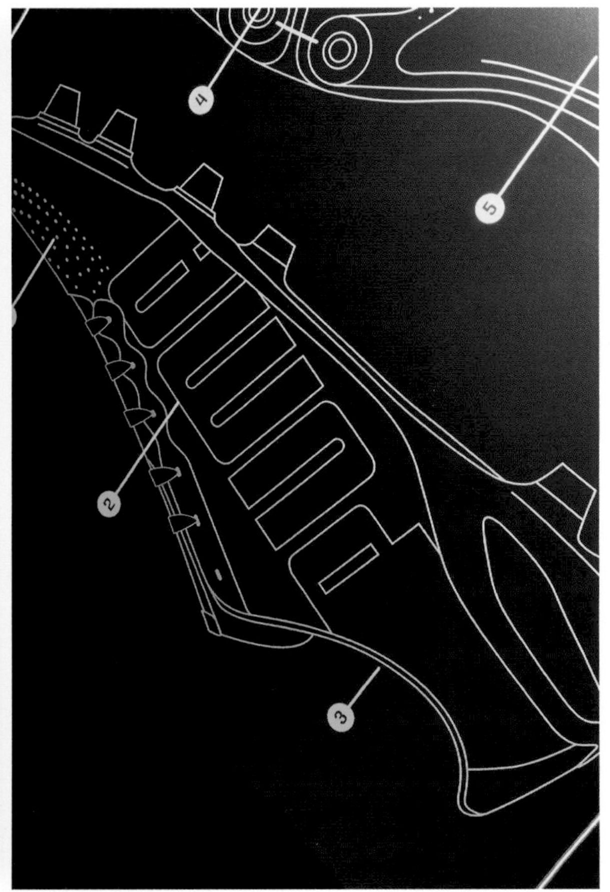
2
3
4
5

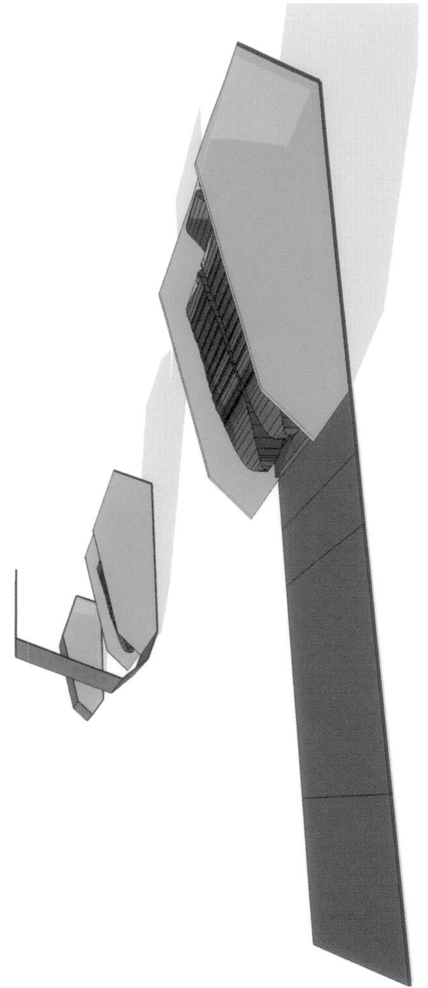

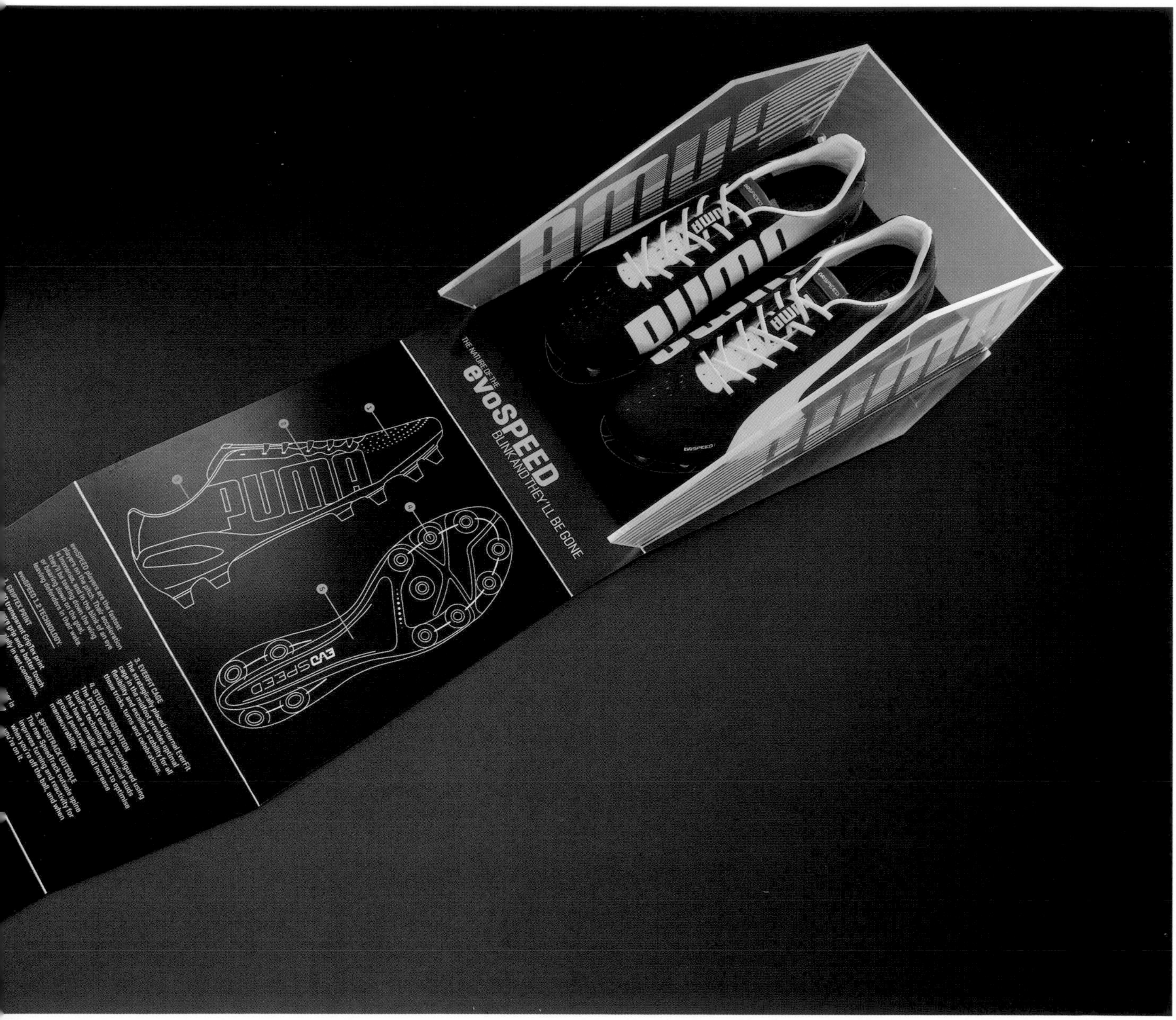

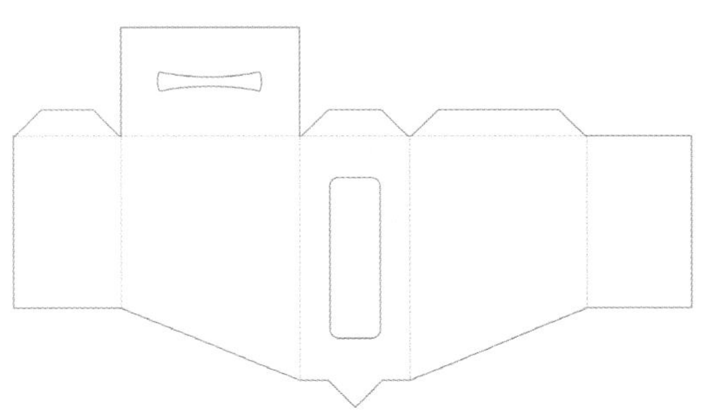

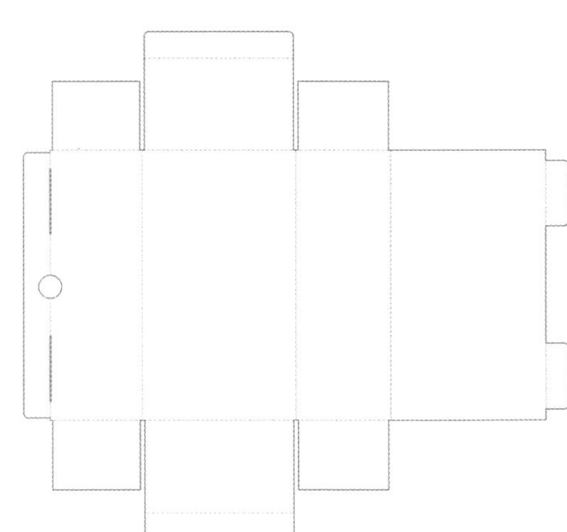

Boom Bap Shoes Packaging

When shopping for shoes, a combination of box and bag are normally offered by the majority of shops to allow customers to carry their items home, and, sadly, the bags are usually made from plastic. Combining box and bag together is the key concept behind this project, allowing the box to become the carrying bag. The box with an integrated handle houses the shoes, while the paper lid "dresses" the box downward, but leaves the handle accessible at the top. Made of natural kraft card and kraft paper with a handle of natural fibers, this packaging is eco-friendly and offers a practical design for reuse. Despite the eco-friendly colors, the marketing factor was not forgotten. Logos and slogans can be seen through cutouts and in other spaces, highlighting the green tint against the natural kraft color.

Client
Boom Bap Wear

Designer
Pedro Sousa

Material
Kraft paper, kraft card, fabric

Size
350mm x 200mm x 122mm

Completion
2014

fuck
you me off

fuck
you me off
BOOM BAP
FRENCH KICK ASS BRAND
FOLLOW
US

FOLLOW
US

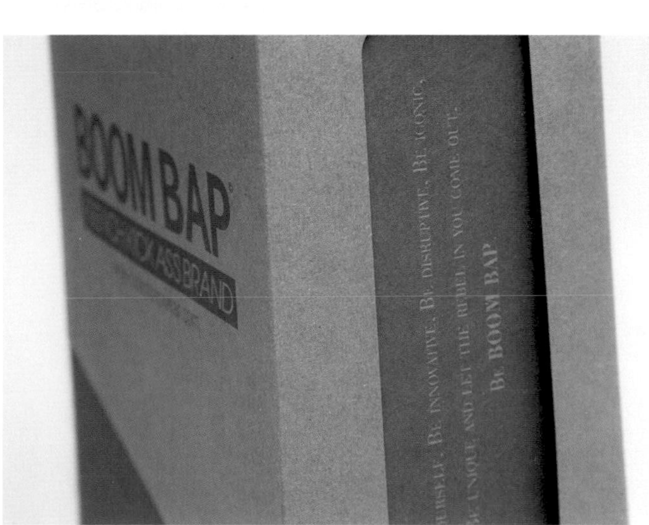
BOOM BAP
FRENCH KICK ASS BRAND
Be BOOM BAP

Puma EvoSpeed SL Superlight PR Packaging

Name & Name was commissioned by Puma in Germany to design the launch packaging for Puma's lightest-ever boot, the EvoSpeed SL Superlight. The box design was itself superlight, being made from light foam and thin card. To illustrate the EvoSpeed theme of giving great speed, a clear slip-case printed with lines slides off the box containing the shoes and printed with the product name. As the lines slide across the product name, also made of lines, an effect of fast movement is created as the design shimmers and flickers. The box uses the colors of the soccer boots: bright red and dark blue.

Client
Puma Germany

Design Agency
Name & Name

Designers
Ian Perkins, Aja Lee, Christine Tseng, Tasha Chen

Material
Cards, plastic

Size
350mm x 250mm x 150mm

Completion
2015

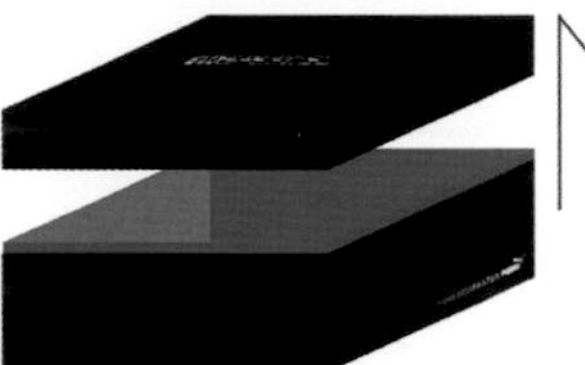

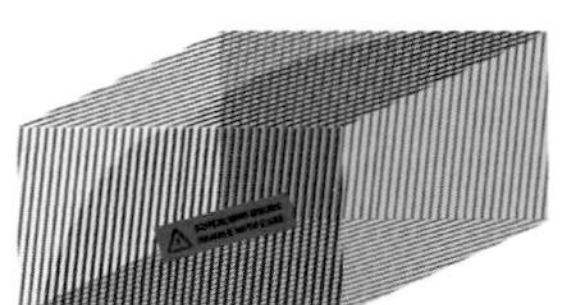

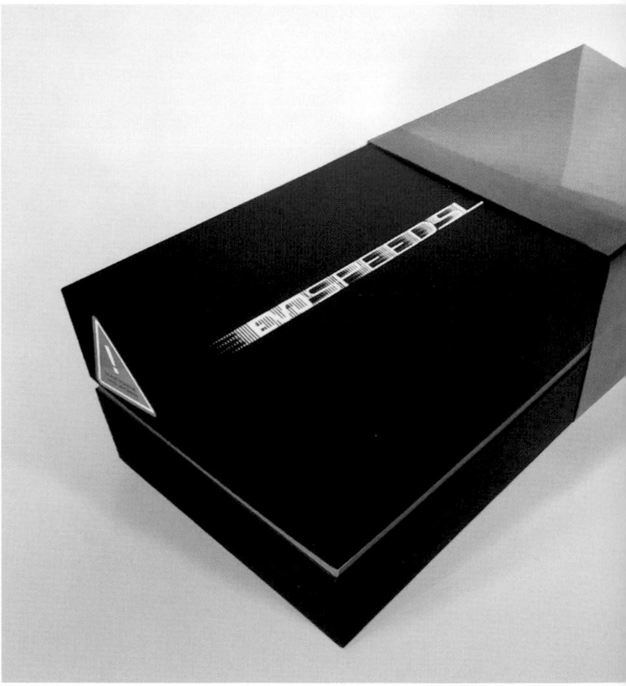

FOREVERFASTER PUMA

Van Gils 65th Anniversary Packaging

Van Gils is a brand known for its high-quality menswear. Since 2013 marked the brand's 65th anniversary, Van Gils seized the opportunity to introduce a limited-edition shoe: the buckskin "Brothel Creeper" in black and white. To attract customers' attention, design agency Frank Agterberg/bca developed a premium shoe box with a twist for the occasion.

Sharing Van Gils' sense of innovation in service, the design agency decided to add some useful extras. Of course the shoe box itself has an appealing design, namely, a white box with contrasting high-gloss embossing that elegantly closes with a magnet. But inside the box, a raised bedding of black velour foam includes cut-away zones that house the gift-pack extras: a matching belt, a set of laces, a set of cufflinks, and a buckskin polishing brush. As consumers will never buy what they haven't seen, the agency added another extra feature that turned the shoe box into a multipurpose tool. With some subtle interventions like a dotted footprint, it became an in-store presentation pedestal, beautifully highlighting the anniversary Brothel Creeper.

Client
Van Gils

Design Agency
Frank Agterberg/bca

Material
Cardboard, white paper

Size
400mm x 300mm x 150mm

Completion
2013

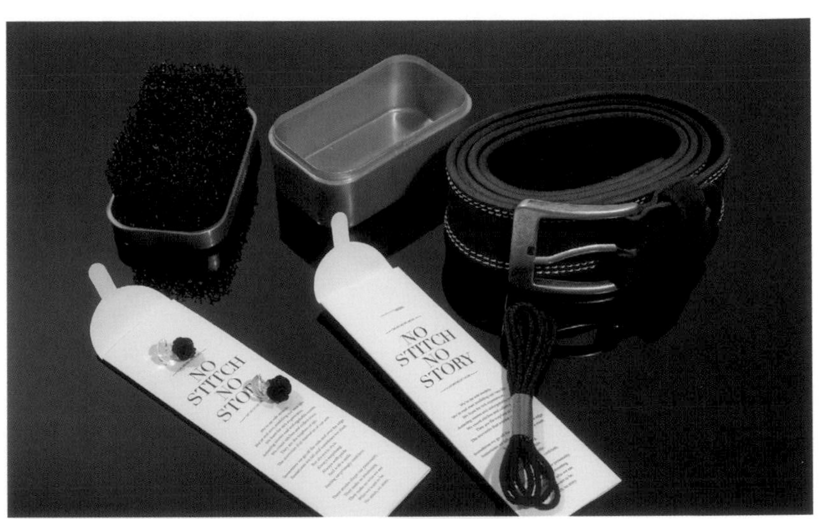
NO
STITCH
NO
STORY

65 YEARS
ANNIVERSARY
LIMITED
EDITION
NO
STITCH
NO
STORY
65 years ago, with Van Gils, men stepped out of line to find their confident self.
Ever since that day Van Gils has been known for its innovative design and looks, providing the ultimate suit for those who aren't afraid to live life to the fullest, the occasional scars included.
Made of classic black-and-white nubuck and based on a distinctive double layer sole, this limited edition Brothel Creeper is a worthy representative to celebrate Van Gils' anniversary.
Ready to add stitch to the story.
Van Gils

NO
STITCH
NO
STORY
65 years ago, with Van Gils, men stepped out of line to find their confident self.
Ever since that day Van Gils has been known for its innovative design and looks, providing the ultimate suit for those who aren't afraid to live life to the fullest, the occasional scars included.
Made of classic black-and-white nubuck and based on a distinctive double layer sole, this limited edition Brothel Creeper is a worthy representative to celebrate Van Gils' anniversary.
Ready to add stitch to the story.
NO
STITCH
NO
STORY
Van Gils

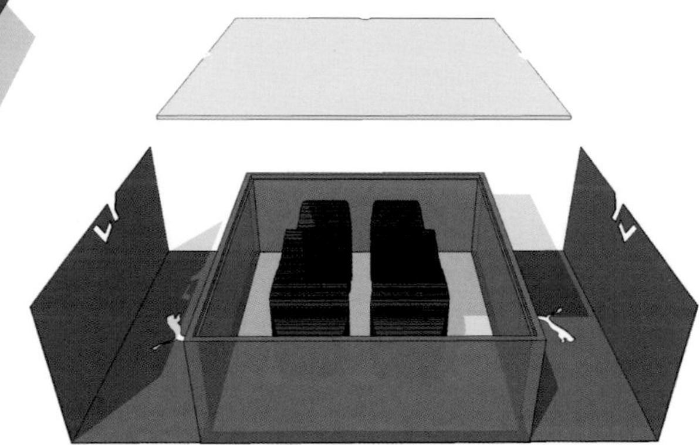

Puma King Luxury Limited Edition Packaging

To launch the new Puma King Luxury Edition football boot, designers Alan Watt and Jonathan Coleman were commissioned to create limited-edition packaging that was a contemporary twist on a traditional presentation case. Limited to just 999 pairs, the Puma King Luxury Edition is a modern interpretation of Puma's premier heritage boot, the King, which has long been associated with some of the greatest players in football history. To reflect its regal status, the King Luxury Edition presentation case is constructed from premium materials. A black anodized aluminum outer case with laser-etched graphics opens to reveal a mirrored, gold-and-black, smoked Perspex interior. The opening of the case and revealing of the boots was designed to have an almost ceremonial feel.

Client
Puma

Design Agency
Everyone Associates

Designers
Alan Watt, Jonathan Coleman

Material
Anodised aluminum, Perspex

Size
325mm x 365mm x 135mm

Completion
2013

THERE
CAN
ONLY
BE
ONE
KING

THERE
CAN
ONLY
BE
ONE
KING

The Nature of
Performance

CHUPL

The CHUPL brand makes footwear whose soles are made of repurposed vehicle tires, and the task for designer Niteesh Yadav was to design box packaging, hang tags and display stands that reflected the raw and handcrafted aspects of the brand. As a designer, it was his responsibility to comply with the brief, but he came up with a creative spin on it, and his solution involved combining all three requirements into one. The shoe boxes became the display and the hang tags were created from a cutout of the box, thus reducing waste of materials and aligning perfectly with the company's focus on sustainability. Two boxes work together to convey the brand's story; the cutouts in the boxes also give direct access to the shoes, so that customers can look at and touch the product without needing to open the packaging.

Client
Tim Sebastian

Designer
Niteesh Yadav

Material
Recycled paper

Size
320mm x 215mm x 110mm

Completion
2015

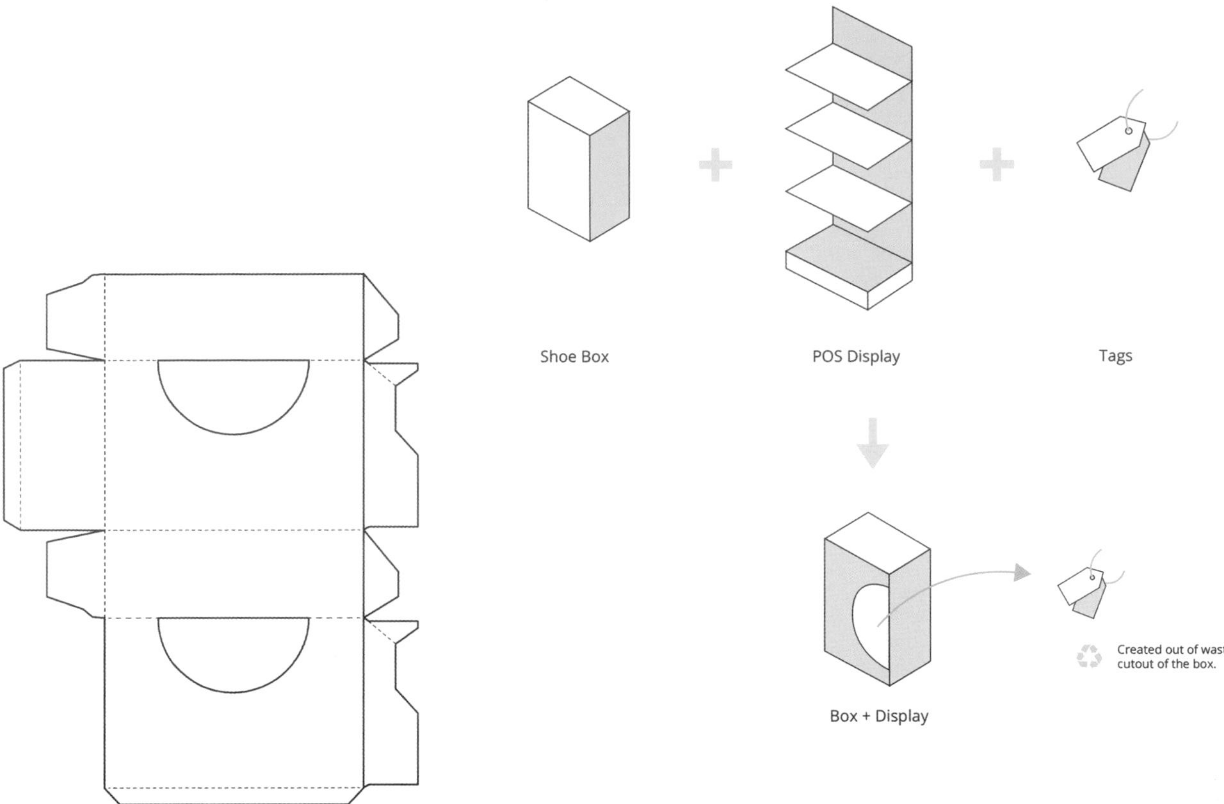
Shoe Box
POS Display
Tags
Box + Display
Created out of waste cutout of the box.

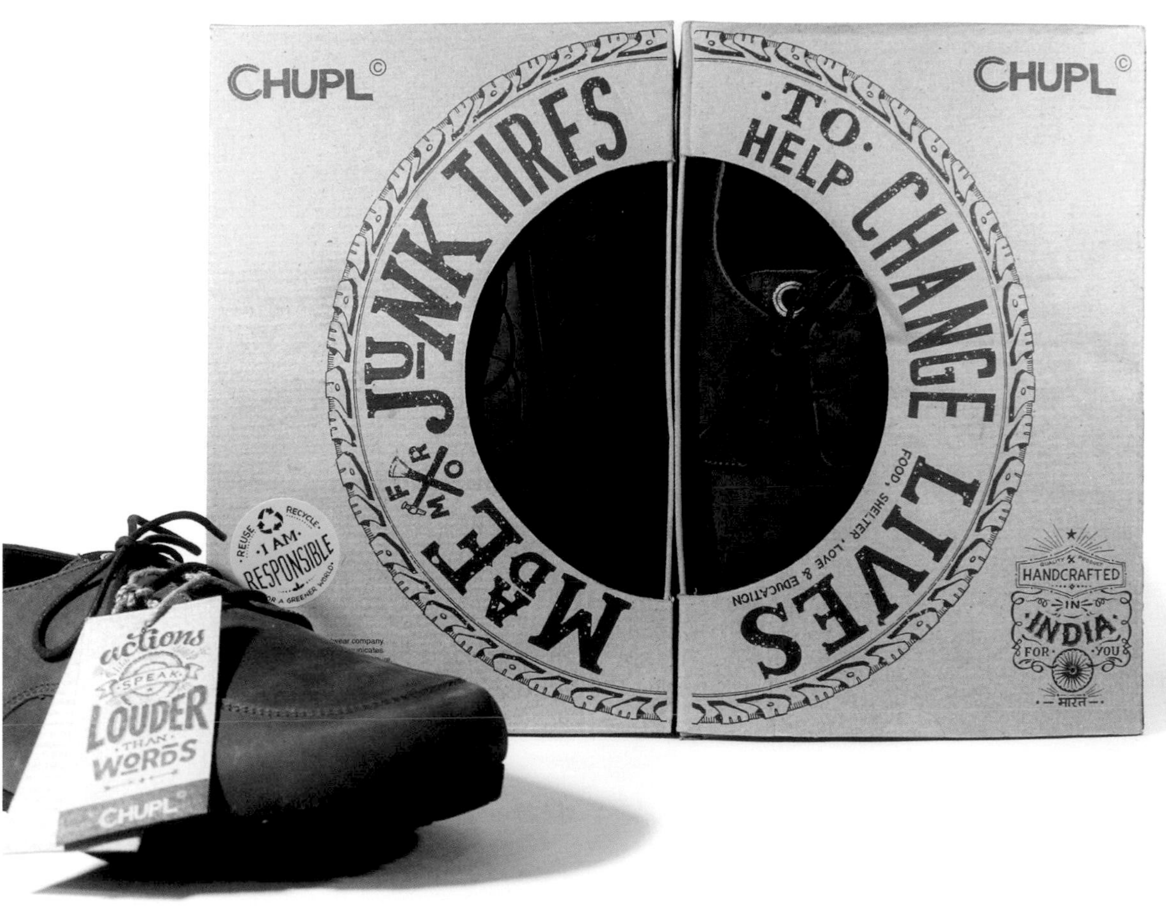
CHUPL©
CHUPL©
MADE FROM JUNK TIRES
TO HELP CHANGE LIVES
FOOD, SHELTER, LOVE & EDUCATION
REUSE RECYCLE
I AM RESPONSIBLE
HANDCRAFTED IN INDIA FOR YOU
actions SPEAK LOUDER THAN WORDS
CHUPL

Puma Tricks 2014 FIFA World Cup Special Packaging

The battle to stand out at the 2014 FIFA World Cup in Brazil was fierce. Puma set out to make a statement on the pitch by being the first brand to have its players wearing mismatched boots—the Puma Tricks Collection. To launch the collection, designers Alan Watt and Jonathan Coleman were asked to create limited-edition presentation cases for the star Puma players who wore the boots, including Mario Balotelli, Cesc Fàbregas, Sergio Agüero, Marco Reus, and Yaya Touré. Being such major football figures, it was important that the case made as stylish a statement as the boots. To reflect the unique appearance of the boots and the energy of Brazil, the designers created a vibrant hinged box that splits open vertically to present the pink and blue boots. Using a combination of contrasting matte and gloss print finishes, the personalized outer sleeve slides off to reveal the boots, jewel-like against a graphic background featuring the names and coordinates of the 12 World Cup stadiums.

Client
Puma

Design Agency
Everyone Associates

Designers
Alan Watt, Jonathan Coleman

Material
Perspex, promolyte

Size
360mm x 210mm x 210mm

Completion
2014

PUMA

EVOSPEE
BRAZZZZZZiiiiiiLLLLL
12_06_14 - 13_07_
#STARTBELIEVI

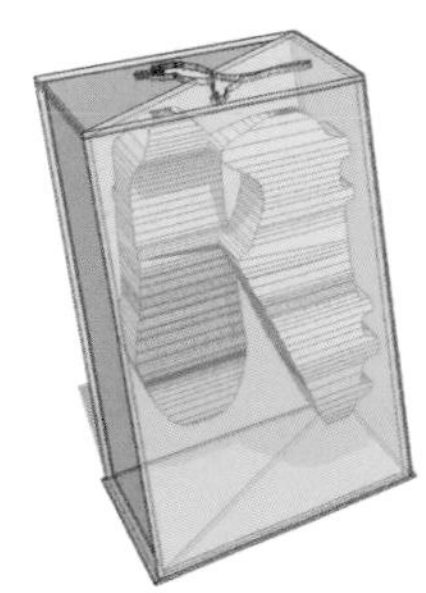

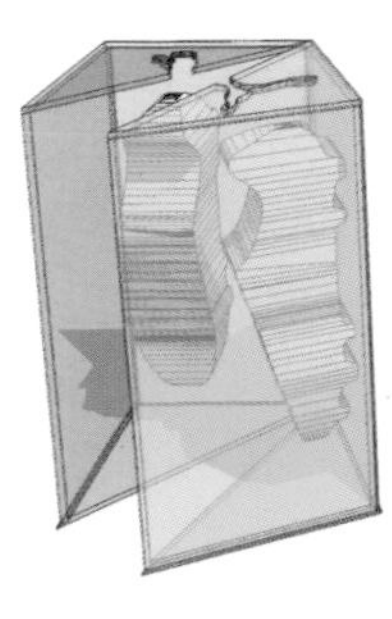

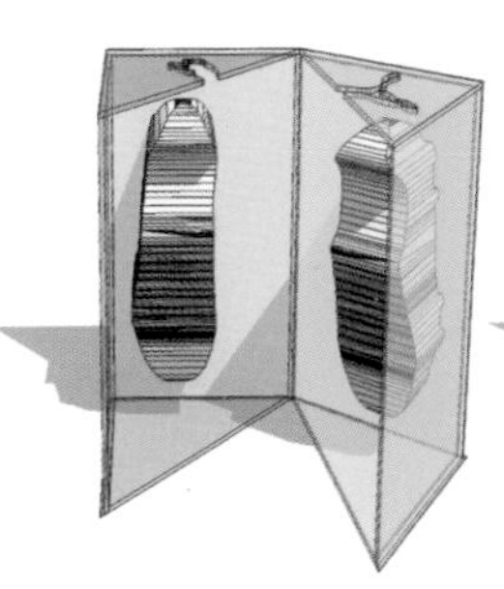

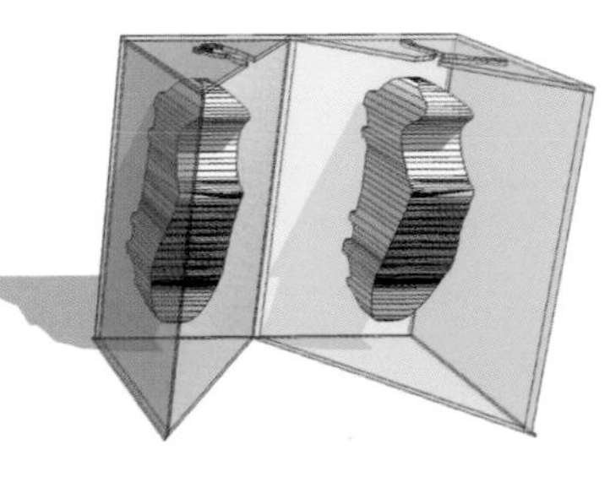

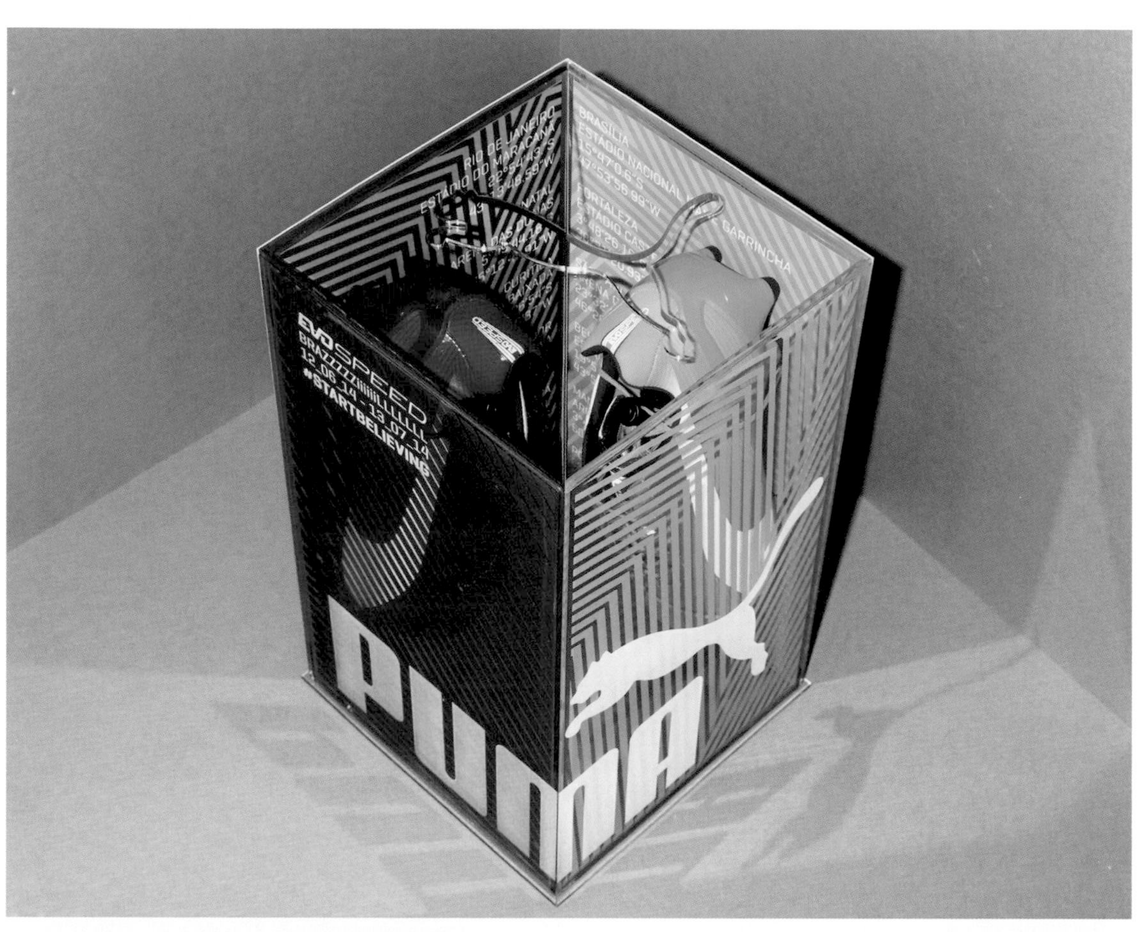
RIO DE JANEIRO
ESTÁDIO DO MARACANÃ
BRASÍLIA
ESTÁDIO NACIONAL
47°53'56.99"W
FORTALEZA
EVOSPEED
BRAZzzzziiiiiiLLLLLL
12_06_14 - 13_07_14
#STARTBELIEVING
PUMA

RIO DE JANEIRO
ESTÁDIO DO MARACANÃ
15°47'0.6"S
47°53'56.99"W
FORTALEZA
ESTÁDIO CASTELÃO
ARENA CORINTHIANS
EVOSPEED
BRAZzzzziiiiiiLLLLLL
12_06_14 - 13_07_14
#STARTBELIEVING

15°47'0.6"S
47°53'56.99"W
FORTALEZA
ESTÁDIO CASTELÃO
3°48'26.16"S
38°31'20.93"W
SÃO PAULO
ARENA CORINTHIANS
23°32'43.91"S
46°28'24.14"W
BELO HORIZONTE
ESTÁDIO MINEIRÃO
19°51'57"S
43°58'15"W
MANAUS
ARENA AMAZÔNIA
3°4'59"S
60°1'41"W
PORTO ALEGRE
ESTÁDIO BEIRA-RIO
30°3'56.21"S
51°14'9.91"W

35°12'49.91"W
CURITIBA
ARENA DA BAIXADA
25°26'54"S
49°16'37"W
SALVADOR
ARENA FONTE NOVA
12°58'43"S
38°30'15"W
CUIABÁ
ARENA PANTANAL
15°36'11"S
56°7'14"W

Redberry

Redberry is a shoe store looking to adopt the typical American footwear retailer and outlet store vibe. The idea of the store is to introduce the American concept of providing branded footwear at affordable prices for the general public. Design agency Anagrama's branding proposal took off from the store's name, Redberry. The agency designed an iconic logo based on the simplification of a raspberry's unique shape, while the typographic style and main single-color selection within the identity contribute to defining the brand as one with an industrial and modern style. A friendly approach was applied to the packaging developed for the brand to provide customers with accessible footwear and a pleasant shopping experience.

Client
Redberry

Design Agency
Anagrama

Material
Cardboard

Size
300mm x 140mm x 180mm

Completion
2014

SHOES-
ON THE
GO
BY
REDBERRY

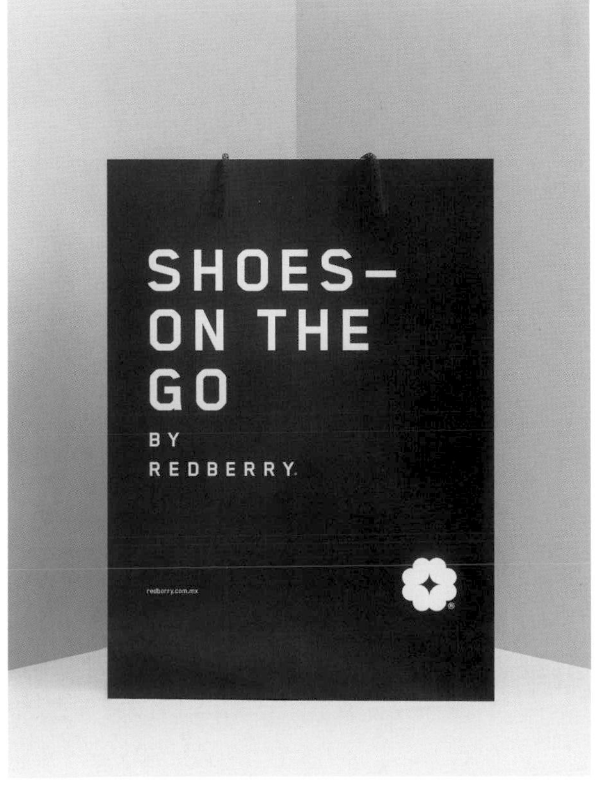
SHOES-
ON THE
GO
BY
REDBERRY

adidas Messi Icon Packaging

The brief was to improve the design and engineering of the adidas Messi Icon packaging. The new concept is based on "Gambeta," which is the term used in football to define the way Messi dribbles against his opponents in perfect zigzag movements. A zigzag line features on the outside of the box, created by two openings on the top of the box: a full-size lid and a smaller lid with two flaps that slot into the larger lid, thereby closing the box.

The new construction makes the shoe box cleaner and very sleek. Joints and folds have been designed to avoid any hinges or unnecessary parts that were visible on the previous designs. Overall, the concept aligns perfectly with Leo Messi's way of playing, and the graphics are inspired by the boots' external construction.

Client
adidasAG

Design Agencies
Markmus Design, adidas AG, AMJ Studios

Collaborators
Marcos Aretio (Design), Joe Stothard (Graphics), Herbert Bartl (Development), Daniel Felke (Project Management)

Material
Cardboard

Size
280mm x 190mm

Completion
2015

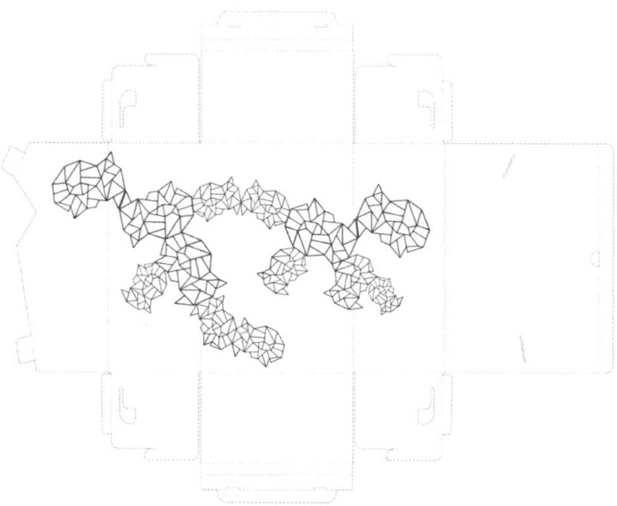

"NO HE GANADO NADA, HASTA QUE HAYA GANADO TODO"
"I'VE WON NOTHING UNTIL I'VE WON EVERYTHING"

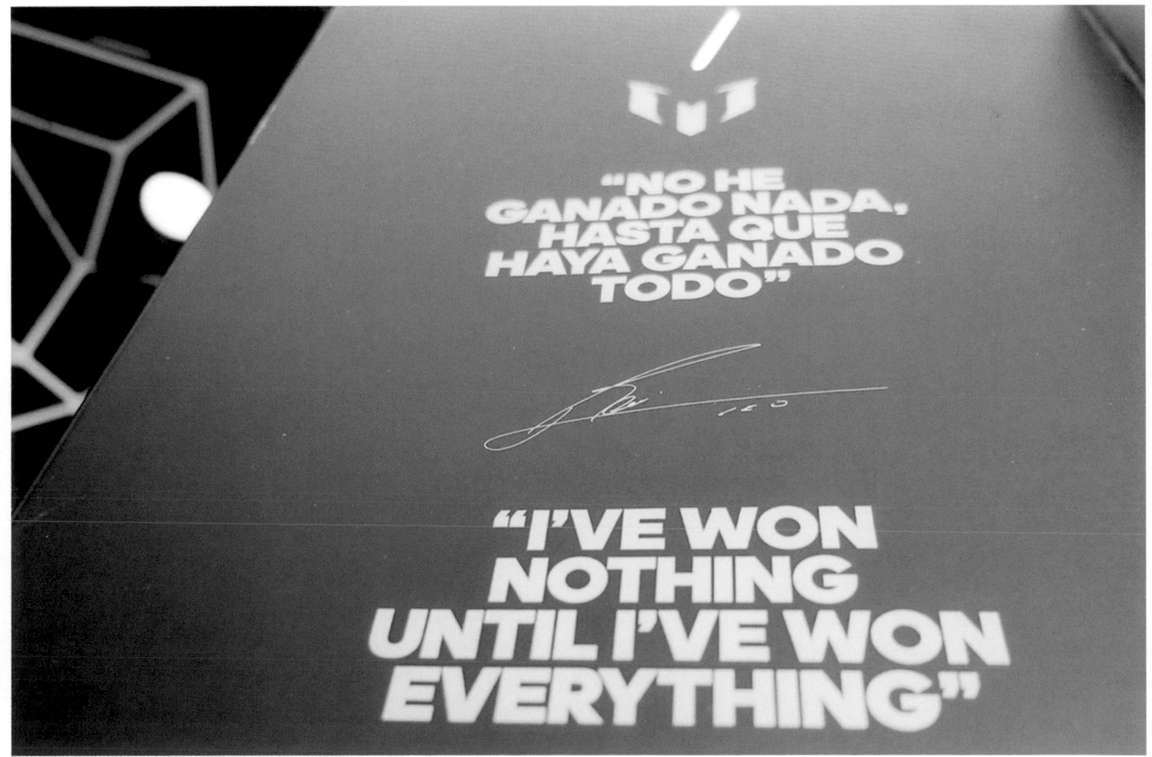
"NO HE GANADO NADA, HASTA QUE HAYA GANADO TODO"
"I'VE WON NOTHING UNTIL I'VE WON EVERYTHING"

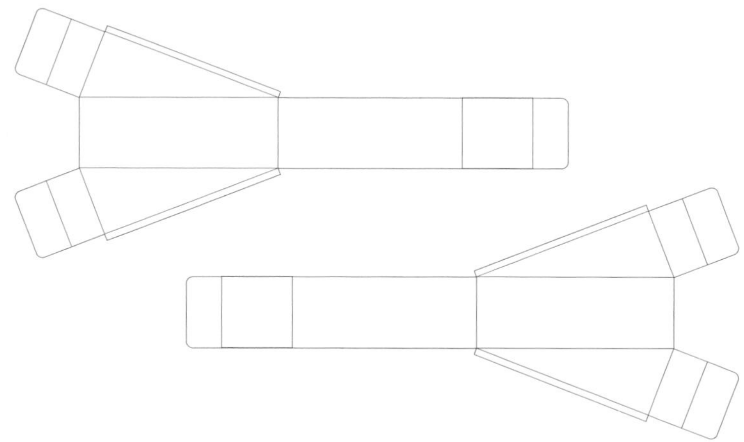

Sneaker Packaging Design

This sneaker packaging design aims to make people feel more comfortable when they're carrying sport footwear in their bag. The packaging has two parts: "banana peel" describes the outer layer, which is made of sturdy cardboard for easy transportation of the shoes. The second part, made of flexible rubber, is called "orange slices"; it divides the shoes into two triangular packages, so that users can easily change the box shape to fit the space in their bag. Unlike other shoes packages, this one will not just be kept in stores or at home; it's also very convenient to take it places. Another advantage is that it protects clothes from the bad odor of shoes after they've been worn to play sport.

Designer
Migle Sciglinskaite

Material
Cardboard, rubber

Size
300mm x 120mm x 120mm

Completion
2014

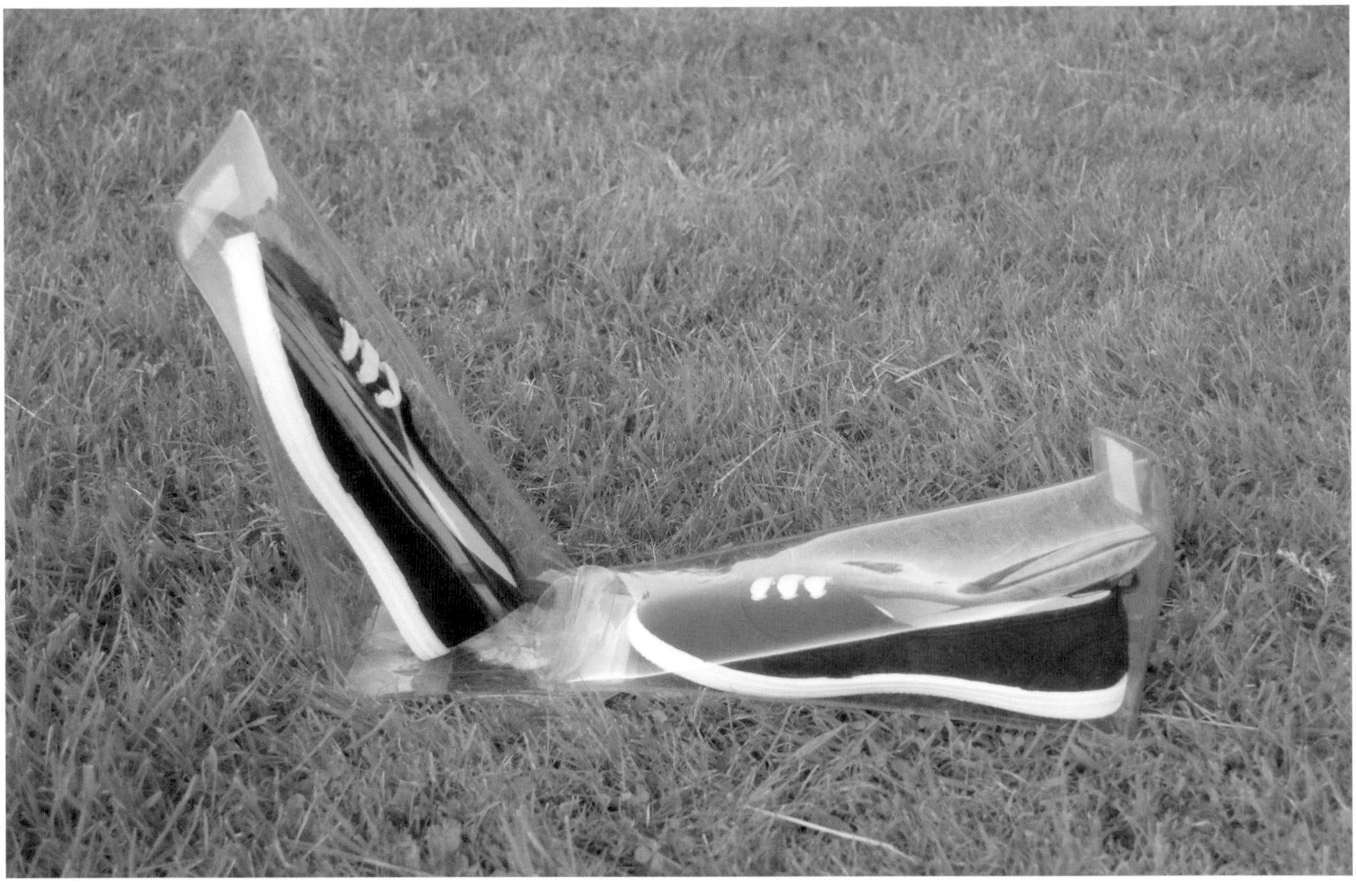

SPORTINIAI BATELIAI
8
UK 7
555301 060

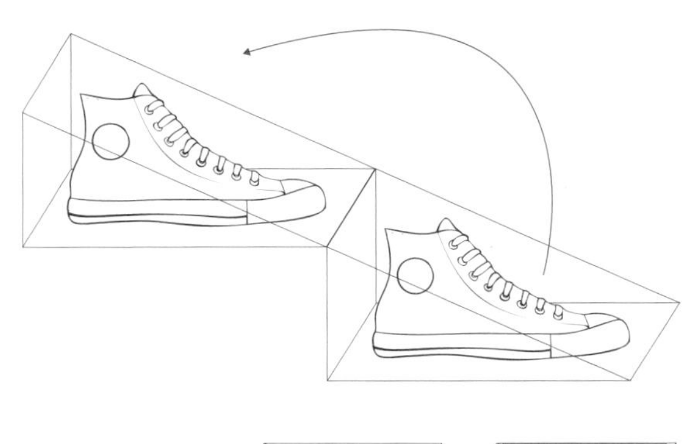

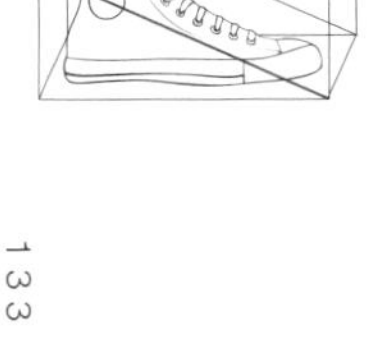

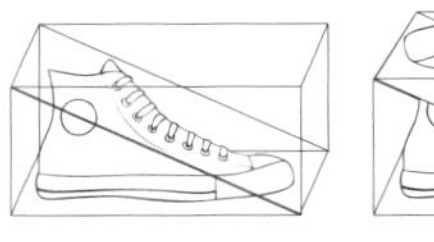

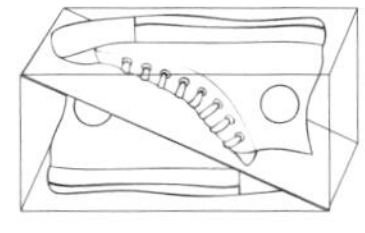

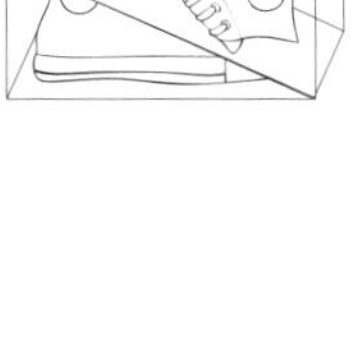

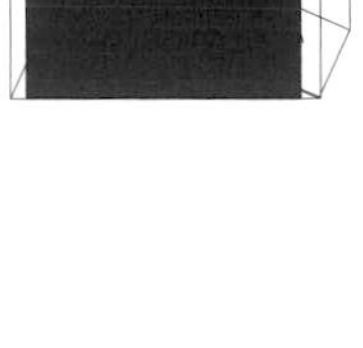

Merrell Shoe Box Package Design

The use of contrasting warm colors—orange and brown—and diagonals on this shoe box is a nod to mountainous slopes, the outdoors, and the adventurous spirit of the Merrell brand. Designed to be a triangular flip-top box, this packaging stands out against the standard horizontal/vertical haptic motion of other shoe boxes.

Client
Merrell

Designer
Shaily Shah

Material
Textured paper

Size
305mm x 159mm x 152mm

Completion
2014

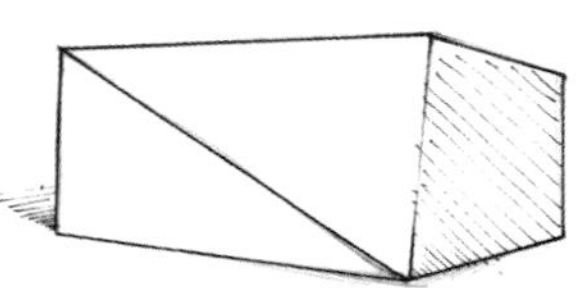

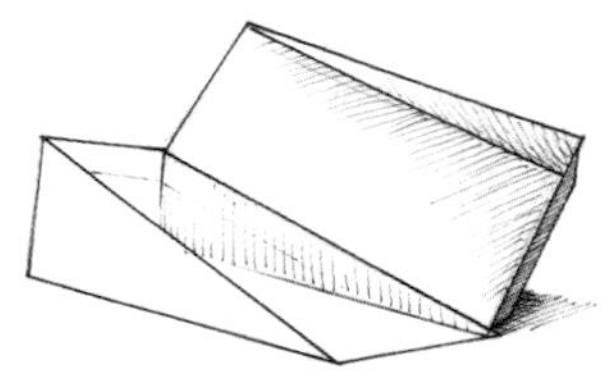

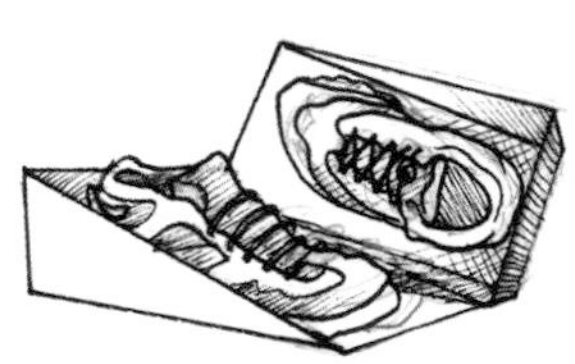

MERRELL
WILDERNESS: THE ORIGINAL
S M L XL
Thank you for shopping!
www.merrell.com

MERRELL

Project ReBoot—Barrick

The Barrick encompasses the most significant functions and styling details derived from the luxurious driver's shoe and the utilitarian cowboy boot. The result is a semiformal, suede leather, outdoor shoe with a full-calf enclosure.

With a cohering urban-cowboy style, the robust shoe bag is made with durable cotton canvas and matching suede leather straps. Polished steel buckles, D-rings, and rivets ensure a stylish and rough look, offering a range of capabilities combined with durability. The multipurpose bag wraps around itself and has no compartments, allowing customers to use the bag as they desire. Beyond carrying shoes, the bag can feature as a small travel bag for accessories, snap to a bike when on the go or have a strap attached to it to become a functional day-to-day satchel.

Client
Adventure Sports

Designer
Diderik Severin Astrup Westby

Material
15oz cotton canvas, 4oz suede leather, polished steel hardware

Size
690mm x 480mm

Completion
2015

Technical Drawings. Barrick Shoebag.

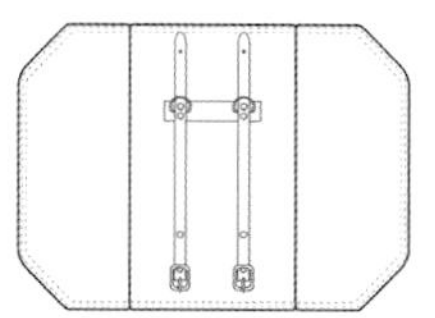

Exterior & Hardware 1/8 Scale

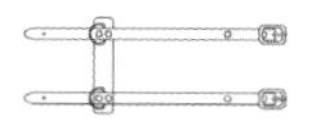

Interior 1/4 Scale

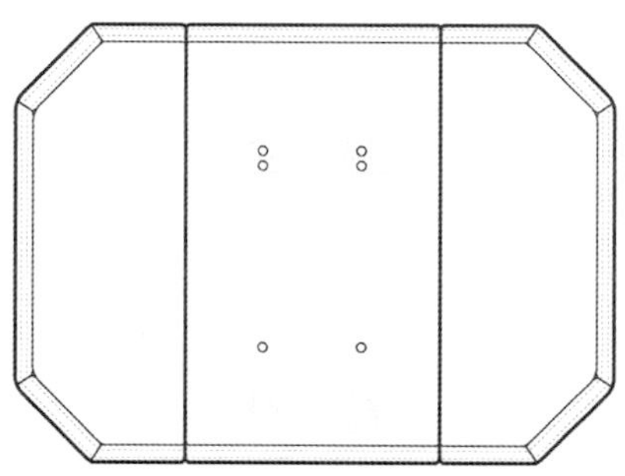

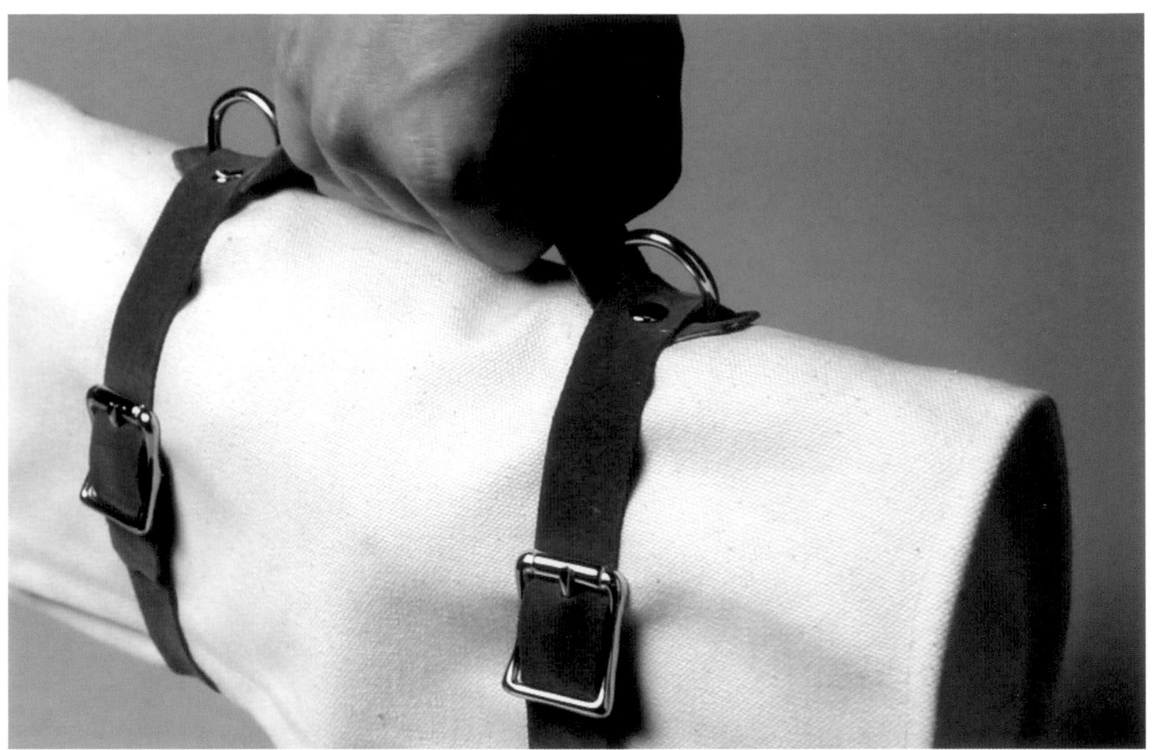

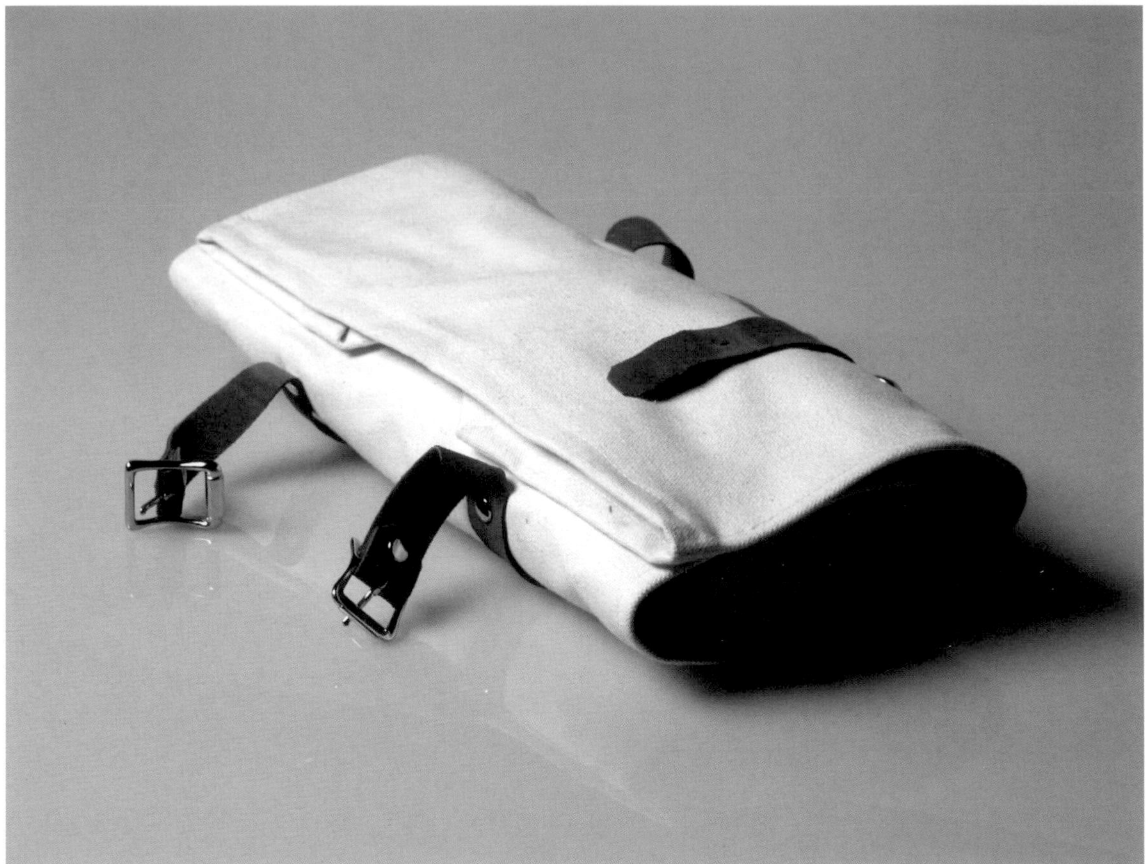

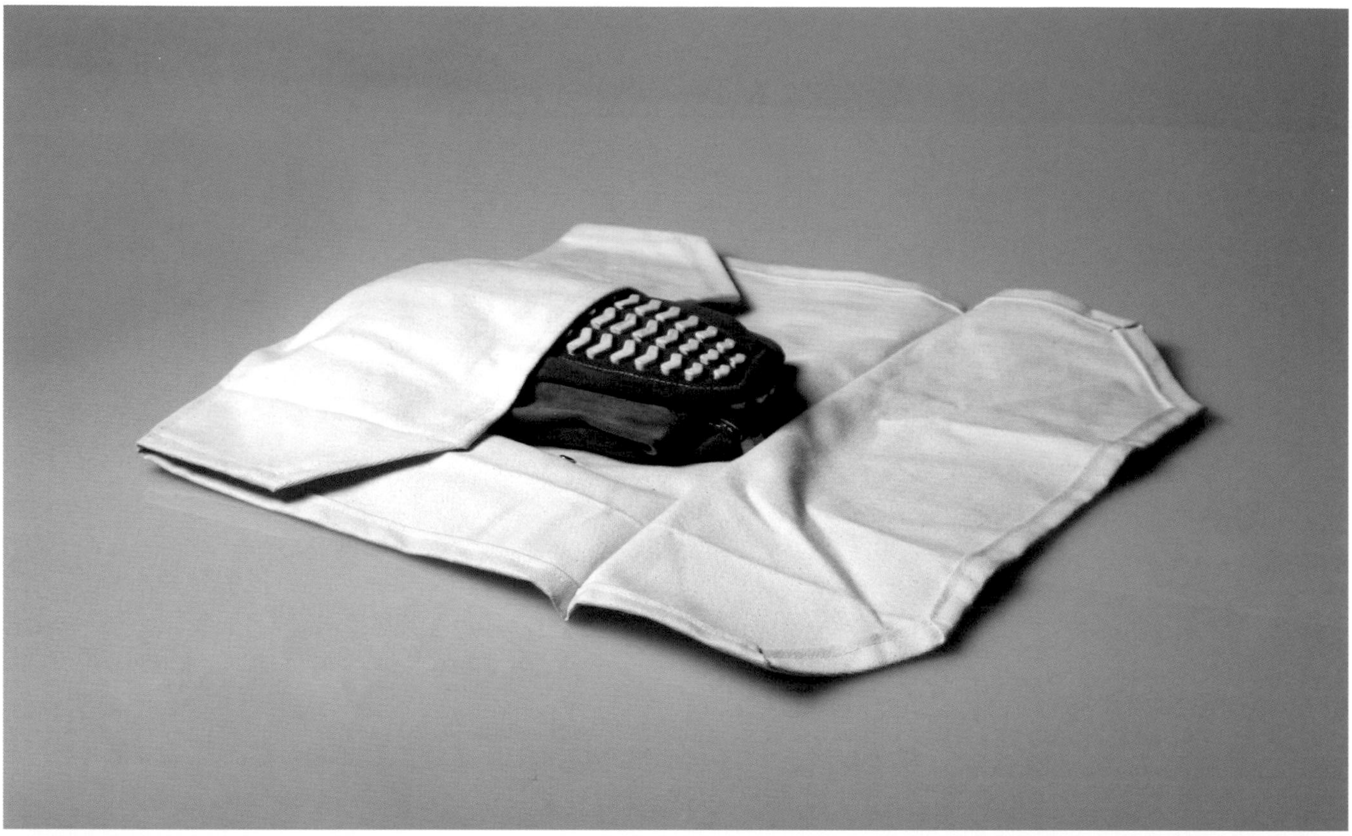

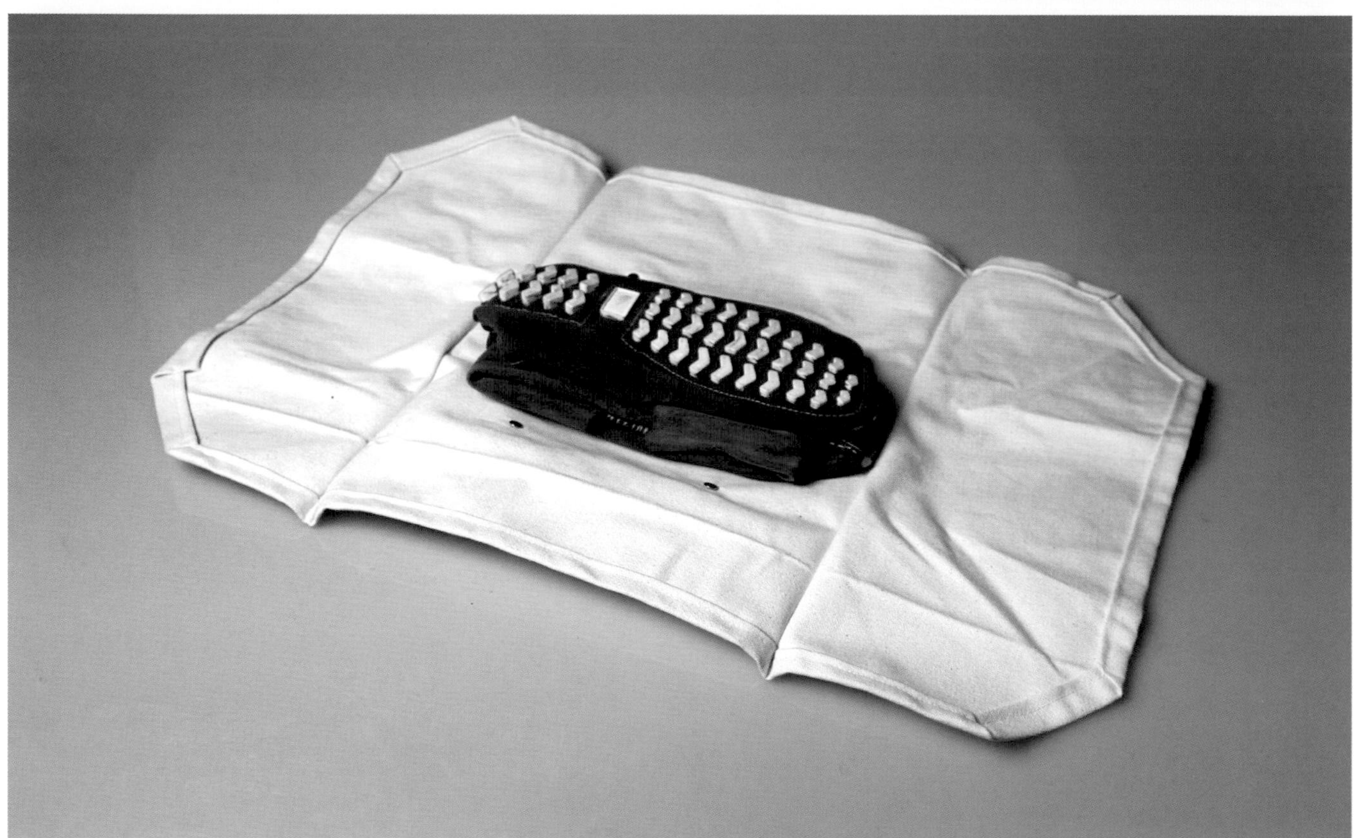

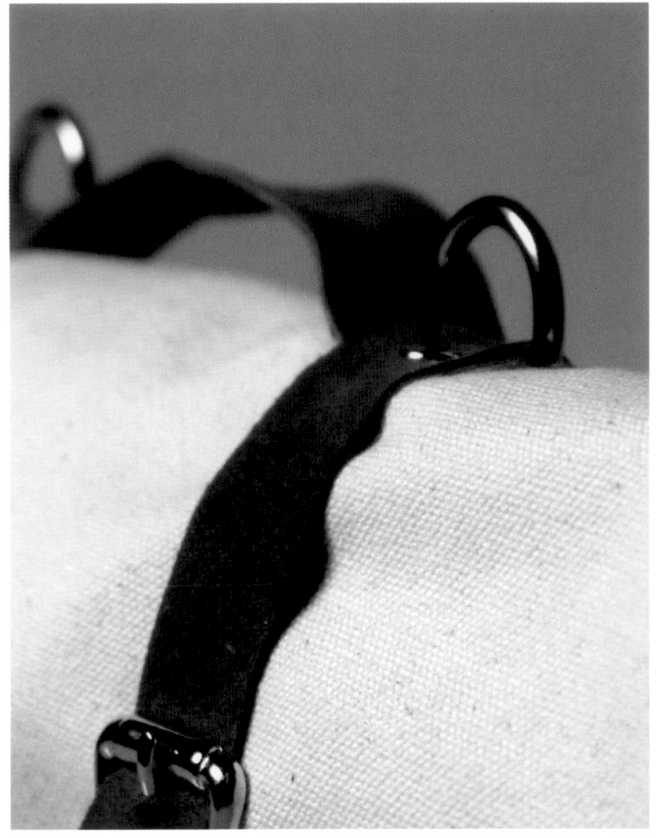

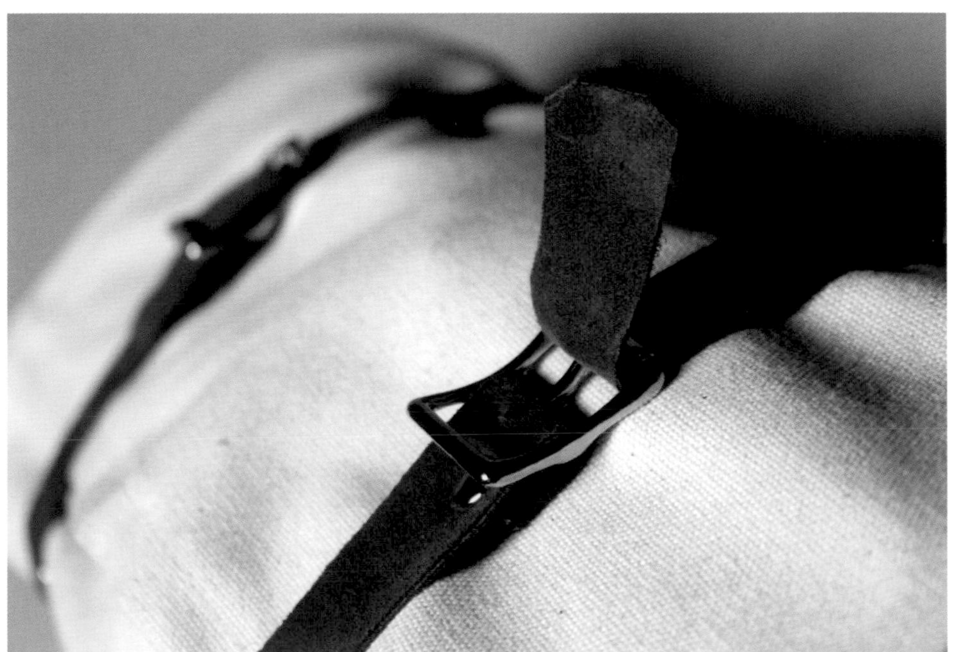

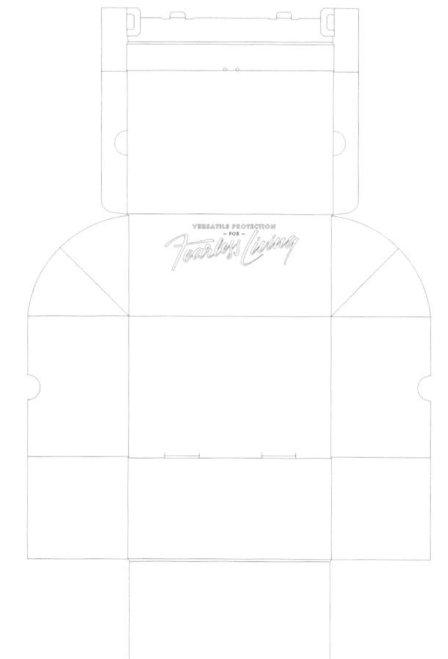

Nike x SNS—Fearless Living

The idea with the Fearless Living project was the creation of a sneaker that can handle rain, snow and hiking in countries with more harsh environments. A sneaker cleaning kit (brush, cloth, and spray) was included with the shoes to enable customers to take care of them so they'd last longer. The package designer wanted to make a versatile product that could also be used as a display in stores or at home. He needed some kind of holder for the accessories so that they wouldn't just be loose in the box, so he developed a way to incorporate the holder inside the actual cardboard box and came up with the idea of making a fold-out shelf that could hold the sneakers as well as the included kit.

Client
Sneakersnstuff, Nike

Designer
Mattias Lundin

Material
Cardboard

Size
160mm x 230mm x 330mm

Completion
2015

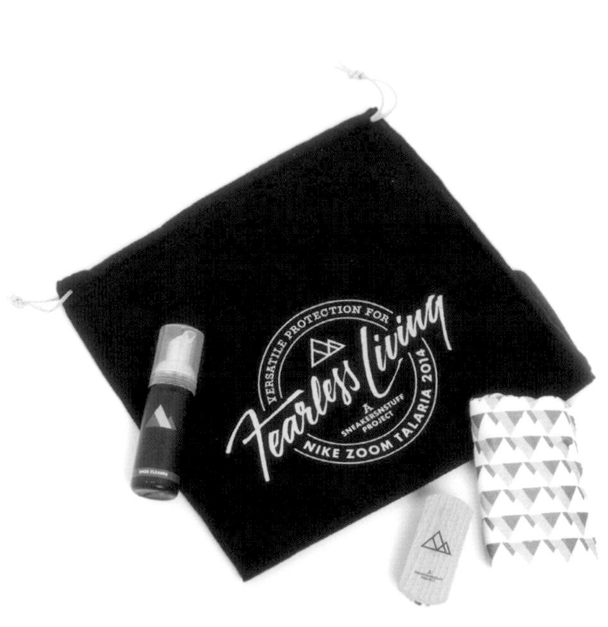
VERSATILE PROTECTION FOR
Fearless Living
A SNEAKERSNSTUFF PROJECT
NIKE ZOOM TALARIA 2014

VERSATILE PROTECTION
– FOR –
Fearless Living

VERSATILE PROTECTION
– FOR –

INSTRUCTIONS

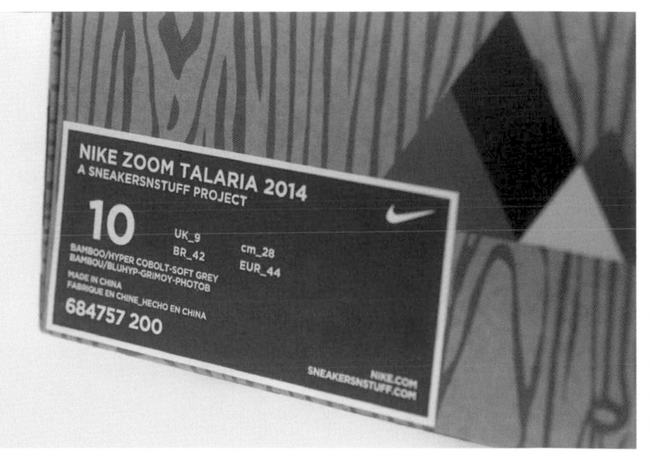
NIKE ZOOM TALARIA 2014
A SNEAKERSNSTUFF PROJECT
10
UK_9
BR_42
cm_28
EUR_44
684757 200
NIKE.COM
SNEAKERSNSTUFF.COM

Color Texture Sport

Color Texture Sport is exclusive packaging created for the spring/summer 2015 seasons of Spanish brand Gioseppo's new colorful sneakers. The main idea for the graphic design and packaging was to convey the explosion of textures and vibrant colors inherent in the sneakers—there were nine different types in all—while keeping the sport shoes fashionable. The packaging is an automatable box that opens up completely so that the buyer has a full, colorful view of the shoes. Not only that, the opened box also reveals the other sneakers in the series.

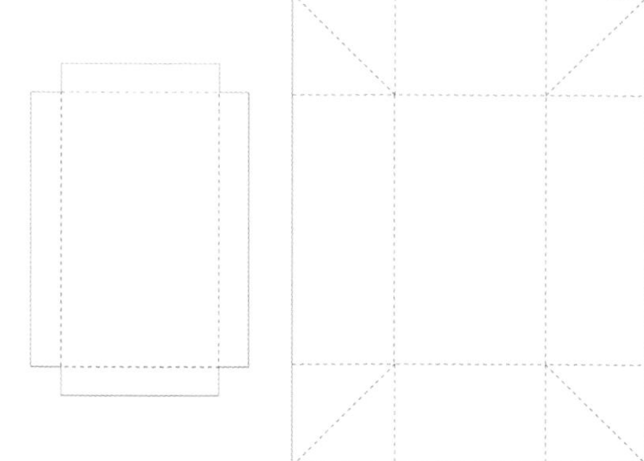

Client
Gioseppo

Designer
Fran Berbegal

Material
Recycled carton box

Size
295mm x 185mm

Completion
2015

Feel the City

The Nike Hyperfeel shoe is designed to move like the human foot, and it provides a minimal layer between the runner and the ground, allowing the runner to "feel" even more while they run. The packaging design features a skateboard grip tape as the outer layer to convey the different textures the shoe allows you to feel. Each pack was individually personalized with the recipient's name. It also included a bespoke map of a city, which highlighted varying terrains to try out the Hyperfeel shoe.

Client
Nike

Design Agency
Marilyn & Sons

Material
Griptape, cardboard

Size
340mm x 130mm x 130mm

Completion
2013

Underwear & Socks Packaging

The Wonderful Socks Packaging

The Wonderful Socks black box is a simple piece of packaging suitable for socks and caps. The design mission was to create a smart package capable of catching customers' eyes and strengthening the company's market position. This is a package that's made to travel around the world. Its peculiar triangular shape and dimensions were wisely conceived for all sorts of shipping, as it's easy to stack a multitude of these boxes in a small space. Assembled from a sheet of thick black paper, the box was made without using any paperclips or glue. A white silk-screen printing highlights the logo.

Client	Material
The Wonderful Socks	Paperboard
Design Agency	Size
ZUP Design	620mm x 270mm
Designer	Completion
Andrea Medri	2015

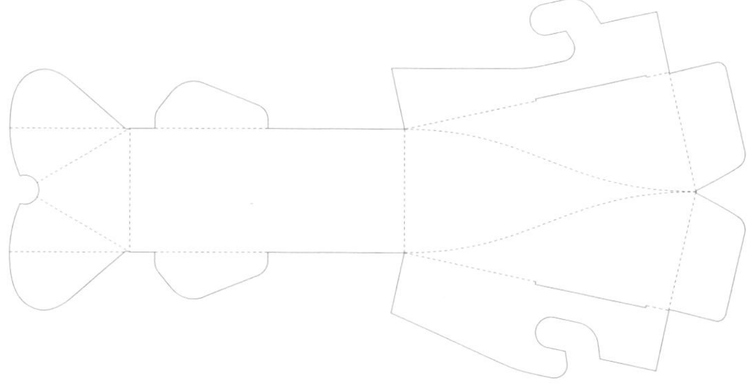

THEWONDERFULSOCKS

SOC Tokyo

SOC is a Japanese brand of socks whose slogan is "An inspiration born from your foot." This packaging has been designed to contain socks of all sizes and to display the different styles. It was created according to the art of traditional Japanese folding, so that it may be opened without destroying the packaging. The form is compact and uses a minimum of paper, is reusable after purchase, is inexpensive to produce, but is still attractive: much like the values of the SOC brand itself.

Client	Size
Old Fashioned Co., Ltd	180mm x 350mm
Designer	**Completion**
Keiko Akatsuka	2014
Material	
White paper	

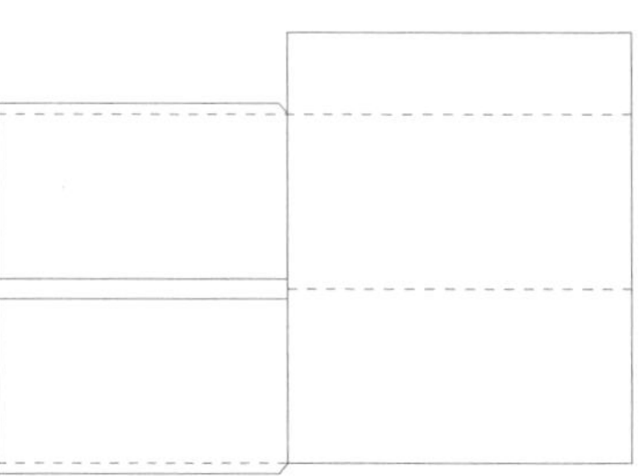

SOC
TOKYO
SOC
SOC TOKYO

SOC
TOKYO
S O C

Chocolate Socks Package

This project was a special "love edition" for Valentine's Day for South Korean sock company Sockstaz. Designer Eun Woo Kim took inspiration from vintage chocolate packaging, and produced two versions of "milk chocolate" and "dark chocolate" socks. Each package contains two pairs of different-colored socks that have a chocolate scent—achieved using a kind of new nanotechnology—which, unsurprisingly, resulted in increased sales. The inner silver packaging is made using embossing technology, and demonstrates a sense of quality. This packaging is especially loved by female customers.

Client
Sockstaz

Size
275mm x 120mm

Designer
Eun Woo Kim

Completion
2013

Material
Aluminum, paperboard

Dark
CHOCOLATE
FLAVOURED
SOCKS
WITH
Delicious
COCOA
ORIGINAL RECIPE FROM SOCKSTAZ
CHOCOLATE SOCKS

SOCKS
WITH
Delicious
COCOA
ORIGINAL RECIPE FROM SOCKSTAZ

Sockstaz Clutch-Bag-Style Packaging

The new packaging for sock company Sockstaz was produced in 2013. Designer Eun Woo Kim was inspired by the clutch bag, a popular fashion item, replacing paper as the material for the packaging with plastic paper. Her original illustrations are printed on the packaging, which comes in two sizes; the special shape and lovely illustrations garnered plenty of attention in the sock industry and helped increase sales. A rubber band is used as a fixed device, and the dyeing process used on the packaging contributes to a more complete and elegant overall design. Customers who pay attention to design love this packaging.

Client
Sockstaz

Designer
Eun Woo Kim

Material
Plastic paper

Size
300mm x 150mm

Completion
2013

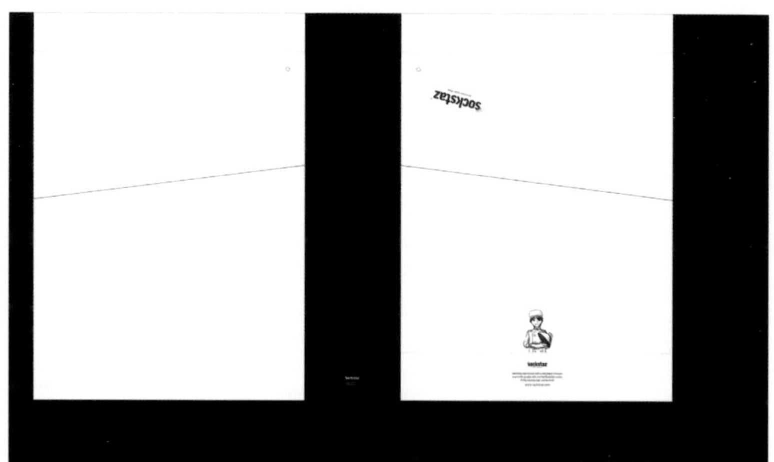

sockstaz

Undergarment—Basic Body Stuff

All kinds of undergarments can fit into a small box, but everything usually gets messed up. The idea for this project was to create a package for underwear that customers could not only carry the product in, but that they'd also want to use to organize and color-code their garments at home.

The design process of the box was quite interesting. The shape needed to be modular in order for it to be stacked in stores and at home, in drawers or on shelves, so designer Martina Ferreira decided on the triangle as the most efficient shape for the Undergarment packaging. But it also needed to connect with the consumer at the point of purchase. The designer learned that people generally like to feel the fabric of what they are purchasing when it comes to clothing; this is especially true of undergarments as they are directly related to personal comfort. This knowledge brought about the lid design for this packaging: it's frosted and transparent to show the product color, and it features a cutout that allows users to feel the garment without over-handling it.

Designer	Size
Martina Ferreira	80mm x 100mm
Material	**Completion**
Plastic	2014

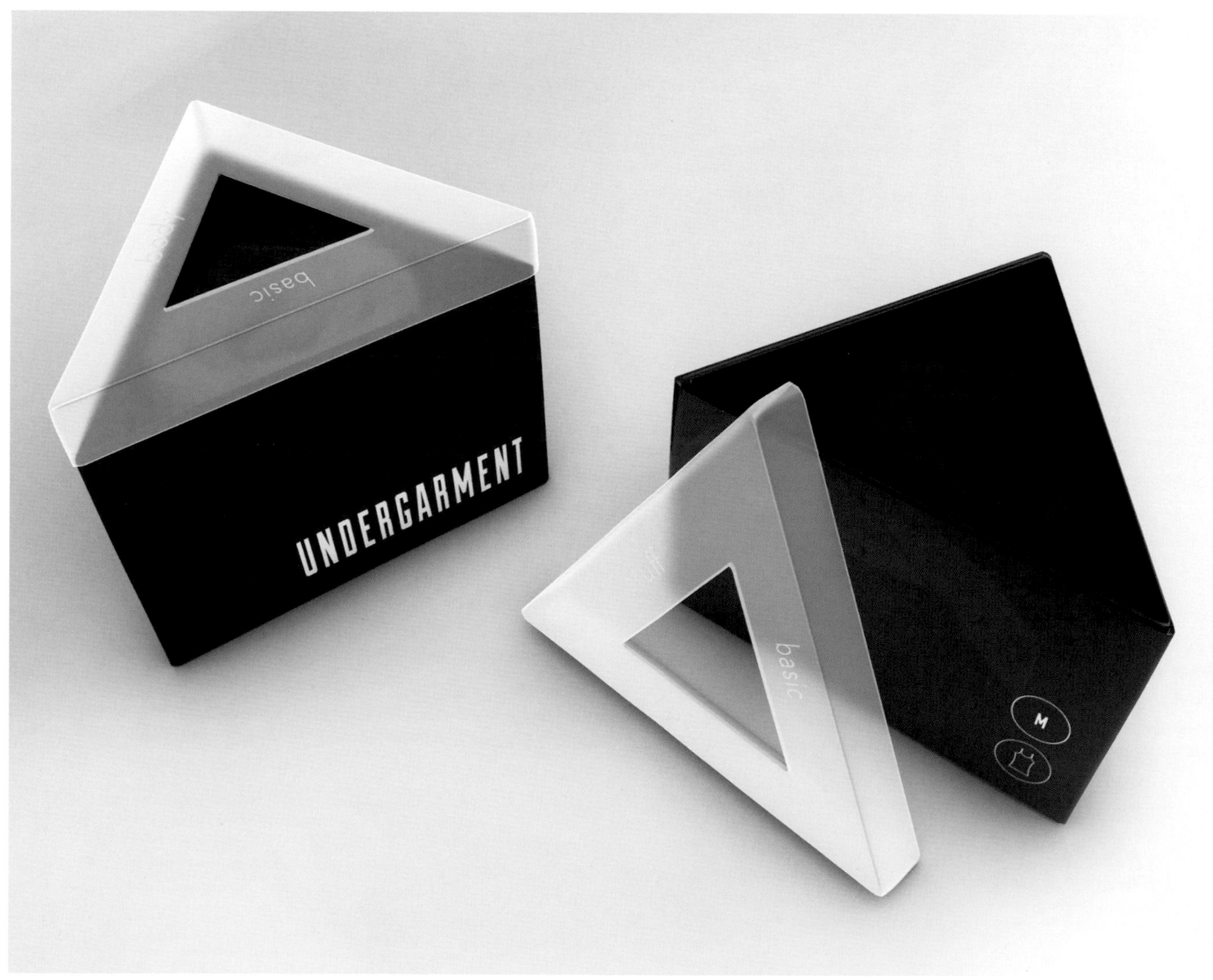

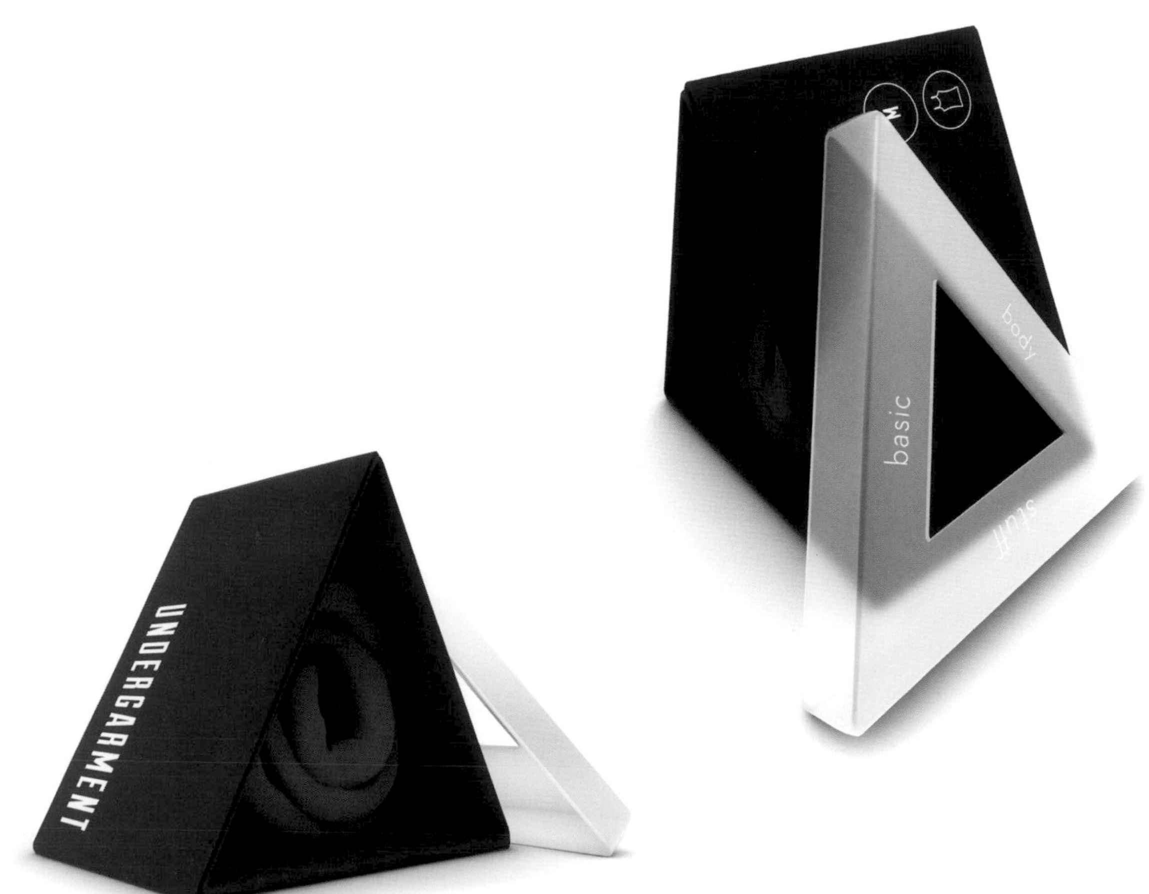
UNDERGARMENT
basic
body
stuff

Oops Panties

As some magazines state, a woman's character might be defined according to the underwear she prefers. This was the thinking of the designers behind Oops Panties, a range of underpants inspired by tattoos, humor and iconic images of Marilyn Monroe. The packaging for the underwear looks like a skirt, and a band with a button holds the packaging together. Different colors were used on the packaging to differentiate the products in the range, which include "Smart Pants," "Fancy Pants," and "Bossy Pants." These slogans are also printed on the actual underpants in a tattoo design, adding another layer of fun and creativity to the product.

Designers
Galya Akhmetzyanova, Pavla Chuykina

Material
Fabric, plastic

Size
62mm x 150mm

Completion
2014

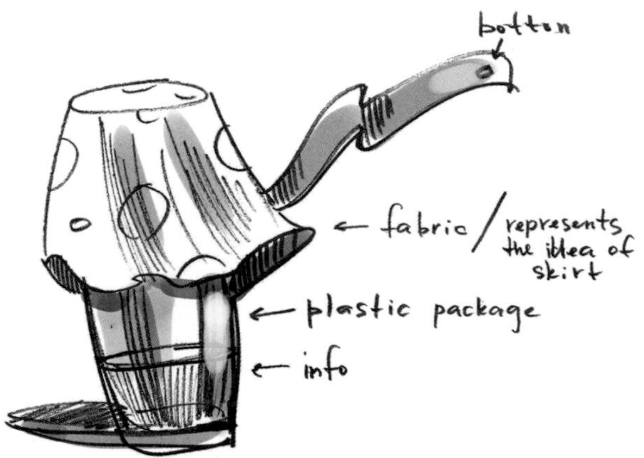

TOP
FABRIC
PLASTIC PACKAGING
BOTTOM

FANCY PANTS
HIGH•QUALITY
COTTON PANTIES
with unique
TATTOO PRINTS
ON THE BACK

WASHING IN WARM WATER
TEMPERATURE NOT OVER 40°C
HIPS
INNER
90 94 98 102
XS S M L

PRODUCT COURTESY
FOR
BOSSY
LADIES
ELASTHAN • 5%
HIGH•QUALITY
COTTON PANTIES
with unique
TATTOO PRINTS
ON THE BACK

Underwearables Packaging

The Underwearables packaging is a reflection of a brand with deep roots in the Scandinavian design traditions of simplicity and quality. Underwearables is based in Copenhagen, a city characterized by neoclassical architecture and iconic design, and these qualities were important to incorporate into the packaging design. The aim was to develop an identity with a contemporary look based on classic refinement and a style that lasts beyond seasons. Combining a monochromatic color scale of black, white, and nudes with classical typography, the Underwearables packaging expresses a brand universe of "poetic minimalism," which evokes a feeling of simplicity and sophistication and speaks in a poetic voice to a global audience of lifestyle consumers.

Client
Underwearables

Design Agency
Spread Studio

Material
Paperboard

Size
160mm x 250mm

Completion
2014

the tank
underwearables
underwearables
WITH COMPLIMENTS FROM
UNDERWEARABLES.COM
UNDERWEARABLES
TO

FRIDAY
IT'S
FRIDAY
DINNERS
DANCES
SATURDAY
SATURDAY
NIGHT FEVER
LONG WALKS
SLOW TALKS
SUNDAY

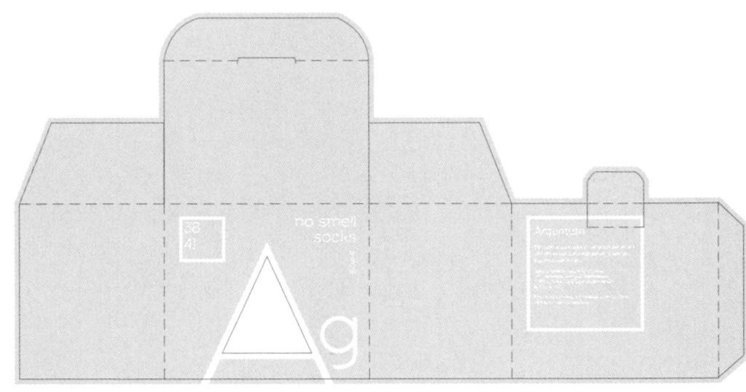

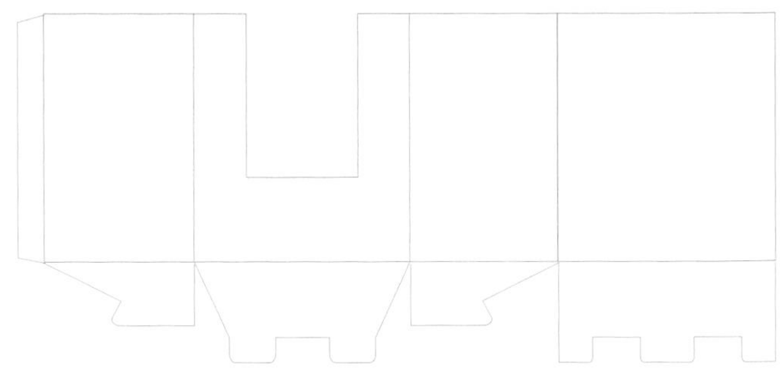

Argentum Socks

Art of Socks, a Russian sock shop, was looking for creative branding ideas for its new special line of socks, Argentum Socks. These contain an antibacterial silver yarn that, the company claims, prevents foot odor. Branding agency Svoe Mnenie built its design concept on a contradiction: the packaging, inspired by the periodic table, looks scientific, complete with the chemical name Ag, but it encourages shoppers to be silly and have fun by sniffing the "no-smell" socks through a special cutout. The designers proposed a bright gradient package for the initial "gray" line of socks to make them look more creative and fit the company's style. The line of silver socks turned out to be so successful that the company launched multicolored socks with patterns in a reserved black package soon in addition to the "gray" line.

Client
Art of Socks Ltd.

Design Agency
Svoe Mnenie

Collaborators
Andrey Kugaevskikh (Creative Director), Maria Solyankina (Designer)

Material
Cardboard

Size
100mm x 110mm x 70mm

Completion
2014

42
45
no smell
socks
silver
Ag

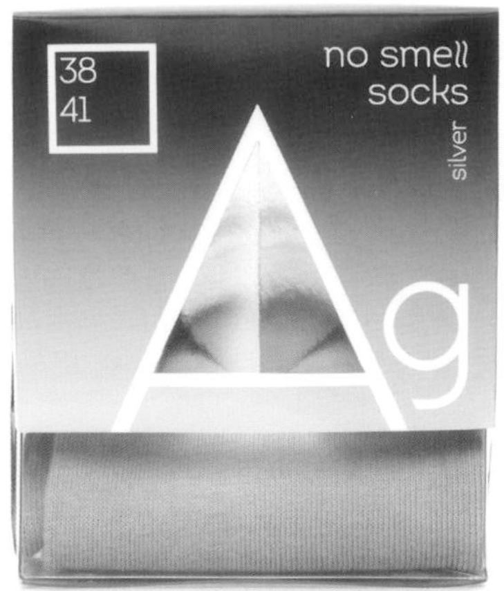
38
41
no smell
socks
silver
Ag

42
45
no smell
socks
silver
Ag

38
41
no smell
socks
silver
Ag

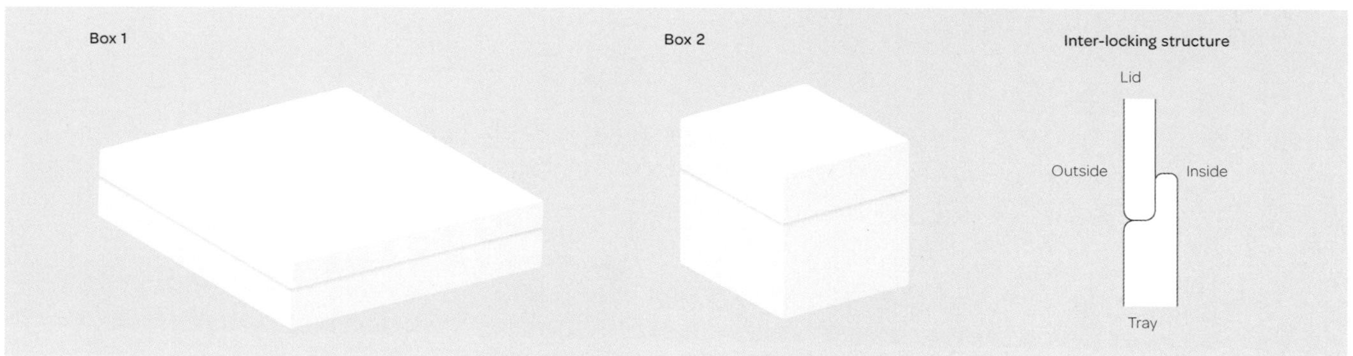

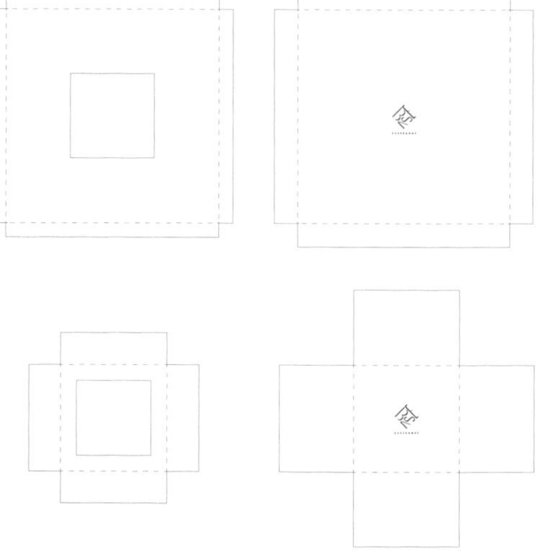

Baserange Boxes

Baserange is a womenswear brand based in Toulouse and Copenhagen. It designs both seasonal collections and a "basics" collection consisting of pieces that are constantly available. For this packaging, the designer wanted to apply a visual language that would be hard to date. The logo, featuring the fragmented letters from the word "BASE," borrows heavily from 1980s' Japanese logo designs, finding itself in the exciting twilight zone between ornament and function.

The aim with the stationery was to make it look like it had been created by a designer schooled in Bauhaus, incorporating the art of the modernist grid, but using an old typewriter as the only tool. Crafted but casual, even vernacular at times, is the combination the designer presents in Baserange's collections.

Client
Baserange

Designer
Michael Thorsby

Material
3D-embossed card and paper

Size
228mm x 228mm x 40mm;
114mm x 114mm x 144mm

Completion
2016

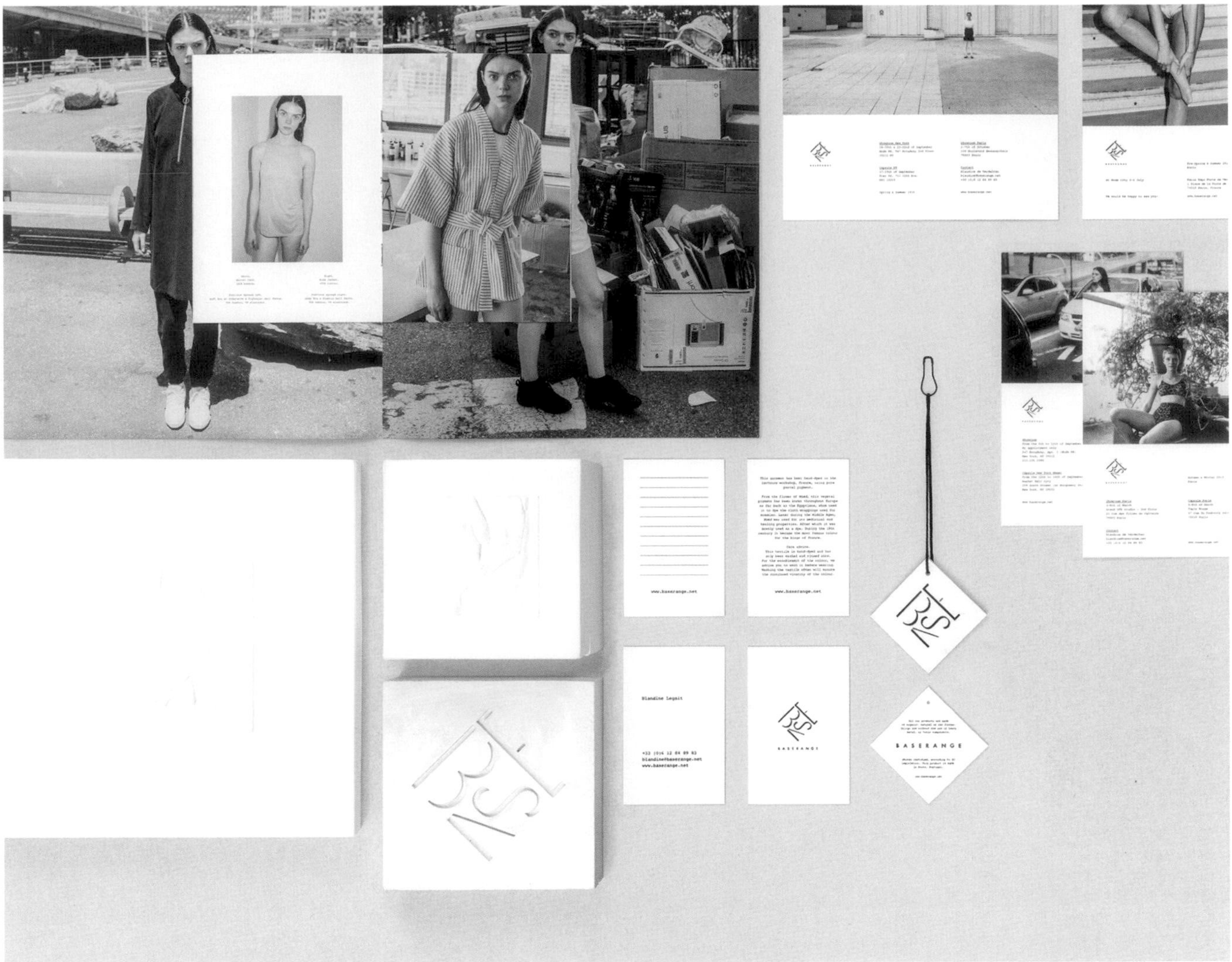

Mini 2 Mini

Mini 2 Mini is a fictional aid organization that sells baby products in developed European countries, and its profits go toward helping children in developing African countries. High-quality products designed with care is the focus of the brand.

The packaging is neutral and simple so as to be appealing to many different people. The bright yellow color symbolizes the good things the organization does, and it's also gender neutral and therefore useful for this kind of product. Both the illustrations on the outside and the pattern on the inside of the packaging are created using the number 2, written in different styles. This is a way of using the brand name, Mini 2 Mini, and it also symbolizes that many children can be helped thanks to Mini 2 Mini's products.

Designer
Sara Petersson

Material
255gsm Billerud Korsnäs white cardboard, yellow tissue paper

Size
110mm x 110mm x 25mm

Completion
2014

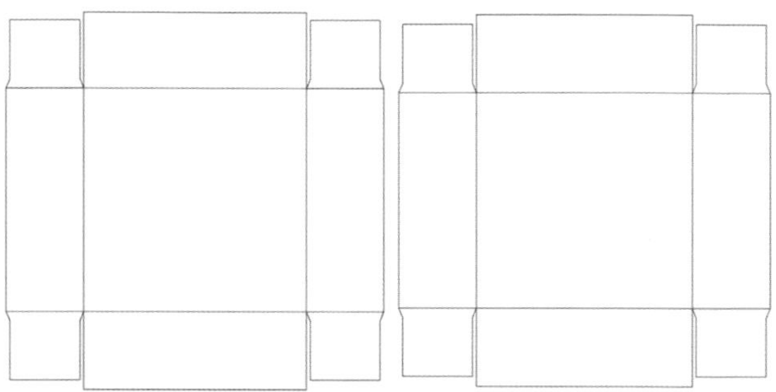

The products were bought from the Swedish stores Polarn O. Pyret and BR Leksaker.

B.shi Branding

B.shi is a Mexican brand of men's underwear, which draws inspiration from the Seri tribe located in the state of Sonora, Mexico. The name is slang in that state and refers to being barely naked or naked. The graphic design was inspired by the decor and colors used for the ceremonies of the Seri tribe. On this occasion, the agency designed stationery, packaging, and the underwear elastic. The recyclable packaging is thin and suitable for shipping, and allows for the product to be partly seen without needing to be opened.

Client
B.shi

Size
200mm x 150mm

Design Agency
Nómada Design Studio

Completion
2013

Material
Kraft paper

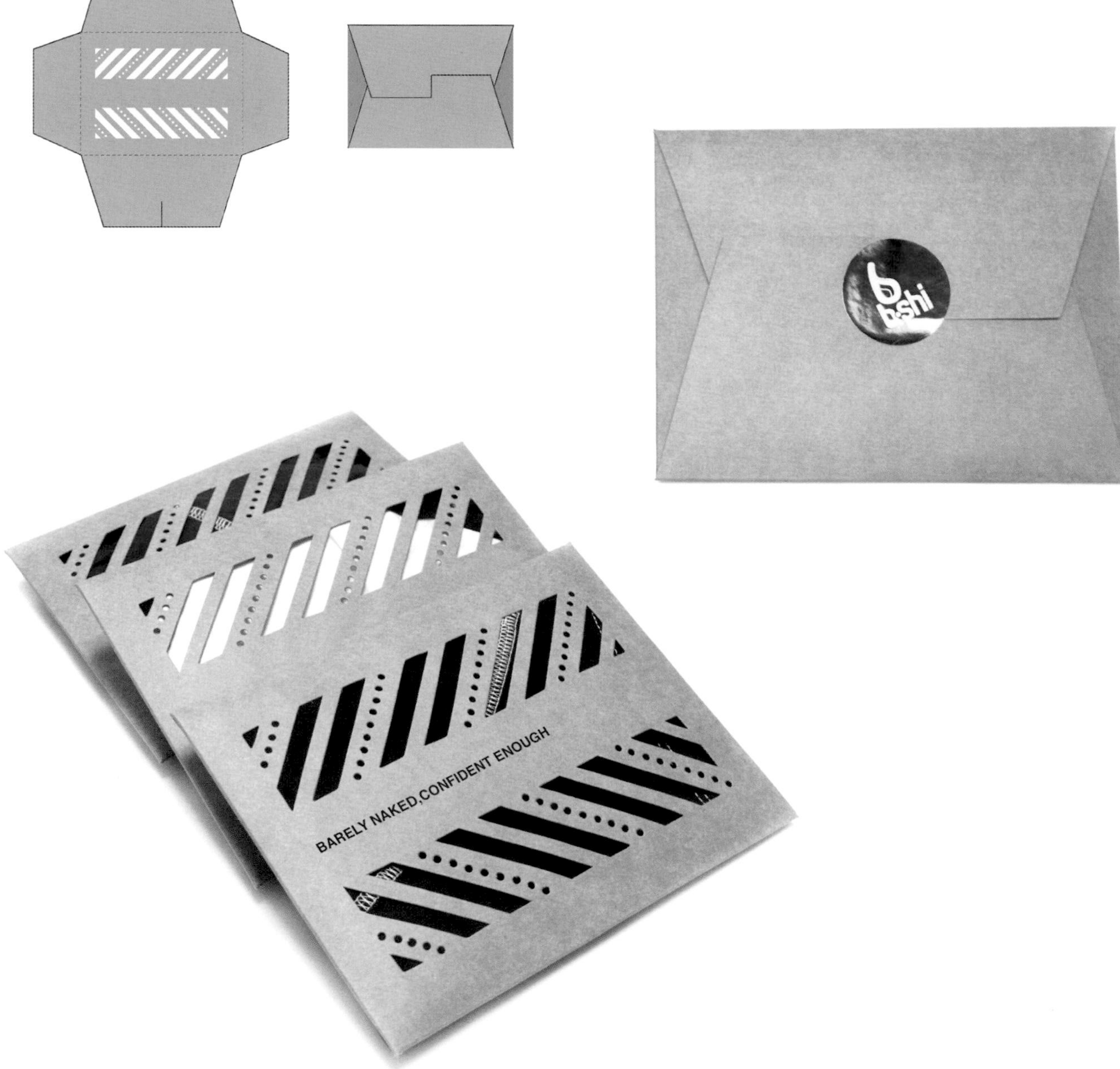

Nonprofit Promotional Package Design

This limited-edition swimsuit packaging promotes the Keep a Breast Foundation's Non Toxic Revolution initiative, which educates young people about cancer-causing chemicals. Inspired by the Keep a Breast logo, which incorporates two overlapping hearts, the designer created a 360-degree display alluding to the feminine figure that holds both pieces of the bikini. The pattern incorporates graphic elements found in the Non Toxic Revolution's campaign materials. This package stands like a tent and is meant to be displayed on a table where consumers can view it from all sides. Information about the initiative is on the front and a QR code peeks out on the back, leading to an interactive experience. The materials used are eco-friendly, recyclable and biodegradable, in line with the Non Toxic Revolution's concept and goals.

Designer
Jessie Michelle Smith-Walters

Material
Chipboard

Size
356mm x 406mm

Completion
2014

ABOUT Underwear Line Packaging

ABOUT is an innovative underwear brand from the Baltics created for everyone who sees beauty in function, and seeks comfort in cuts and materials. A "healthy Fit design" icon invites shoppers to discover the additional qualities of its products, which make a positive impact on people's skin. The clean graphics and hygienic image of the ABOUT underwear packaging embody the concept of the ABOUT product. This simple packaging solution creates a clear visual system for the brand. Product lines are divided by using different colors for the graphics of each collection's packaging. As a result, the whole concept looks very united and organized. As underwear touches skin directly, the designer chose light colors for the packaging in an effort to portray a soft and comfortable user experience.

Client	Material
ABOUT—Baltic Underwear	Laminated paper
Design Agency	**Size**
Ai-Du Branding Studio	150mm x 120mm x 60mm
Designer	**Completion**
Aidas Urbelis	2013

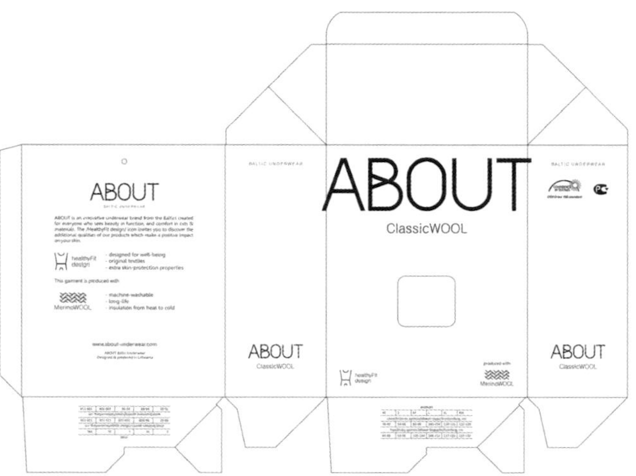

ABOUT
sense
woman
healthyFit
programme
SilkPROTEINS

ABOUT
/Trend/
woman
healthyFit
programme
AloeVERA

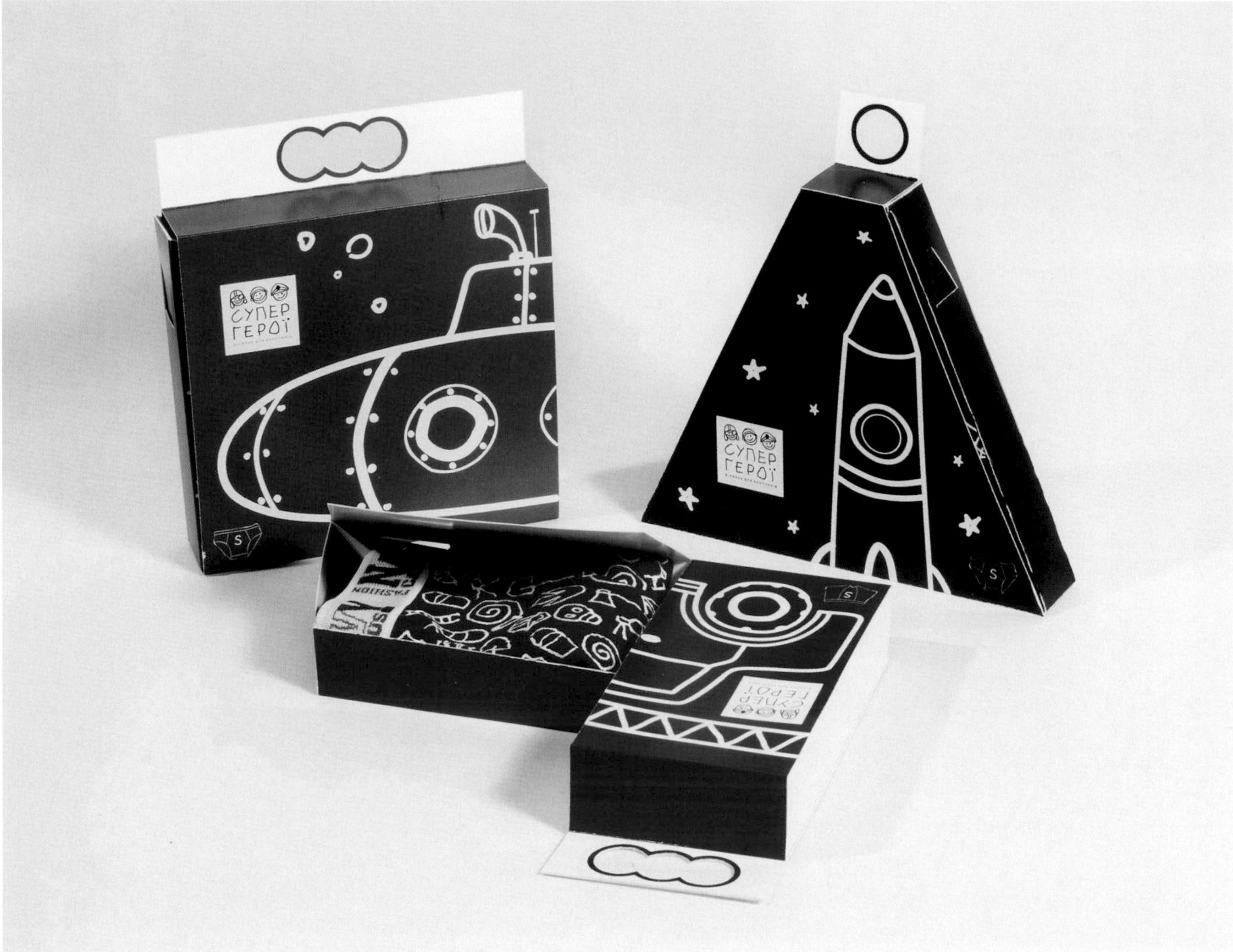

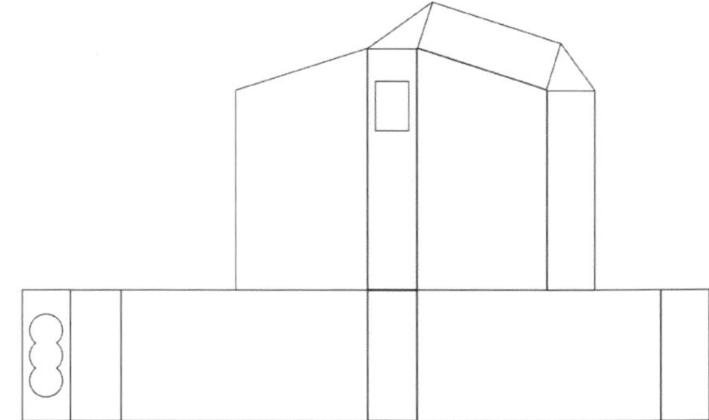

Superheroes

This packaging project for the "Superheroes" range of children's underwear consists of three different containers. Each one is made of cardboard, with additional sheets involved in the construction to form extra internal compartments, according to the number of products in each box. Graphics and the titles play up to most children's dreams of being an astronaut, a firefighter or a diver, and the illustrations look like children's drawings, each one corresponding to the theme of the package. Built into the design is a carrying handle and holes for easy opening.

Client
Children's Clothing Store

Designer
Alona Zdorova

Material
Paperboard

Size
150mm x 150mm;
180mm x 160mm;
150mm x 80mm

Completion
2013

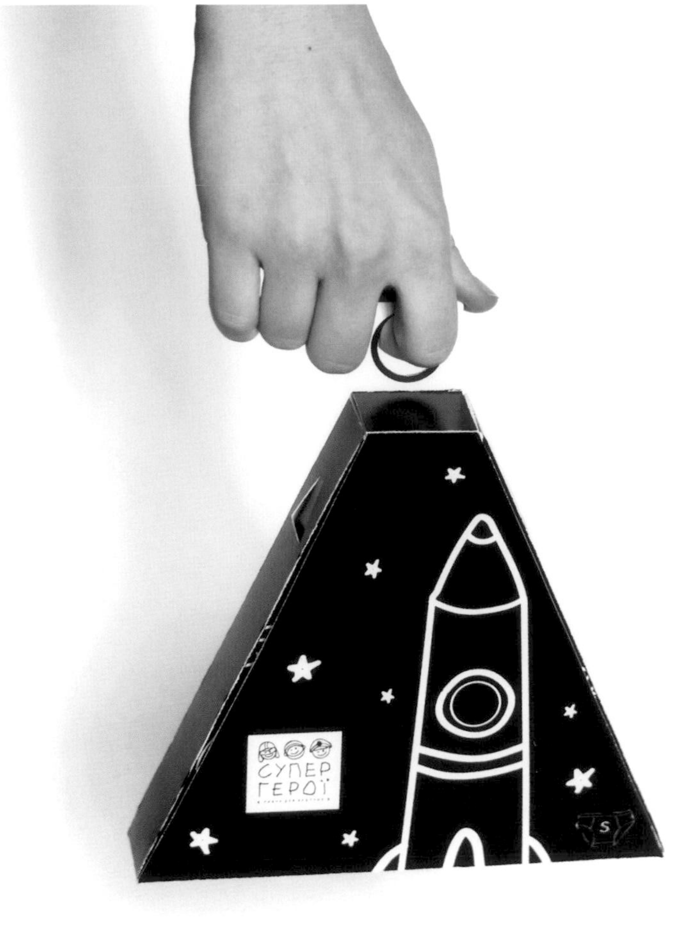
СУПЕР
ГЕРОЇ

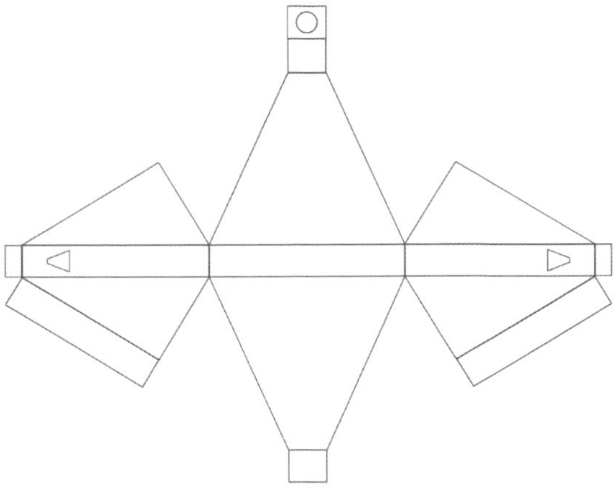

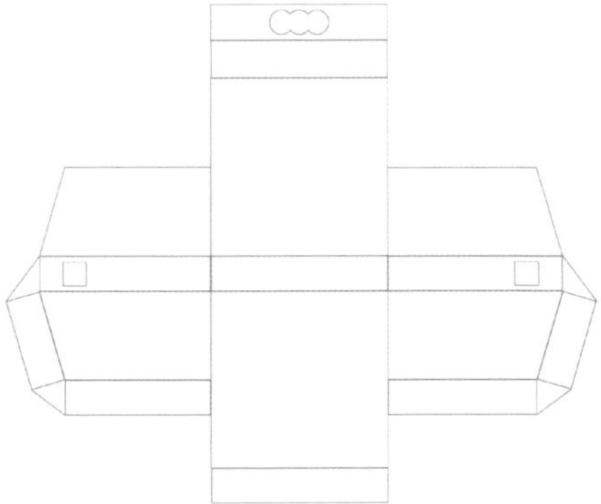

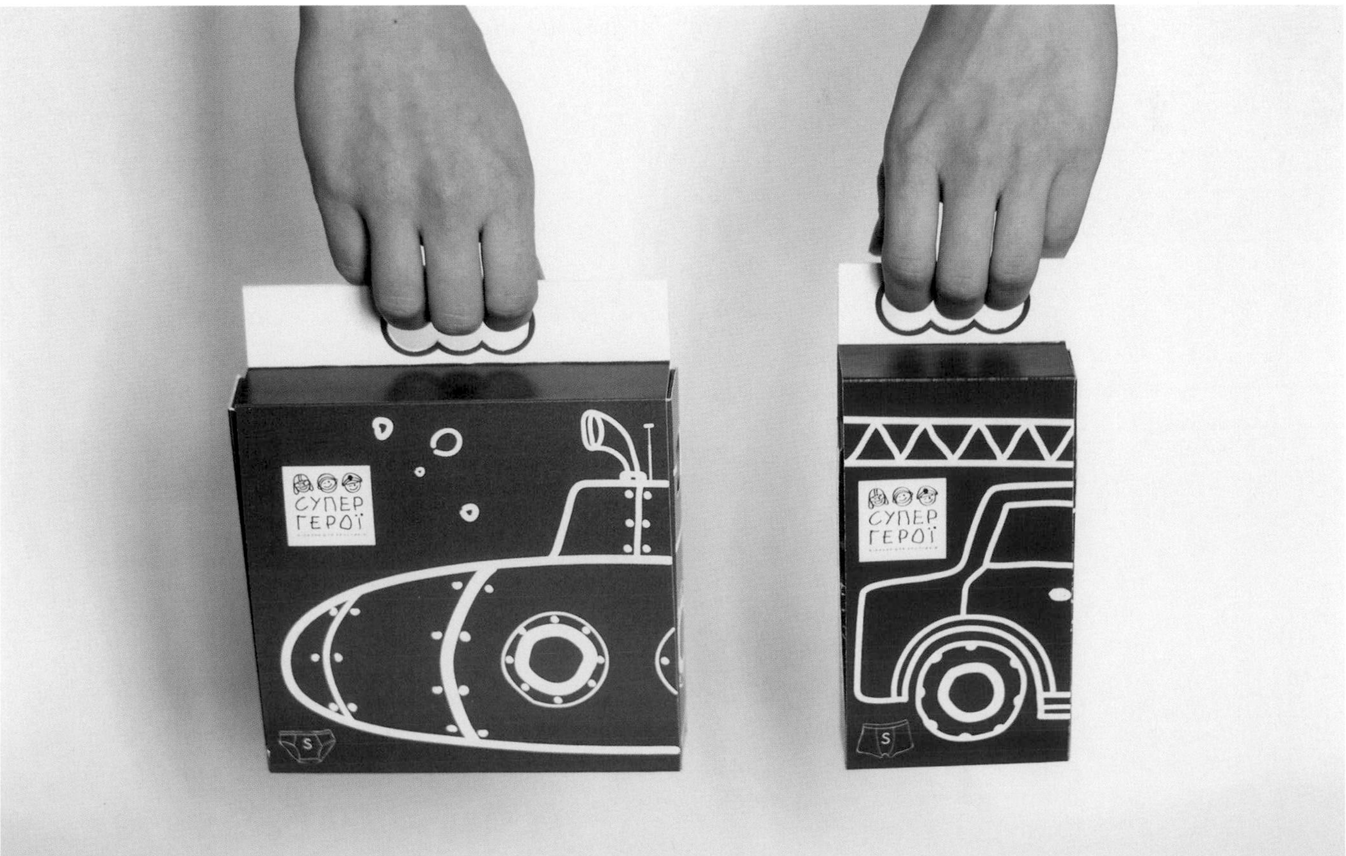
СУПЕР
ГЕРОЇ
СУПЕР
ГЕРОЇ

Packaging for Chuseok

In South Korea, bringing gifts home at festival times, such as for the Chuseok harvest festival, is a cultural tradition. Socks are a good gift choice, because everyone in the family is able to wear them. Designer Eun Woo Kim came up with the packaging for Sockstaz' Chuseok socks, choosing silk to wrap them and paying close attention to the quality of the silk. This unique fabric packaging not only reflects the oriental features of the festival, but can also be used as a handkerchief after the present is unwrapped. The packaging also includes a postcard printed with a pattern that is inspired by the moon. A high-quality label reflects the stores' inherent values.

Client
Sockstaz

Designer
Eun Woo Kim

Material
Cloth

Size
275mm x 120mm

Completion
2014

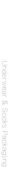

Tippy Toes

Tippy Toes is sustainable and cute packaging for baby socks. The package is reusable, and can either be used as a hanger or to store socks. Animal shapes aid in motivating children to help out with chores, encouraging a sense of curiosity. Information on the package is kept simple and easy to read to avoid taking attention away from the hanger itself, and to reduce clutter and open up the composition. A variety of designs are incorporated (alligator, lion, caterpillar), differentiating the sock sizes to aid usability and avoid confusion. The design also successfully eliminates the need for small plastic tags, which are normally used to keep socks together or attached to the packaging.

Designer
Jennifer Wilson

Material
Mason board, vinyl stickers

Size
Caterpillar / 444mm x 292mm
Alligator / 406mm x 279mm
Lion / 406mm x 292mm

Completion
2014

TIPPYTOES™
0-6 MONTHS
3 PAIRS

TIPPYTOES™
6-12 MONTHS
2 PAIRS

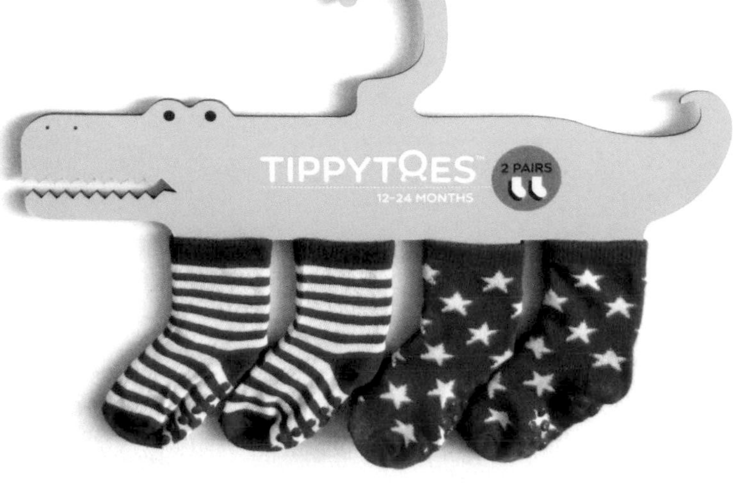
TIPPYTOES™
12-24 MONTHS
2 PAIRS

Topman Underwear Packaging

This Topman underwear packaging looks like "business on the outside" and a "party on the inside." The outside of the packaging is plain and businesslike, while the inside is vibrant, pushing the concept of the designer, who tried to rely on a user experience to drive the design. This concept was combined with a South African visual language: the inside features a typical South African pattern, as well as three removable characters, and each pair of underwear is wrapped in a poster featuring a South African pattern or design. The packaging is made out of recyclable cardboard and the posters are meant to be reused. There are also three Perspex characters included in the box, intended to be displayed with the pop-out characters.

Designer Casper Schutte	Size 180mm x 210mm
Material Cardboard, Perspex, paper	Completion 2015

TOPMAN

WE GOT YOU BACK
TOPMAN

Pom Pom

Pom Pom is a modern and stylish lingerie brand created by design agency Reynolds & Reyner for a Los Angeles-based fashion designer. In each package, there are two kinds of pants in individual boxes that resemble diagonally cut cubes in shape. The first type is more comfortable and simple, meant for everyday use at work or when working out; the second offers a more creative and interesting lingerie type intended for evenings and nights, parties and leisure. The two-piece set is reflected not only in the packaging and the brand's slogan—"Work hard, play hard"—but also in the brand name. A "pom-pom" can refer to an ornamental ball on a hat or other piece of clothing, as well as to objects that American cheerleaders hold during sporting events, such as basketball or American football matches. The dual brand name perfectly conveys the idea of lightness and brightness shown by cheerleaders and also refers to the idea of combining the two types of lingerie in a single set.

Client
Kristine Hardig

Design Agency
Reynolds & Reyner

Designers
Alexander Andreyev, Artyom Kulik

Material
Cardboard

Size
200mm x 200mm

Completion
2015

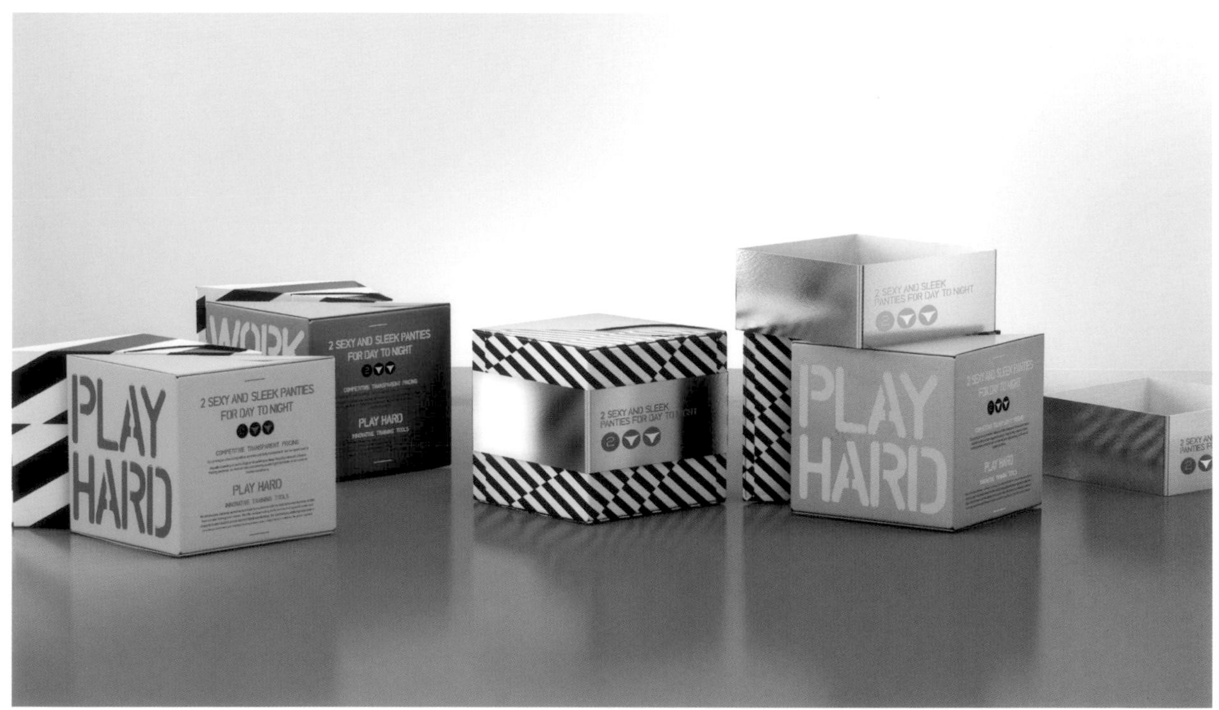

PLAY HARD
2 SEXY AND SLEEK PANTIES FOR DAY TO NIGHT
PLAY HARD
WORK
2 SEXY AND SLEEK PANTIES FOR DAY TO NIGHT
PLAY HARD
2 SEXY AND SLEEK PANTIES FOR DAY TO NIGHT
PLAY HARD
2 SEXY AND SLEEK PANTIES FOR DAY TO NIGHT

HARD
KRISTINE HARDIG
LOS ANGELES
KRISTINE HARDIG
LOS ANGELES
KRISTINE HARDIG
LOS ANGELES

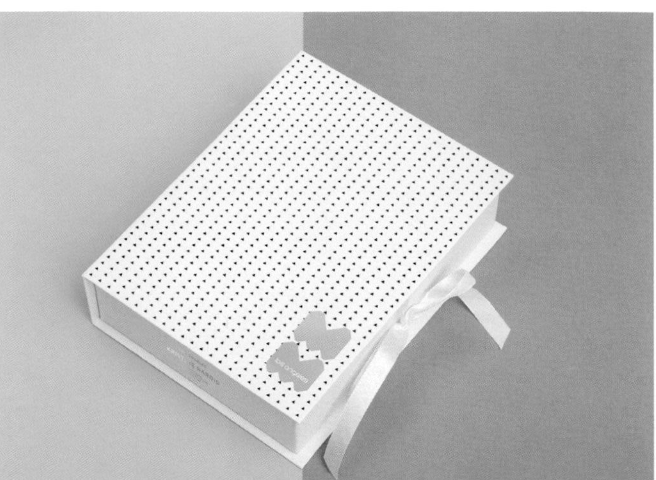

WORK HARD

USA
LOS ANGELES

los angeles

Flashtones

Flashtones is a fresh, Czech Republic brand producing colorful socks. The main goal of this project was to simplify in-store customers' experience and help them choose their desired colors quickly and easily. "Single pack" designs were based on a recycled cardboard box with a rounded opening on the top, making it easy to see the color of the socks inside. The company's branding is printed in gold on the boxes. In addition to the single packs, designer Petr Kudláček was asked to design a "mystery pack," which would contain 14 randomly colored socks. Tissue boxes were the inspiration for this idea, but instead of tissues, randomly colored socks are pulled out–solving the dilemma of deciding which socks to wear today!

Client
Flashtones

Designer
Petr Kudláček

Material
Recycled cardboard

Size
80mm x 80mm x 10mm

Completion
2015

F
T
FLASHTONES

French Cancan Packaging

This packaging project was inspired by the paintings of Toulouse-Lautrec. There are two lines of packaging for leggings, tights, stockings, and socks. Casual black items are housed in colorful packaging for contrast and brightness, while seasonal, colorful items have a white background so as not to distract the buyer from the color of the product. Customers can see the texture and color of the goods through the cutout legs on the packaging, which look like the legs of a woman dancing.

Designer
Elena Bychinina

Material
Cardboard

Size
Socks /
70mm x 120mm
Tights /
120mm x 120mm
Leggings /
120mm x 180mm

Completion
2013

L-4
100 DEN
ЛЕГГЕНСЫ
XS-1
100 DEN
ЛЕГГЕНСЫ

КАН
КАН
100 DEN
ЛЕГГЕНСЫ
XS-1
СКИЙ
КАН-К
S-2
КОЛГОТКИ
40 DEN
ЧУЛКИ
XL-5
XS-1
100 DEN
ЛЕГГЕНСЫ

ФРАН
ЦУЗ
СКИЙ
КАН
КАН
40 DEN
ЧУЛКИ
XL-5
ФРАН
ЦУЗ
СКИЙ
КАН
КАН

Be Girl Empower Panty

Be Girl, a social enterprise that makes reusable menstruation products, required packaging for its 2015 Kickstarter marketing campaign. Consumers who purchased the high-performance Empower Panties would provide a sponsorship of Be Girl menstruation products for girls in need around the world. As the company produces environmentally conscious products, the packaging had to reflect these values as much as possible. As such, the design features a glueless enclosure, single-ink printing on cardboard, and no additional inserts for extra information (this is printed on the panels of the box instead). The playful diecuts of the women effectively display the product, add color to the design, and speak to the company's agenda for women's empowerment.

Client
Be Girl

Designers
Victoria ChienYun Spriggs, Diana Sierra

Material
Cardboard

Size
170mm x 100mm

Completion
2015

YOU
ARE MAKING A DIFFERENCE
GET ONE, GIVE ONE
WHY
MENSTRUATION MATTERS
250 MILLION GIRLS
LIVE IN EXTREME POVERTY, LACKING ACCESS TO SAFE AND BASIC MEANS TO MANAGE THEIR MENSTRUATION WITH DIGNITY.
PHYSICAL IMPRISONMENT
Every EmpowerPanty is an investment in Womankind!

YOU
ARE MAKING A DIFFERENCE
GET ONE, GIVE ONE
HER
YOU
EMPOWERPANTY

Be. EMPOWERPANTY
THONG
HIPSTER
BIKINI
HIGH-WAISTED BRIEF
SIZE CHART (U.S.)
XS 34 - 36" hips
S 37 - 39" hips
M 40 - 42" hips
L 43 - 45" hips
XL 46 - 48" hips
Made in Colombia
Cotton and nylon blend
GET ONE, GIVE ONE
SOFT & LIGHTWEIGHT
SEAMLESS DESIGN
STRETCHY FOR PERFECT FIT
RESPONSIBLE MANUFACTURING
ENVIRONMENTALLY CONSCIOUS
BeGirl.org

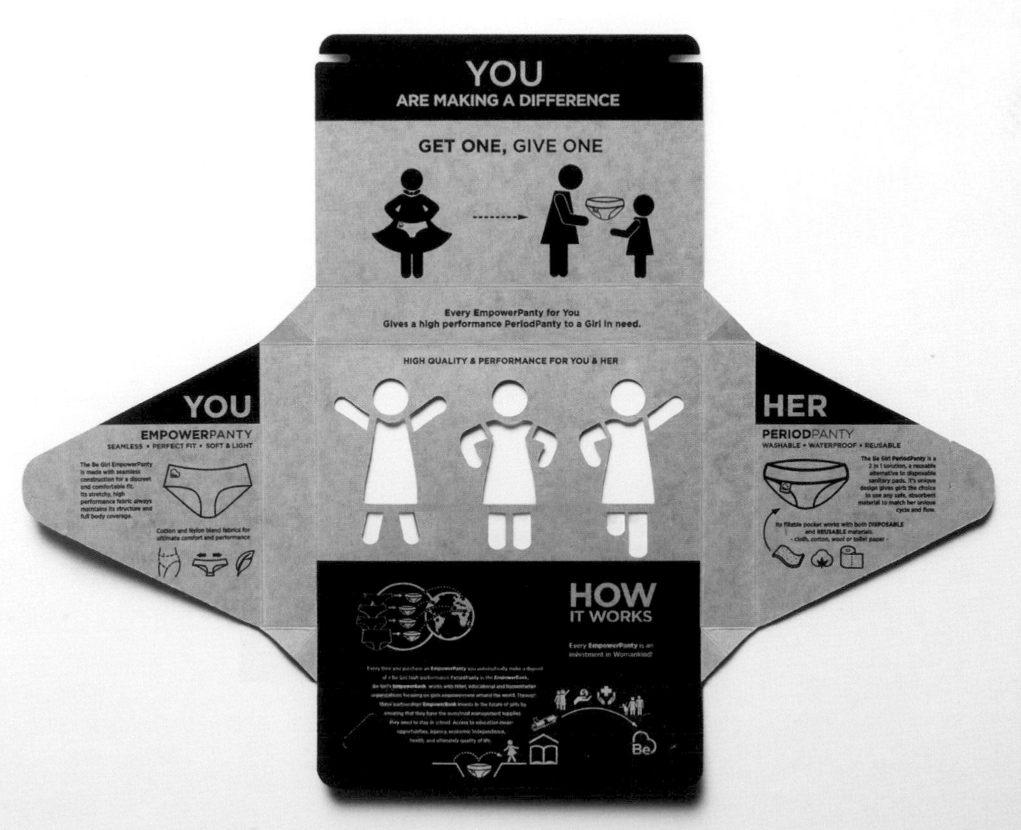
YOU
ARE MAKING A DIFFERENCE
GET ONE, GIVE ONE
Every EmpowerPanty for You
Gives a high performance PeriodPanty to a Girl in need.
HIGH QUALITY & PERFORMANCE FOR YOU & HER
YOU
EMPOWERPANTY
SEAMLESS • PERFECT FIT • SOFT & LIGHT
The Be Girl EmpowerPanty is made with seamless construction for a discreet and comfortable fit. Its stretchy, high performance fabric always maintains its structure and full body coverage.
Cotton and Nylon blend fabrics for ultimate comfort and performance
HER
PERIODPANTY
WASHABLE • WATERPROOF • REUSABLE
Its fillable pocket works with both DISPOSABLE and REUSABLE materials.
- cloth, cotton, wool or toilet paper -
HOW
IT WORKS
Every EmpowerPanty is an investment in Womankind!

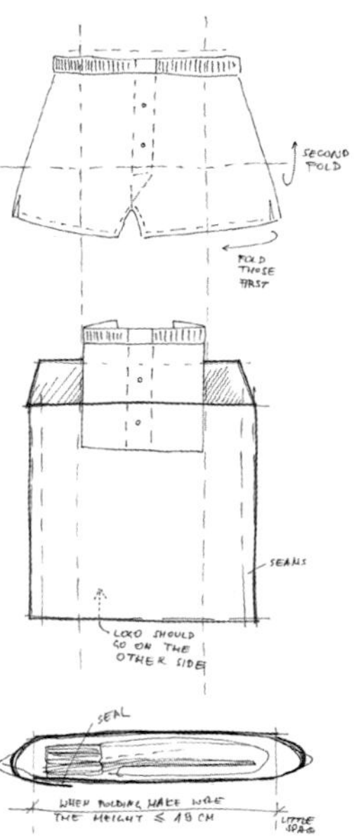

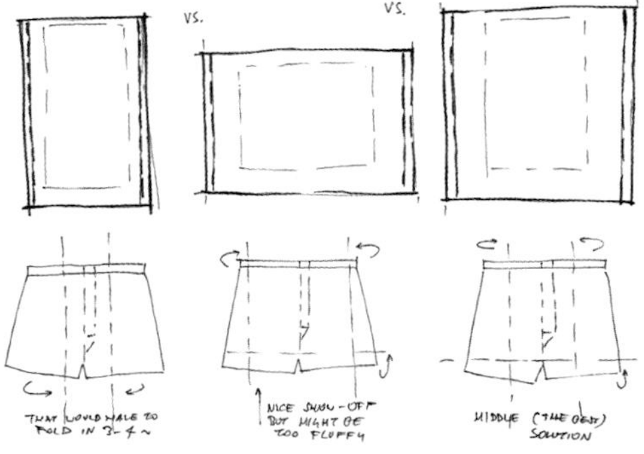

Unerdwear Packaging

Unerdwear is a brand of high-quality boxer shorts with colorful, geeky patterns. The company's branding concept and name was based on geek culture and addressed to the tech community. This packaging, made from opaque, metallic foil, was inspired by the glossy, metallic-foil envelopes that hardware computer elements are sold in for protection. It is a square envelope with a peel-and-seal adhesive closure to fit one pair of neatly folded boxers. The logo is screen-printed on the front with matte-black paint, which contrasts nicely with the glossy foil background. Gold foil was chosen by the designers to match the design details on the boxers' gold tag and gold buttons. The flat packaging allows the product to be shipped in envelopes, which lowers the cost of delivery to online customers.

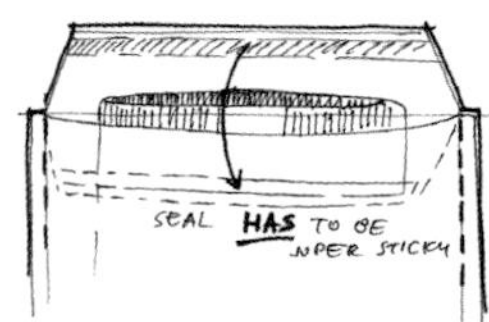

Client
Unerdwear

Designers
Katarzyna Bojanowska, Joanna Socha

Material
Gold foil

Size
220mm x 220mm

Completion
2013

Merrell Socks Package Design

This packaging structure was designed to launch Merrell's summer campaign, encouraging people to explore the great outdoors with the new product range. Two-ply wood veneer was used to give the socks-holder a distinct outdoorsy feeling. It is shaped as a quarter oloid, slips snugly inside a pair of Merrell shoes, and can be used to put rolled-up socks inside, making it a must-carry item when traveling.

Client
Merrell

Size
165mm x 51mm

Designer
Shaily Shah

Completion
2014

Material
Wood

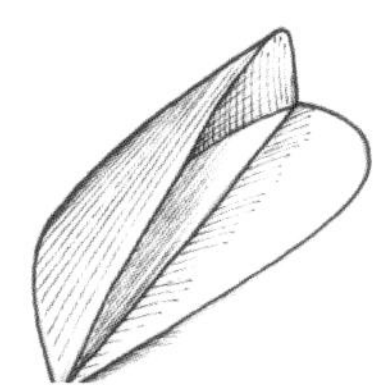

SILVER
ENGINEERED WITH PATENTED XT2® FIBER TECHNOLOGY, WHICH BLENDS SILVER PARTICLES WITH PIMA COTTON FOR THE MOST LUXURIOUS AND ANTI-MICROBIAL PERFORMANCE UNDERWEAR.
MACKWELDON.COM

Mack Weldon

In the spring of 2014, Mack Weldon launched its Silver underwear collection, which features X-static® XT2™ cutting-edge fiber technology. The addition of the precious metal helps deliver a new level of benefits to men's underwear. Blackrose was asked to create a distinct brand identity for this new collection, including visual identity, packaging, brand video, copy and voice, and on-product marketing. The goal was to differentiate it from existing products and enhance Silver's technologically advanced attributes. The logo's type is a takedown from the original MW logo, thinned and stenciled for a modern, utilitarian feel. The color palette, like the product, is created from dark gray and black. The bags are flooded in matte-black ink and UV spot varnish is used on the logo.

Client
Mack Weldon Silver Collection

Design Agency
Blackrose NYC

Material
PE with matte OPP lamination

Size
Underwear packaging / 178mm x 203mm
T-shirt packaging / 279mm x 356mm

Completion
2014

BY MACK
UNDER
TH PATENTED XT2 FIBER TECHNOLOGY, WHI
PARTICLES WITH PIMA COTTON FOR THE MO
D ANTI-MICROBIAL PERFORMANCE UNDERWEA
WELDON.COM

SILVER
BY MACK WELDON
BOXER BRIEF
SILVER
BY MACK WELDON
T-SHIRT
SILVER
BY MACK WELDON
BOXER BRIEF
SILVER
BY MACK WELDON
SILVER
BY MACK WELDON
BOXER BRIEF
SILVER
BY MACK WELDON

Accessories Packaging

Light Gauze Muffler Zipangu Color

This book-shaped paperboard packaging can be regarded as a "memorial book" associated with the gentle touch that these "gauze mufflers" (scarfs) offer. The book concept was inspired by the notion of a traveler wearing their favorite scarf and stopping by an old, secondhand bookstore in a small town to buy their favorite book in memory of their journey. Paperboard boxes that complement the warm and gentle prints of the fabric are used as the packaging material, and cutouts are included to highlight the soft touch of the ultrathin, multi-layered gauze mufflers.

Client
Colorsville Co., Ltd.

Design Agency
Grand Deluxe

Designer
Koji Matsumoto

Material
White paper, cardboard

Size
144mm x 202mm x 27mm

Completion
2015

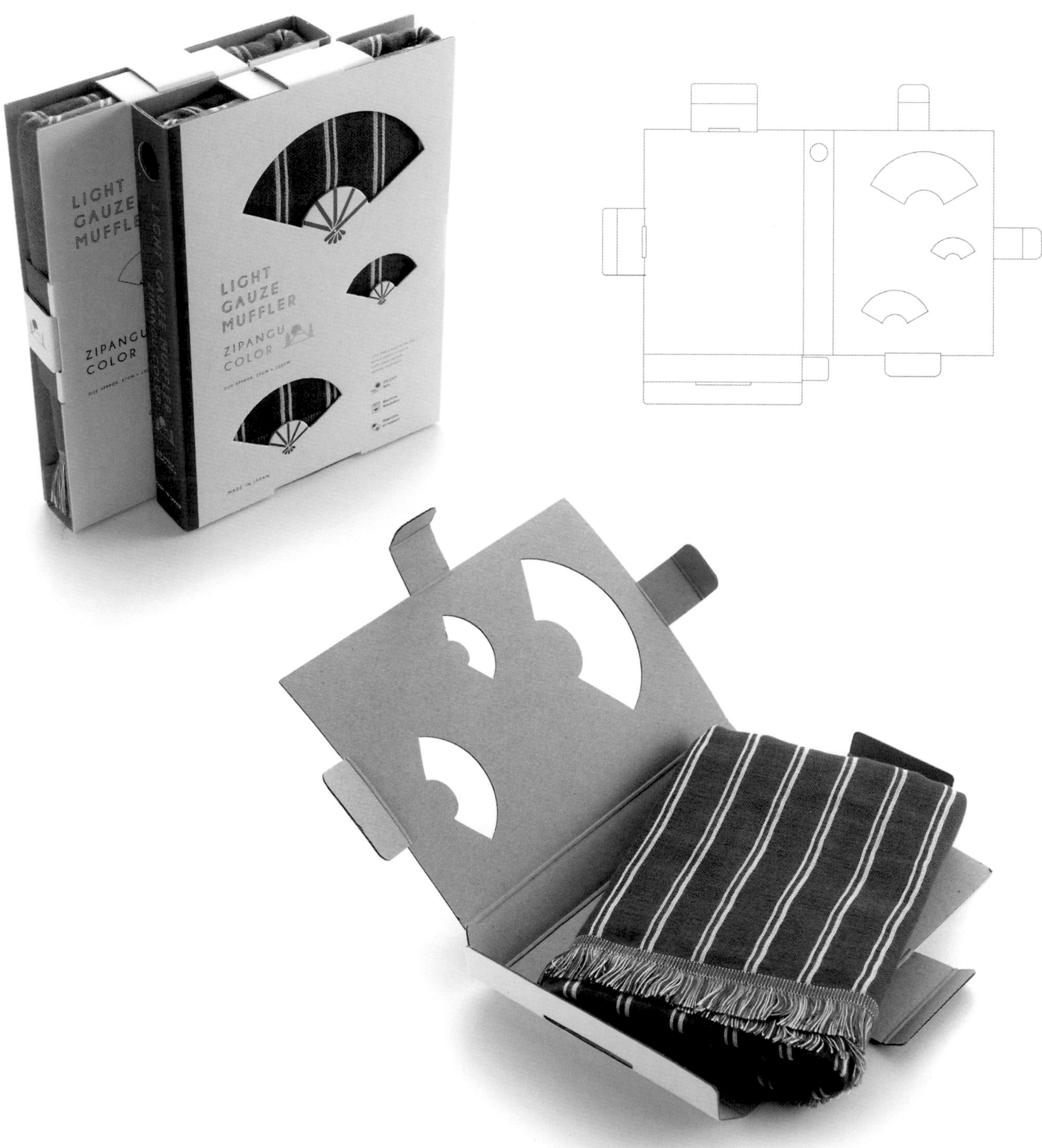

LIGHT GAUZE MUFFLER
ZIPANGU COLOR
SIZE APPROX
27CM × 150CM

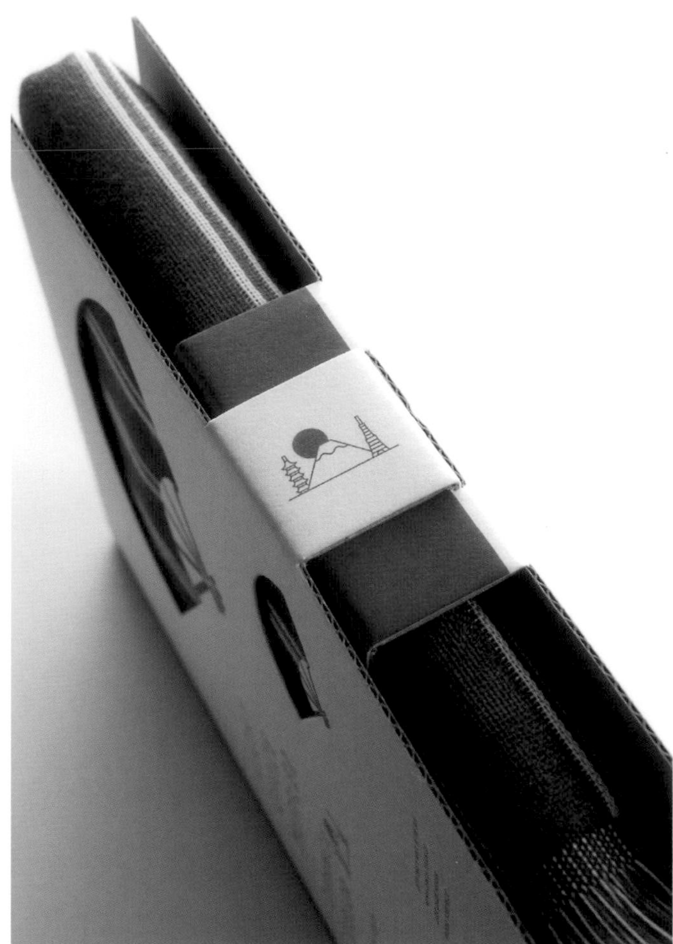

LIGHT
GAUZE
MUFFLER
ZIPANGU
COLOR
SIZE APPROX. 27CM × 150CM
MADE IN JAPAN

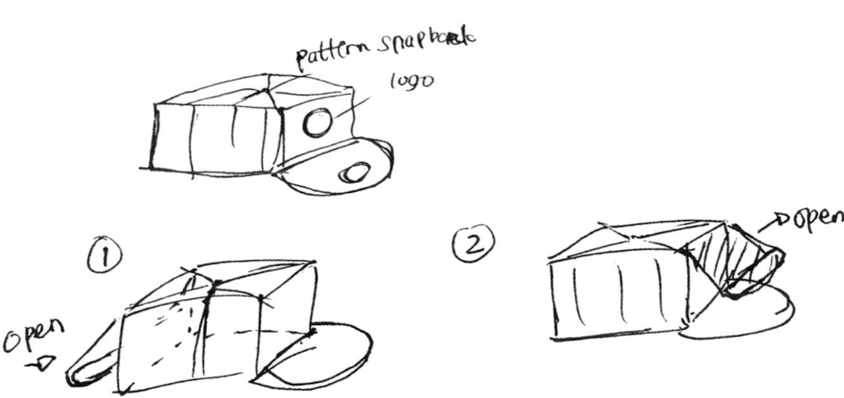

Joel Merch's Papertoy —Snapback Invasion

The original idea was to create an iconic urban paper toy. In order to promote the launch of Joel Papertoy using merchandise, such as T-shirts, hoodies, varsity jackets, snapbacks (adjustable baseball caps), key chains, sticker packs, and so on, there are several packaging ideas that could be created; this snapback packaging is one of them. The packaging has the same patterns as the snapbacks, but is different in shape to fit the snapbacks inside. The fonts are different for each logo, using Debussy, Carnivalee Freakshow, and Arial Condensed Bold.

Client
Joel Papertoy

Designer
Yulia Susanti

Material
250gsm fancy paper

Size
107mm x 50mm

Completion
2014

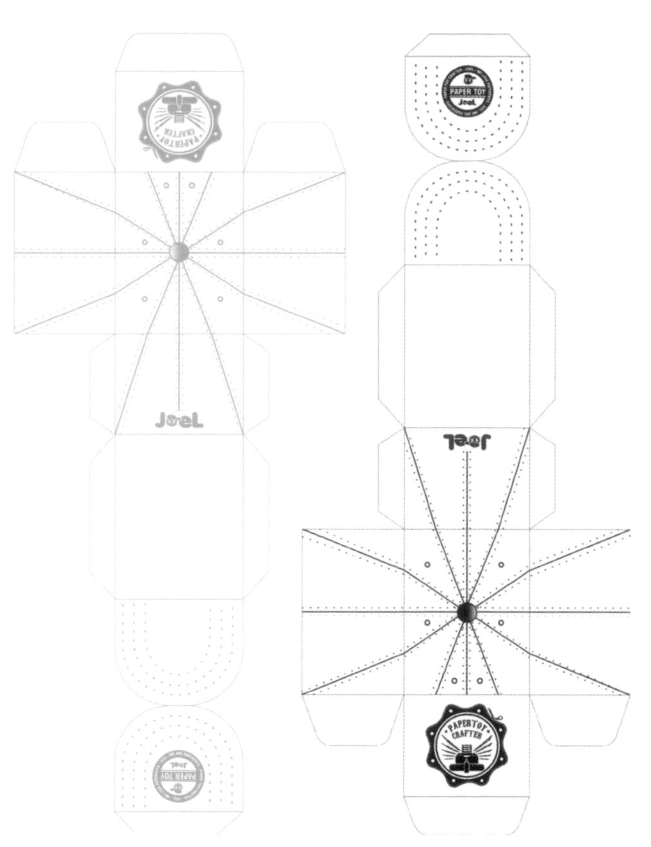
PAPER TOY
JoeL
PAPERTOY
CRAFTER

Papertoy

Men's Neckwear Packaging

In order to update the packaging for a new line of men's neckwear and accessories under the classic Wembley brand for Kohl's Department Store, designer Jon Walters created a fresh design that reflects the brand's rich heritage while modernizing it for contemporary audiences. Walters drew from Wembley's vast archive of mid-century advertising graphics to produce a series of original, vintage-inspired illustrations to adorn the accessory boxes. In addition, he composed playful copes, selected period-appropriate fonts and patterns, and used whimsical diecut windows to round out the design.

Client
Kohl's Department Store

Designer
Jon Walters

Material
Cardboard

Size
Sock & Tie Set /
127mm x 289mm x 57mm
Tie Set /
140mm x 227mm x 25mm
Bow Tie /
76mm x 178mm x 35mm
Bow Tie & Pocket Square /
152mm x 190mm x 35mm
Tie & Sock (Mens) /
140mm x 229mm x 25mm
Tie & Sock (Boys) /
140mm x 203mm x 25mm

Completion
2015

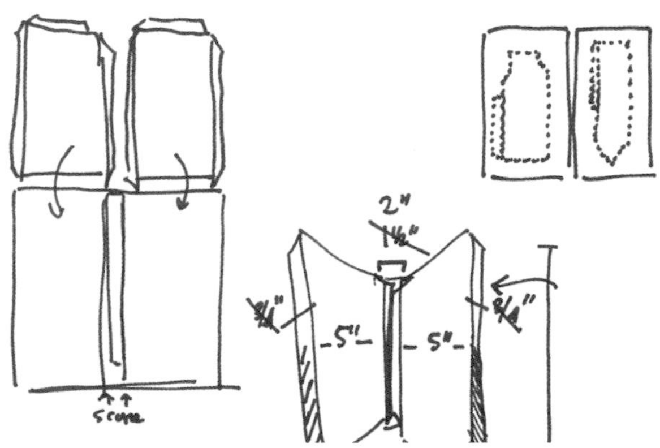

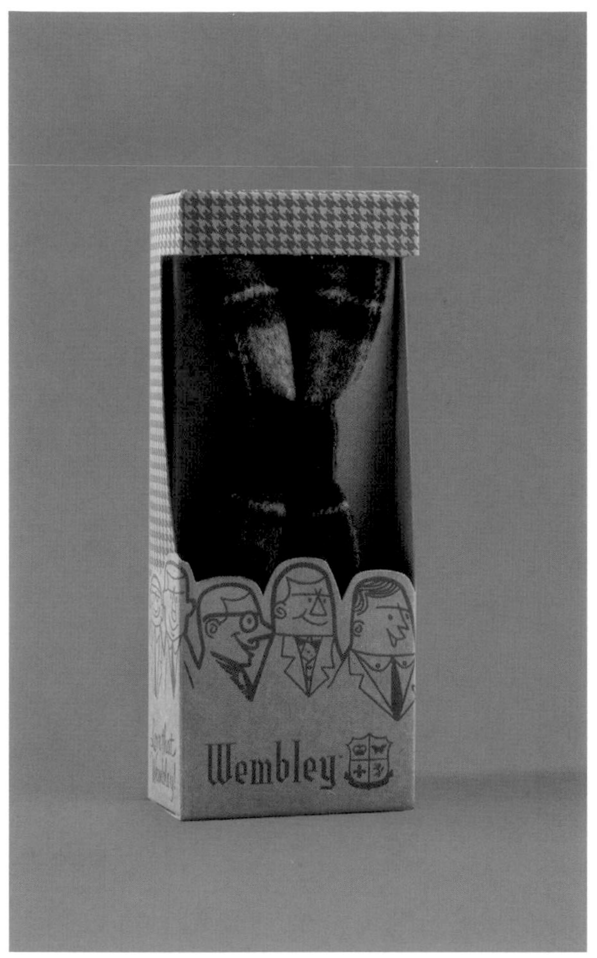
Wembley

Wembley
Bow Tie & Pocket Square Set

How about some swanky socks to finish your dapper look off.
A fancy tie sure would look spiffy with that suit of yours.

Macaw's Packaging

Macaw is a small, Montreal-based fashion brand providing unique marbled accessories. The products are all completely made by hand, from the fabric-printing process, to the jewelry design and the sewing. Macaw's packaging was designed to perfectly fit each accessory; made from expedition tubes and bamboo, it is strong, light, and perfect for shipping. The packaging is printed only with the logo and slogan in black, which makes it simple, natural and eco-friendly. It was also specifically created to be reused as storage for the accessories, protecting the items as well as providing an aesthetically pleasing display.

Client
Macaw

Designer
Audrey-Claude Roy

Material
Expedition tubes, bamboo, Lentra fabric, leather

Size
42-80mm x 75-177mm

Completion
2015

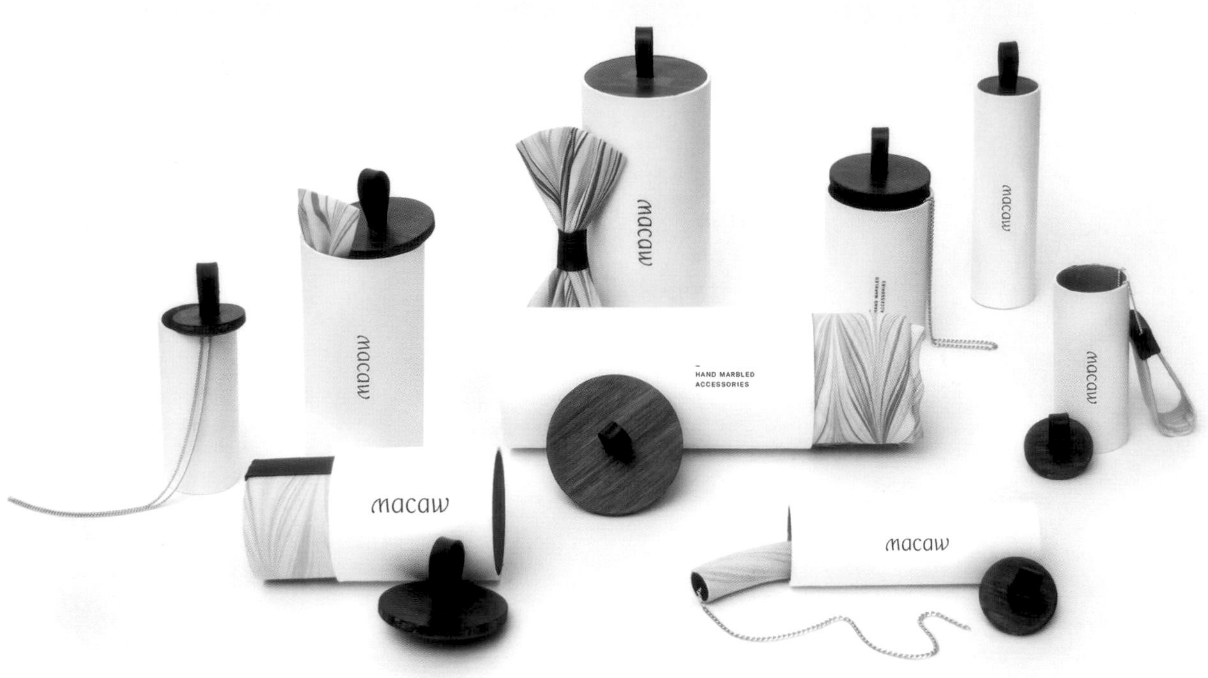
macaw
macaw
macaw
macaw
macaw
macaw
macaw
HAND MARBLED
ACCESSORIES

macaw

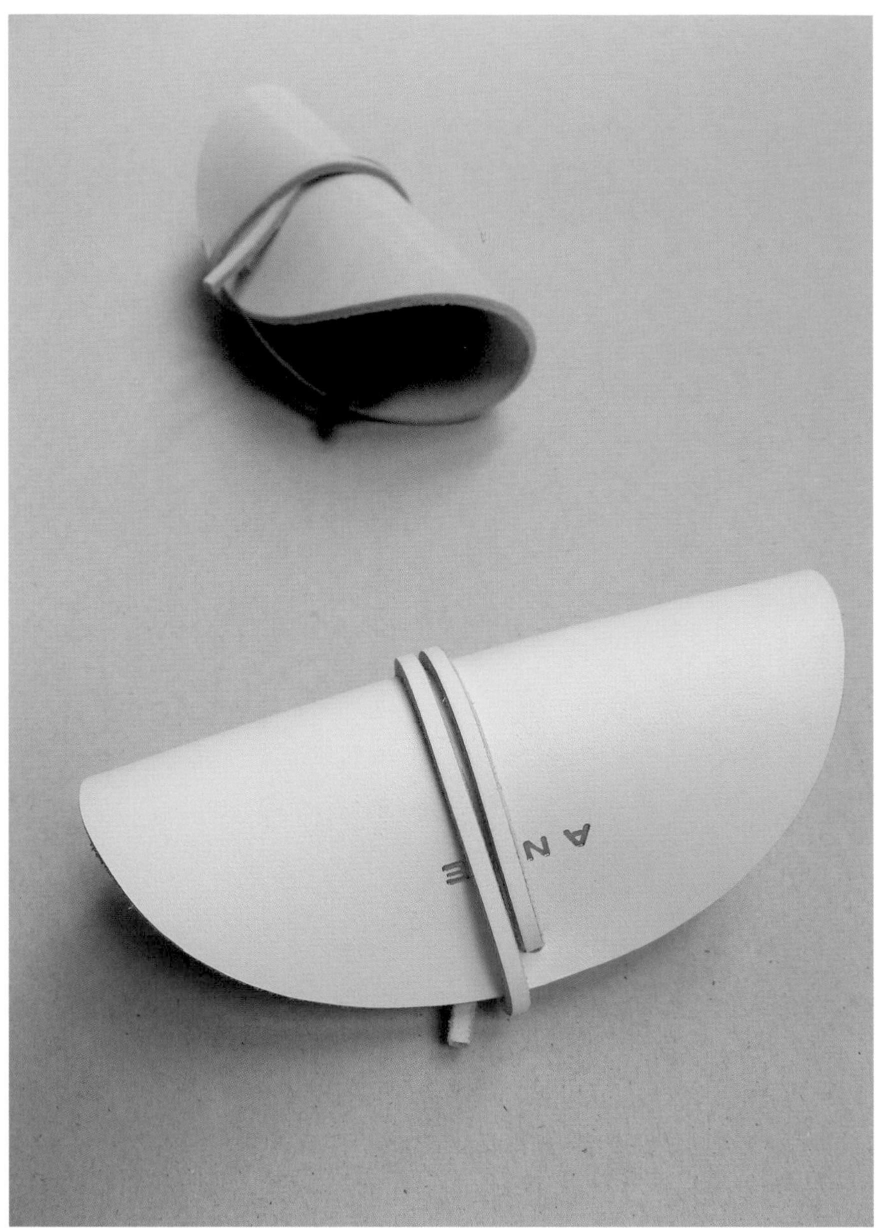

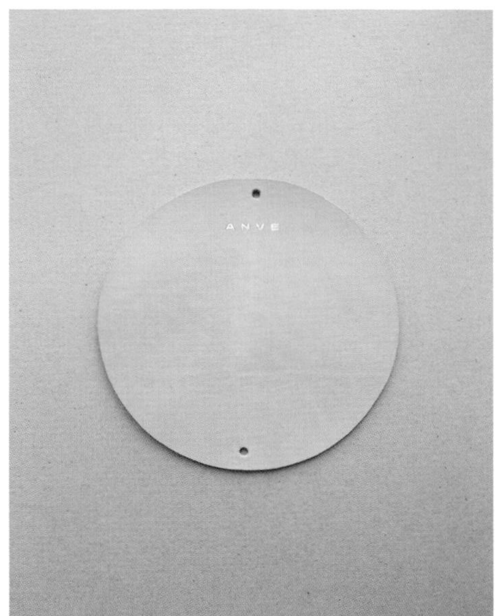

ESTOJO Sunglasses Case

The general idea behind the brand ANVE is to create objects that make daily life more beautiful. Its elegant objects are the result of a minimalistic approach combined with simple functionality. All items are produced in very small editions and are handcrafted or manufactured in small quantities. The idea of the ESTOJO Sunglasses Case was to create simple protection for the sunglasses. Consisting of two pieces, the cases are made of a round piece of leather with two holes and a leather cord with a halved arrowhead at one end. The vegetable-tanned leather is available in three different colors (natural, white, and black) and is cut by hand; the logo is printed by hand with a gold foil. Once the round piece is folded to a half-moon shape and secured by the cord, it fits smoothly into a person's palm.

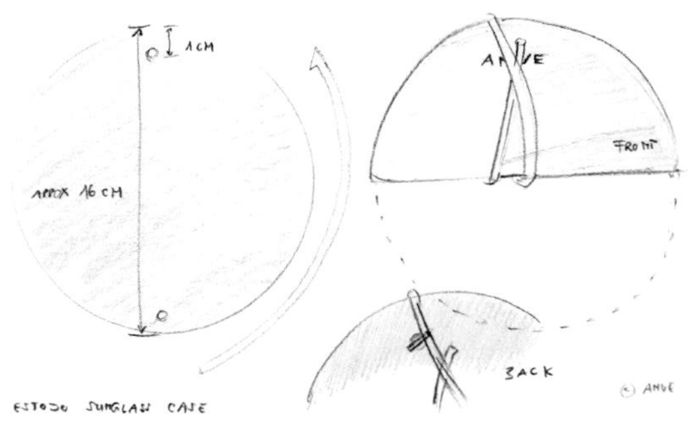

Design Agency	Size
ANVE	165mm x 83mm
Material	Completion
Vegetable-tanned leather	2013

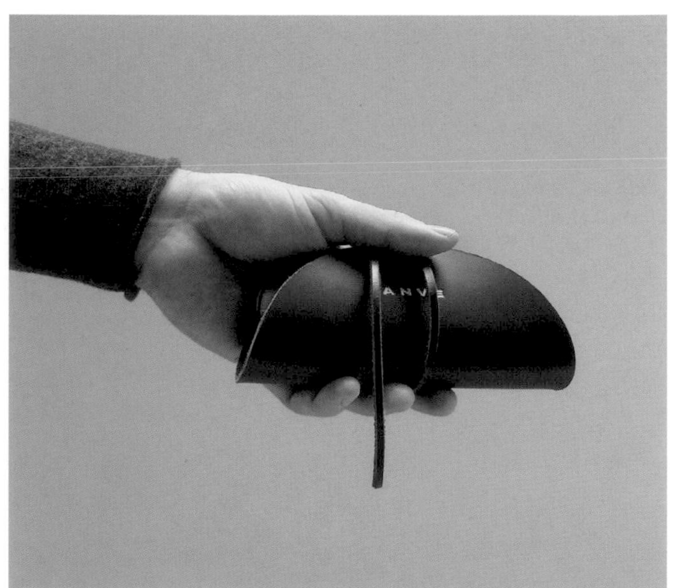

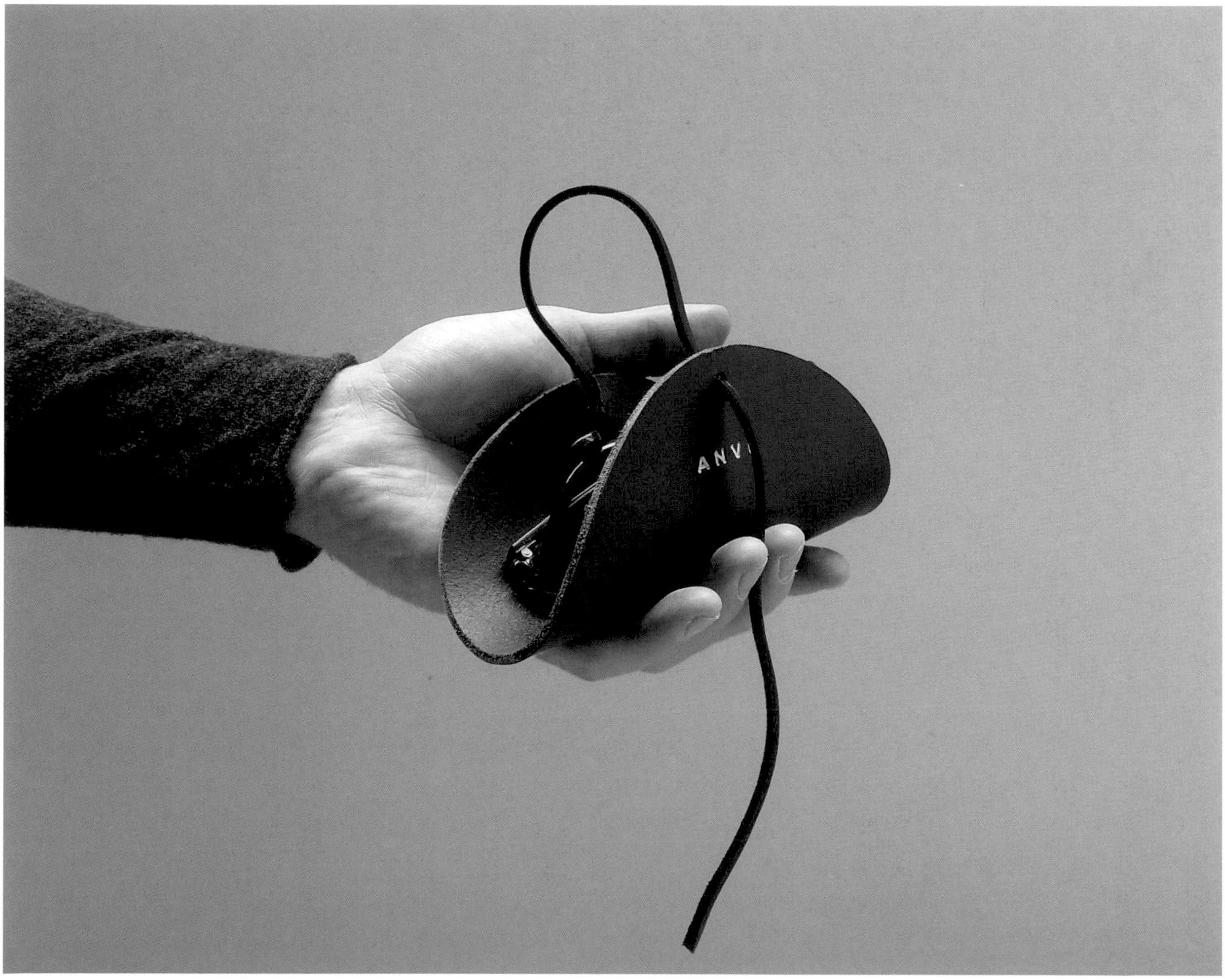

Packaging for Wooden Sunglasses

Kerbholz designs wooden sunglasses frames. Designers David Gibbs and Alisa Sorgenfrei were asked to submit conceptual design ideas for new packaging, keeping production costs to a minimum. Their goal was to achieve this without compromising the design or allowing the packaging to appear cheap.

The company started after the founders took a road trip through Latin America where they were inspired by the local wood. Integrating this travel inspiration and cultural infusion into their design, the designers came up with graphics incorporating little beer bottles and suitcases, which were inspired by the founders' travel anecdotes. They thought about common materials that are easy to access and are generally recyclable as well as sustainable, and finally decided to use cardboard boxes for the packaging. To suit the size of the stylish wooden frames, they redesigned the outer shape, and to reflect the company's unique product, they created a banderole that could be used to seal the box in front of the customer upon purchase.

Client
Kerbholz

Designers
David Gibbs, Alisa Sorgenfrei

Material
Cardboard, paper

Size
150mm x 100mm x 50mm

Completion
2013

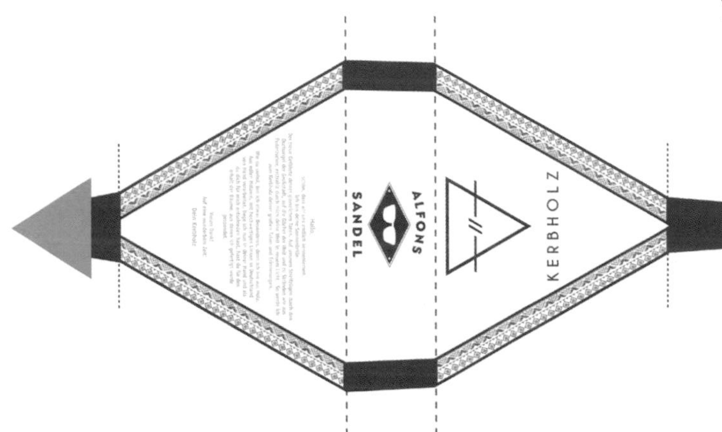

KERBHOLZ

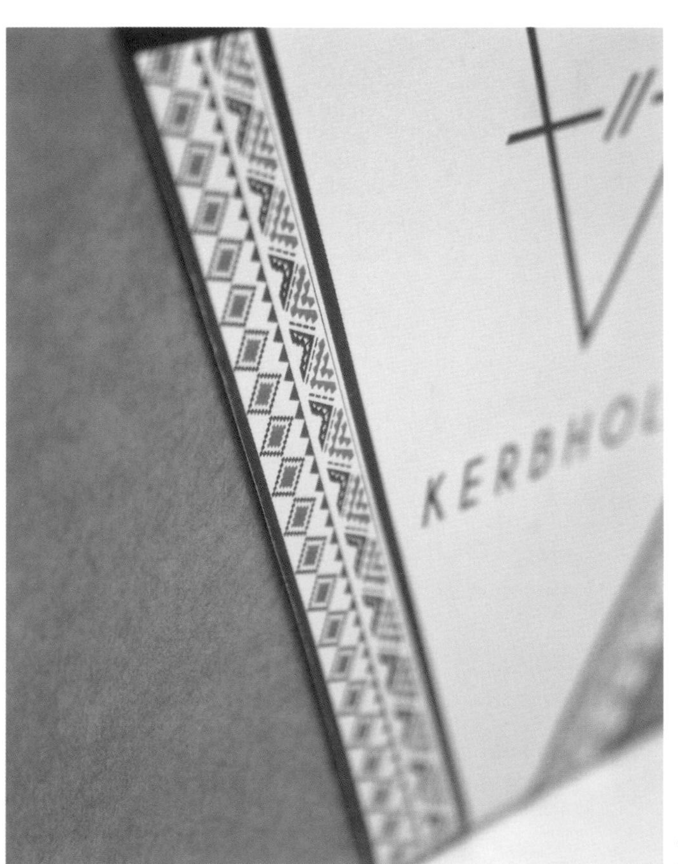

Gloves Verri

From novice to advanced, Verri sports gloves are created for athletic customers with varying needs. Designer Didier Roberti was asked to redesign the packaging of four models of gloves and a belt. Verri needed to be presented to be consistent with its competitors on the shelves of Walmart stores. Gloves were separated into two categories—"Amateur" and "Pro"—and each category required a different concept. The "Amateur" packaging needed to be friendly and to provide a sense of security for customers just beginning in sports practices, thereby generating empathy with the product. "Pro" is aimed at an audience that already plays sport frequently and expects more of the product; therefore, its packaging needed to convey professionalism and superior technology.

It would seem that the "Amateur" line builds trust with customers, while the "Pro" gear retains those customers over time. "Amateur" gear is bright and welcoming, using white, gray, and a robin's-egg blue as its color palette, while "Pro" gloves rely on a more serious combination of mostly gray, white, and splashes of orange. Both types of gloves are packaged in tear-open bags, giving buyers a sense that the product is pristine and new—certainly a state it won't be in later after plenty of use and workouts. The back of the packaging uses graphs and other images to convey information, giving Verri a scientific edge.

Client **Verri**	Size Box / 280mm x 130mm x 11mm Inside packaging / 170mm x 260mm
Designer **Didier Roberti**	
Material **Cardboard, plastic**	Completion **2015**

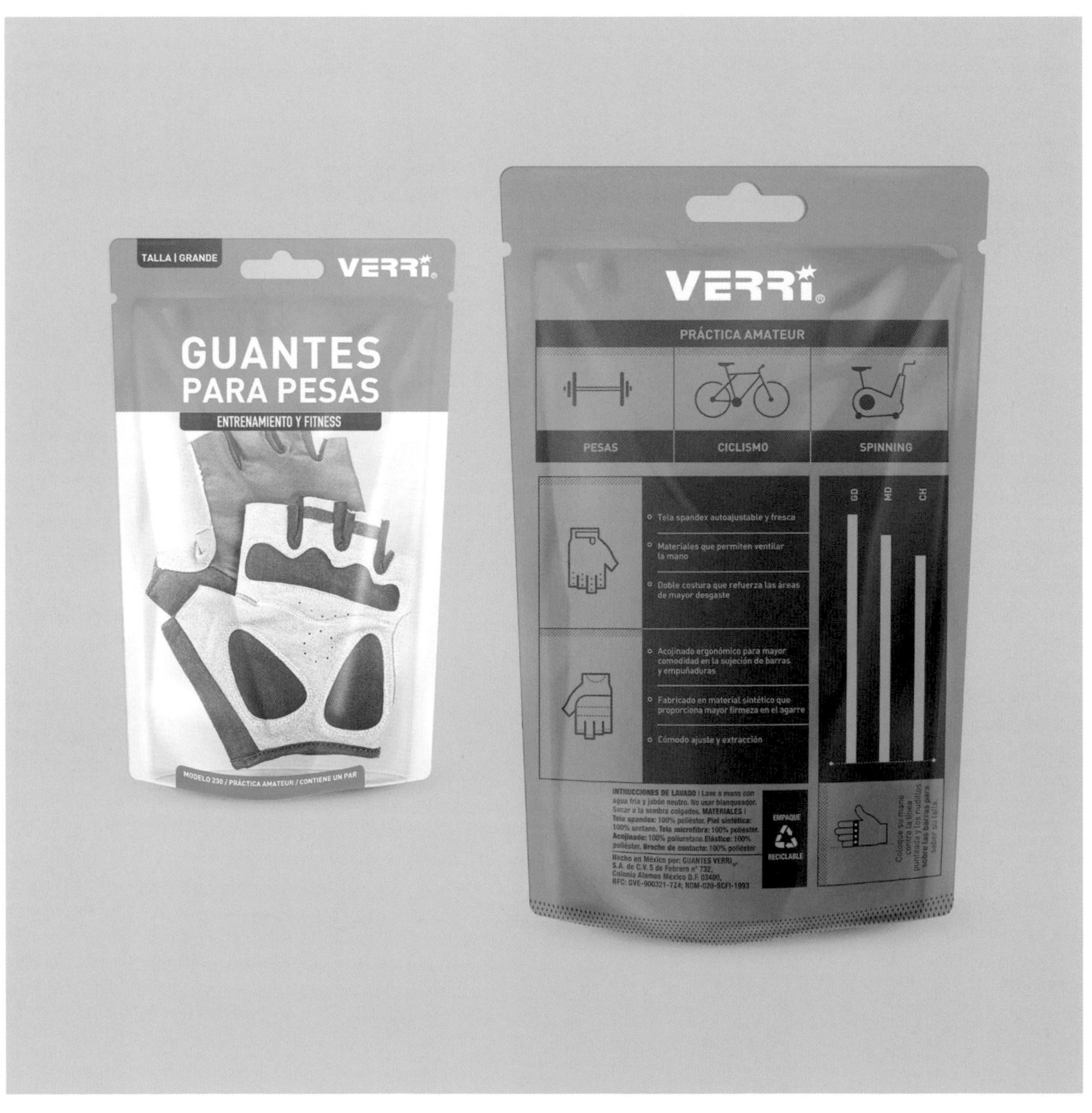

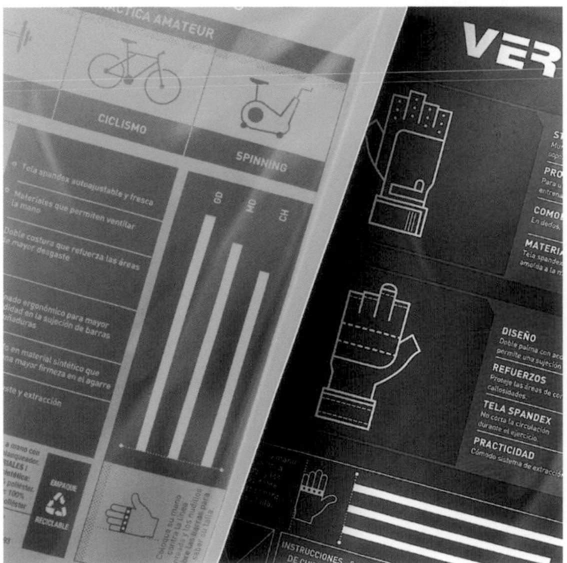
CICLISMO
SPINNING
DISEÑO
REFUERZOS
TELA SPANDEX
PRACTICIDAD

VERRI
CARACTERÍSTICAS

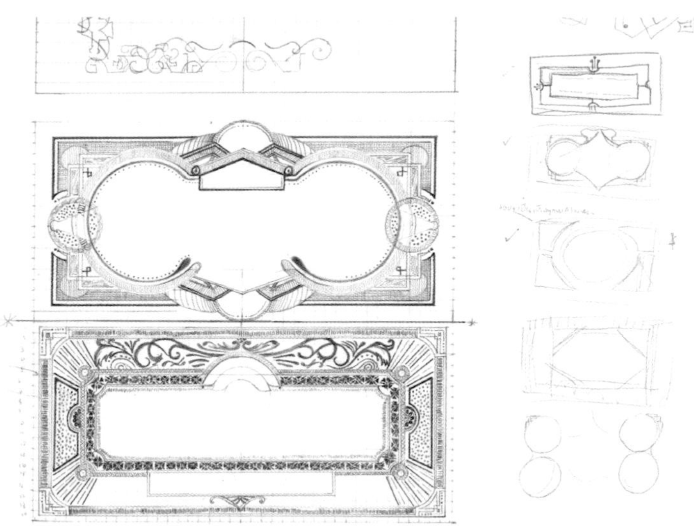

Jida Watt Packaging Design

This project was for the Jida Watt sunglasses brand. Brand creator Som Jida Watt wanted the brand to reflect her personality and values, and as a result, the brand's character is handcrafted, glamorous, feminine and vintage. The typeface used for the logo is a serif font and the illustration on top of the wooden box expresses a handcrafted feel. Moreover, the circle design of the illustration corresponds with the shape of the sunglasses.

Client
Jida Watt

Designer
Nan Napas

Material
Wood

Size
195mm x 95mm x 60mm

Completion
2015

Given name
NAIVE BARBARY
(JI115, gold/brown)
Place of Birth : Japan
Body Material : Titanium
Eyes color : Café Brown
www.jidawatt.com

JIDA WATT
Handcrafted by Japanese Artisans

Kombi Brand Identity

Kombi is a family owned winter accessories company founded in Montreal in 1961. It recently underwent a major brand revamp in an effort to get closer to its clients and open new doors. This resulted in a new logo, signature, packaging, and website (in partnership with Okam), as well as print communication tools, a booth (in partnership with Huma), in-store visuals, and a social media presence. Kombi's new image is inviting and warm, but not just any kind of warm. It's the kind of human warmth that makes you want to go and play outside, creating lifelong memories. The designer used bright colors such as yellow and red to bring the new packaging to life and to help break the stifling atmosphere that can be present on winter days.

Client Kombi	Material Cardboard
Design Agency Polygraphe Studio	Size 233mm x 122mm
Designer Sébastien Bisson	Completion 2015

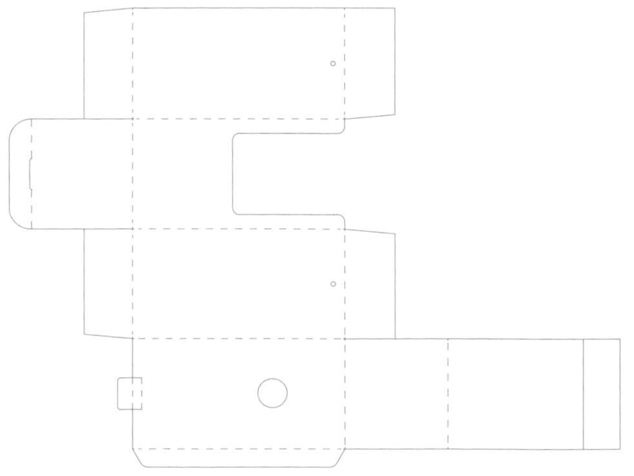

KOMBI
Suspenders.
Bretelles.
KOMBI

Women
Femmes
Hot times
in the city.
Chaleur urbaine.
KOMBI
Men
Hommes
KOMBI

KOMBI
Socks.
KOMBI

Packaging for Kypers Eyewear

Kypers is a brand of sunglasses that needed packaging to reflect its brand identity—a young, brave, and bold image. The packaging was designed using fluorescent colors to create a big impact when it was displayed in stores and to help it stand out from its competitors. It was very important to keep the colors bright and dense in the production process, and the designers used retro patterns to express the boldness and vitality of the brand. Looking at the packages through polarized glasses, customers can witness a fun iridescent effect. The boxes are lined with rigid cardboard and the entire set, including tubes, uses a select range of Pantone shades to create harmony between the individual components.

Client
Kypers

Design Agency
Orange BCN

Designers
Aïda Font, Jordi Ferràndiz

Material
Lined cardboard

Size
167mm x 71mm x 50mm

Completion
2015

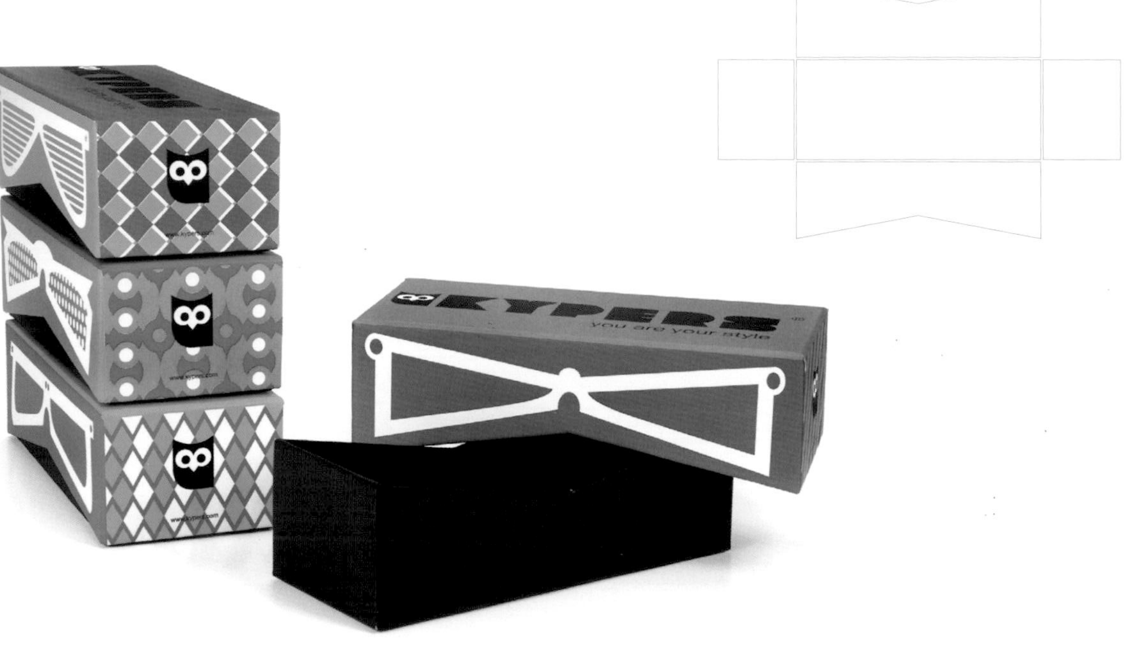

KYPERS®
you are your style

KYPERS®
you are your style

KYPERS®
you are your style

KYPERS®
you are your style

KYPERS®
you are your style
KYPERS®
you are your style
KYPERS®
you are your style
KYPERS®
you are your style

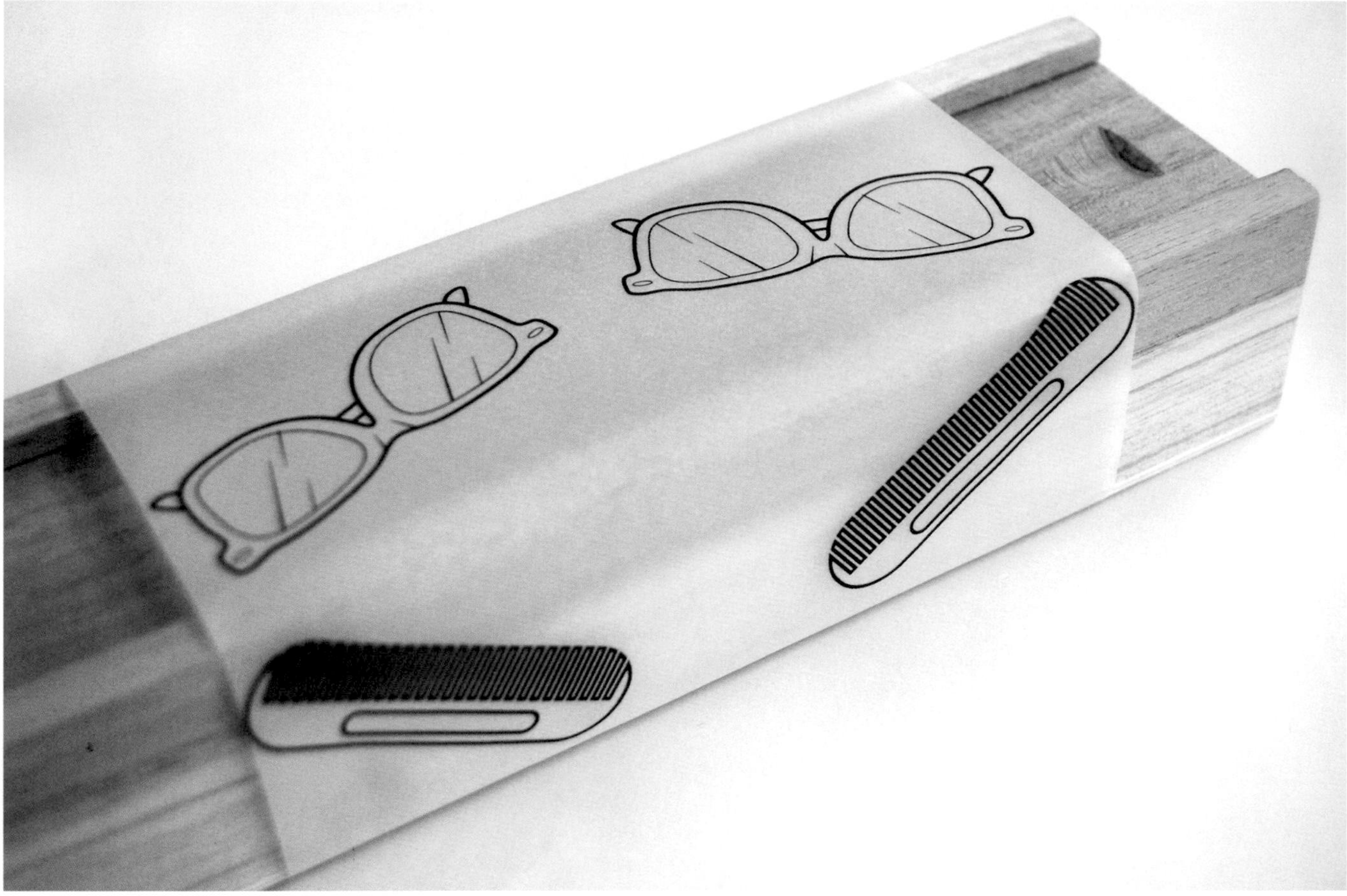

The Man Kit

The brief for this project was to reimagine the packaging for sunglasses in a new and inventive way, based on the idea of the "modern gentleman." After much thought, the designer finally decided to create a "Man Kit," which features a pair of sunglasses, a mustache comb, and a pot of mustache wax. The packaging for the man kit is a box with sliding lid made of a light wood with a smooth finish; laser-etched lettering was added to the surface. A wrap featuring outline illustrations covers the box, providing additional excitement for consumers when they slide it off and unveil the contents. The design also allows for ease of transportation when traveling or commuting.

Designer	Size
Kurtis Weaver	205mm x 65mm
Material	**Completion**
Wood	2014

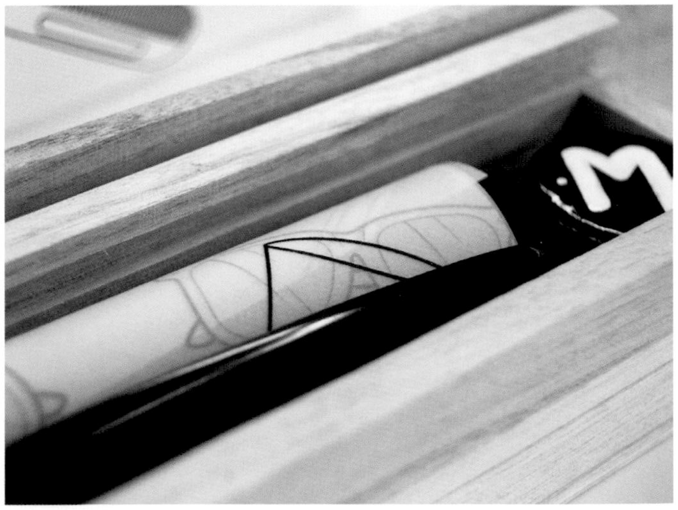

THE
MAN KIT
ORIGINAL

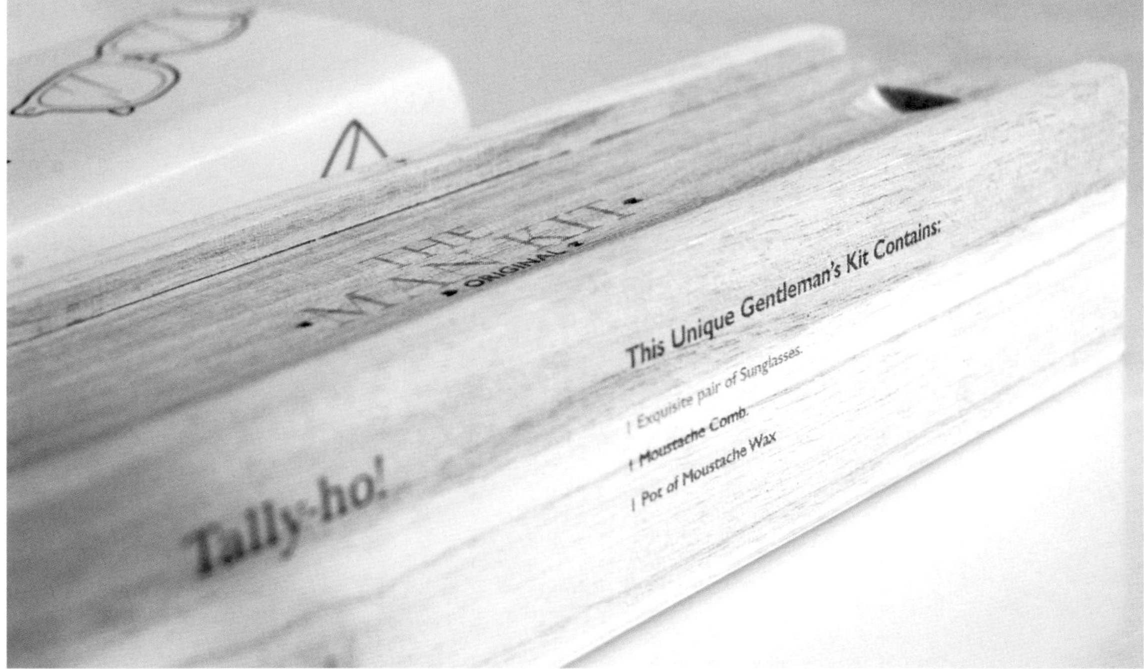
Tally-ho!
This Unique Gentleman's Kit Contains:
1 Exquisite pair of Sunglasses.
1 Moustache Comb.
1 Pot of Moustache Wax

Oysho Packaging

Oysho is a Spanish clothing retailer specializing in women's homewear and undergarments. Whenever the company organizes a Press Day to show a new collection, it gives all attending press people a special gift, in this case, a foulard scarf from the collection. This Fall/Winter Collection was characterized by colors such as white, blue, and gray, and warm pieces with interesting textures and material combinations. The packaging for the special gift reflects this visual universe of sensations by using a metal, white tube, interesting textured paper, and blue foil.

Client
Oysho

Designer
Ingrid Picanyol

Material
Metal tube, white textured paper

Size
600mm x 150mm

Completion
2015

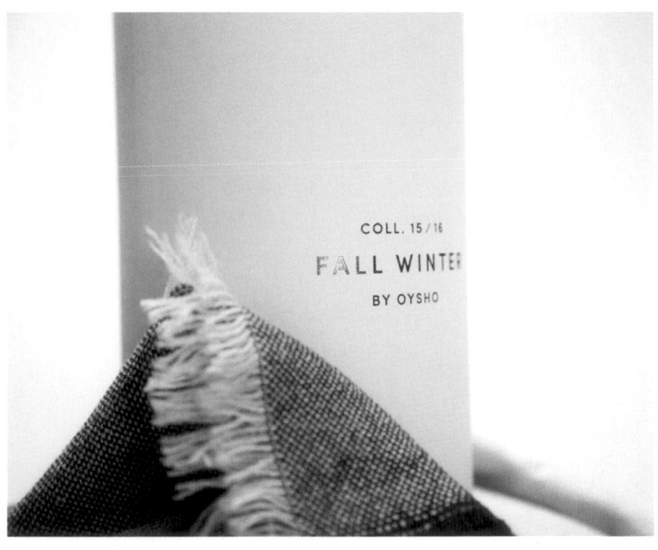
COLL. 15 / 16
FALL WINTER
BY OYSHO

NO. G25013
COLOR
ECNU / TURQUOISE
NEVY / BURGUNDY
SIZE
135X135CM 4X2CM 200GR
QUALITY
100% OYSHO

15 / 16

Collar Hanger & Packaging

Áine is an Irish knitwear brand that sells scarfs, hats, collars, and so on. The brief for this project was to create "something" that would properly display the company's collars in shops causing little or no disruption to the shop, the shop owner, or shop workers; it also needed to double as a unique carrier bag for customers. Designer Nina Lyons came up with the concept of a hanger-bag, but the challenge was to create a hanger small enough to display the collars and a bag large enough to hold a collar and a hat after purchase.

In order to promote the branding, the graphics applied to the packaging were kept simple, with just the new logo sitting in the center. When the hanger-bag arrives in shops, it is flat to save on space. Once the base is popped into position, it takes its full form as a carrier bag. The creases on the base allow the bag to balance when standing, and also give it a slight curve.

Client	Material
Áine	Cardboard
Design Agency	**Size**
Return Studios	270mm x 194mm
Designer	**Completion**
Nina Lyons	2015

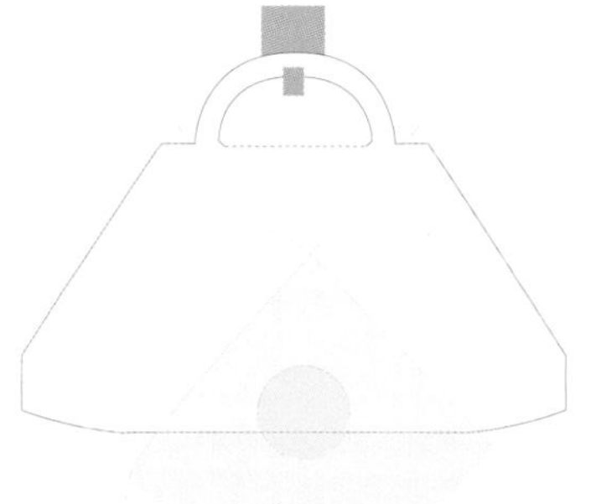

Hanger-Bag Display: Hanging Front View

The hanger-bag can be hung using its handle. A tab is pushed down out of the way, which allows the hanger to be hung on a hook or rack.

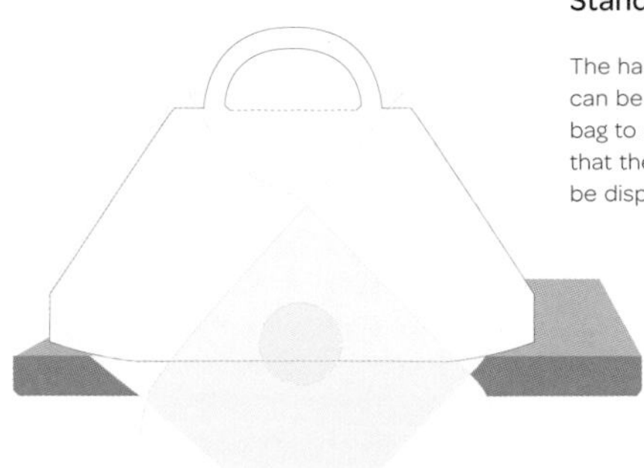

Hanger-Bag Display: Standing Front View

The hanger-bag has a base that can be pushed out, allowing the bag to stand independently so that the neckwear products can be displayed on shelves or tables.

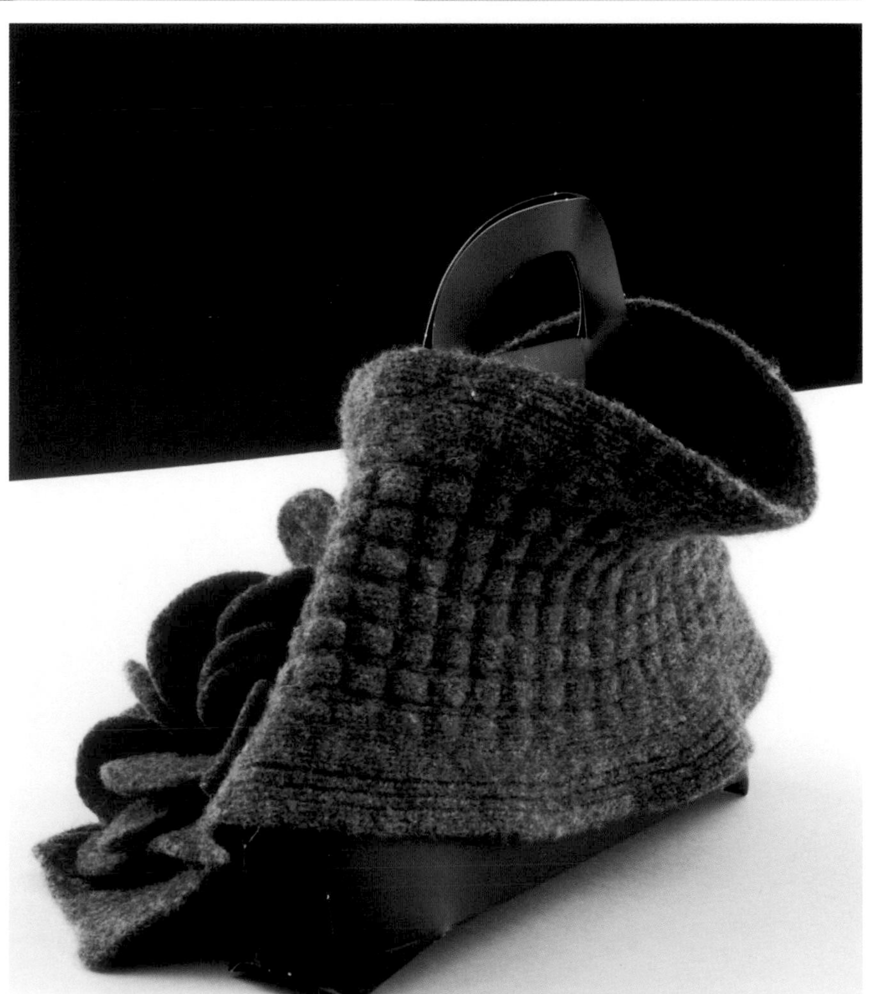

Merrell Gloves Package Design

This gloves package is a vertical, truncated, square pyramid, and has been designed to look like a tent. One of the side flaps can be opened with ease, turning this symmetrical structure into something very handy to carry on a camping trip. The cord on the top can be used to hang the case from a hook on a knapsack or a tent. Drawing on aerial photography, topographic maps and satellite photographs with deep contrasts, scaling diagonals and superimposed textures, the design language reinforces the thrill of adventure inherent in the Merrell brand.

Client
Merrell

Size
108mm x 114mm

Designer
Shaily Shah

Completion
2014

Material
Textured paper

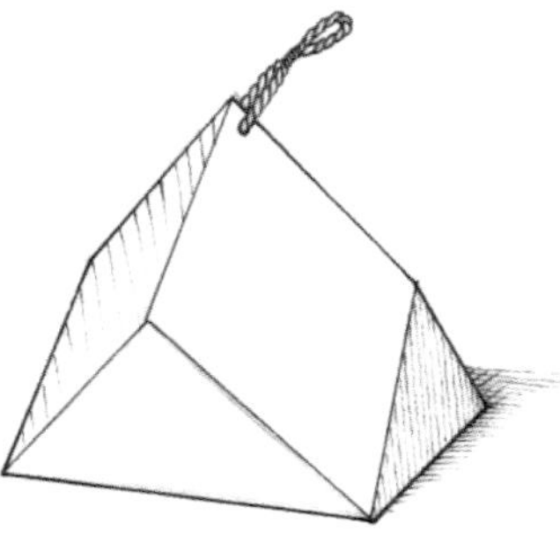

SURVIVE TH

MERRELL

Românico Bordados

Românico Bordados produces fantastic, luxury linen and cotton goods—tablecloths, towels, bedding, and so on—that incorporate embroidery from the northern Portuguese region of Vale do Sousa. The company commissioned VOLTA to create a brand that would highlight the tradition and longevity of the embroidery motifs, which are inspired by Romanesque monuments found in the region and date back to the 12th century. It wanted to emphasize this region's characteristic identity and traditional handmade look to showcase the company's exquisite products.

VOLTA's solution was to create a symbol that reflects both the monuments' and embroidery's motifs and it combined this with a decorative but strong typeface (Estilo Pro by Portuguese designer Dino dos Santos). The designers used kraftlike paper for the tags and product boxes, printing only in one color. They also created the brand's kids' range, Românico Baby. This contrasts with the rest of the range through the use of illustrations by Helena Soares, which are based on animals also portrayed on the Romanesque monuments. The baby range focuses on an animal-specific color palette and geometric shape, allowing for eye-catching packaging and product displays.

Client
Românico Bordados

Design Agency
VOLTA Branding & Design Studio

Designers
Pedro Vareta, Helena Soares

Material
Kraft-paper-lined cardboard

Size
Tube /
325mm x 95mm
Little Box /
245mm x 245mm x 55mm
Big Box /
450mm x 305mm x 55mm

Completion
2014

ROMÂNICO
FOLHA DE PALMA

ROMÂNICO
BABY

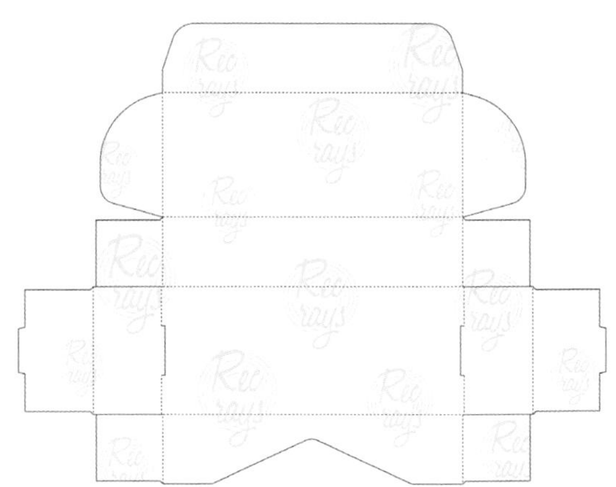

Rec Rays Sunglasses Packaging

Each of the packages for Rec Rays sunglasses was designed to be unique, like the sunglasses themselves. These sunglasses are made of recycled records and wood, and the prints on the boxes are meant to capture the radial properties of these materials. Variable printing on packaging is still something that is relatively hard and expensive to do with more traditional forms of printing such as offset and litho. The packaging was digitally printed on a HP Indigo 30000, using an in-line, opaque, white-ink underlay, and some of the boxes include a hot stamp of the Rec Rays logo in silver holographic foil.

Client
Rec Rays Sunglasses, LLC.

Designer
Brittany Vazquez

Material
Recycled kraft paper

Size
165mm x 70mm x 38mm

Completion
2015

RECYCLED | REISSUED
VINYL SUNGLASSES
RECYCLED | REISSUED
VINYL SUNGLASSES
RECYCLED | REISSUED
VINYL SUNGLASSES

handmade in:
Cleveland, OH
RECRAYSSUNGLASSES@GMAIL.COM
RECRAYSSUNGLASSES.COM
RECYCLED | REISSUED
VINYL SUNGLASSES

Sartor Branding & Packaging

Sartor is a small family business that creates handmade men's clothing and accessories. As it changed hands and evolved, Luminous Design Group was commissioned to create a new image for the brand, bringing it in line with current trends. The agency employed a solid, monochrome design approach in black. Cylindrical packaging was chosen to accommodate the company's bow ties; every bow tie is attached to a card, which folds in order to fit properly into the cylinder and unfolds in order to be hung in a store display. Cubes were designed to house the neck ties, which are folded inside the box and are easily accessible by the way the box opens. Once opened, the interior packaging reveals all the necessary information about the neck tie. Inspired by tailors' spools, the brand's business cards highlight the owner's occupation, leaving no doubt about it.

Client
Sartor

Design Agency
Luminous Design Group

Material
Kraft paper

Size
Cylinder /
108mm x 18mm
Cube /
100mm x 100mm x 100mm

Completion
2015

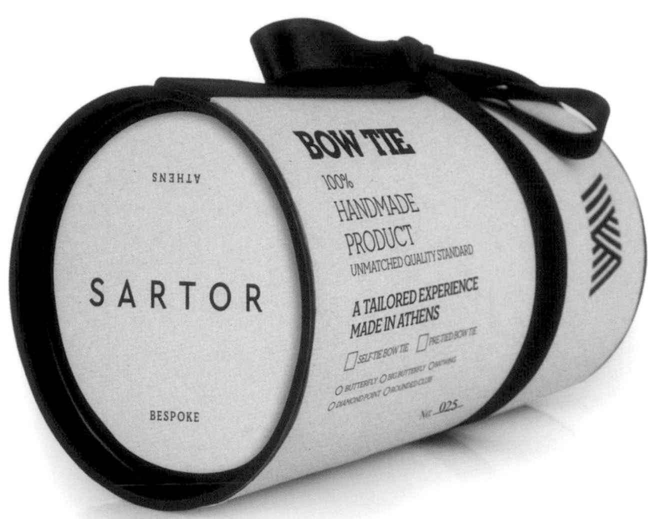
SARTOR
ATHENS
BESPOKE
BOW TIE
100%
HANDMADE
PRODUCT
UNMATCHED QUALITY STANDARD
A TAILORED EXPERIENCE
MADE IN ATHENS

SARTOR
No. 025
ATHENS
BESPOKE
SARTOR
No. 025
BOW TIE
100%
HANDMADE
PRODUCT
UNMATCHED QUALITY STANDARD
A TAILORED EXPERIENCE
MADE IN ATHENS
SELF-TIE BOW TIE
PRE-TIED BOW TIE
BUTTERFLY
BIG BUTTERFLY
BATWING
DIAMOND POINT
ROUNDED CLUB
No. 025

Avoca Spool Scarf Packaging

As part of the "Avoca Nest" scarf-packaging project, designer Annie Brady was tasked with creating an unusual way to display Avoca's knitted and woven scarfs in-store. The idea for the scarf on a spool was inspired by a routine visit by the client to the Avoca mill. There, the walls are always stocked with spools of yarn for imminent use as part of various woven goods. By taking the simple spool structure that holds the product's raw material and using it as a packaging base for the end product, it makes a strong statement about the scarfs' origins and manufacture process, as well as an eye-catching display. The designer was required to create appropriate graphics suitable for each type of scarf, which resulted in tongue-in-cheek designs perfect for the quirky Avoca brand.

Client
Avoca Handweavers Ltd.

Size
130mm diameter

Designer
Annie Brady

Completion
2013

Material
Kraft board, metal rim

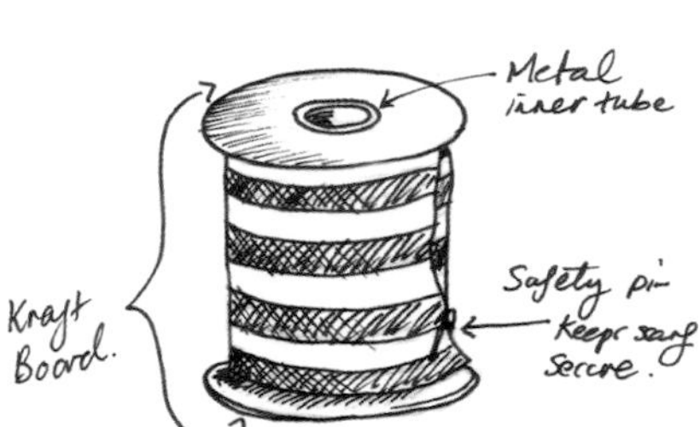

AVOCA ESTABLISHED 1723. 100% COTTON SCARF. ON A SPOOL.
Dedicated to design & quality since 1723. Work hard. play hard. Positive Thinking. Mission: To create joy.

WHICH BREED ARE YOU? * AVOCA * FASHION CLAN SCARF ON A SPOOL -
The Prima Donna
The Perfectionist
The Rebel
The Mad Hatter
The Exhibitionist
The Domestic Diva

AVOCA ESTABLISHED 1723. 100% COTTON SCARF. ON A SPOOL.
Dedicated to design & quality since 1723. Work hard. play hard. Positive Thinking. Mission: To create joy.

AVOCA * FASHION CLAN SCARF ON A SPOOL - WHICH BREED ARE YOU?
AVOCA
AVOCA
AVOCA

Vualé: Versatile Scarfs

Vualé is a Colombian brand of premium silk scarfs. It is known as the most versatile women's apparel item, because the scarfs can be folded and draped in multiple ways, turning into a bandana, bag, skirt, shirt, and more. In addition to the product design, a series of packages was created, including a tubular container and two tin boxes. The tubular container and the square tin box were designed as basic packaging pieces, while the rectangular tin box was conceived as a premium or gift-packaging piece; the latter included a scarf ring, perfect for arranging the scarfs in different ways. In addition, the packages were covered with adhesive-paper designs, resulting in unconventional and engaging containers.

Designer
Carolina Díaz

Material
Adhesive paper, tin

Size
Tube /
150mm x 200mm
Square tin box /
88mm x 88mm x 74mm
Rectangular tin box /
104mm x 165mm x 42mm

Completion
2013

VUALĒ
COLOMBIA

VUALĒ
COLOMBIA

VUALĒ
COLOMBIA

Azede Jean-Pierre FW14 Invitation Packaging

Invitations to the Azede Jean-Pierre Fall/Winter 2014 Collection Runway Show were sent out in a package that included a knitted hat with the date and time of the show embroidered onto it, plus a tag with more details about the event. The package itself is an expandable envelope, which looks like a mailable envelope when it lies flat, but can also stand up vertically to be functional as a bag. Somewhat similarly to how a paper bag folds, the design of the envelope perfectly conceals the somewhat bulky and lumpy contents. A heather-gray cardstock was chosen for the envelope, which was thick and sturdy enough to hold up in the mail, but soft and feminine enough to complement the collection. The envelope was held closed with two small black brads, and a small circular sticker that said "Stay Warm" was placed on the back.

Client
Azede Jean-Pierre

Designer
Joseph Veazey

Material
Cardstock, metal brads

Size
165mm x 241mm

Completion
2014

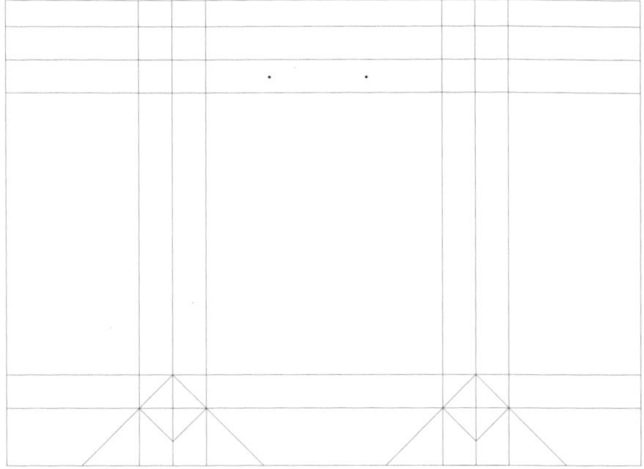

AZEDE JEAN-PIERRE
JOSEPH VEAZEY
1234 1ST ST #1A
NEW YORK, NY 10001

STAY
WARM

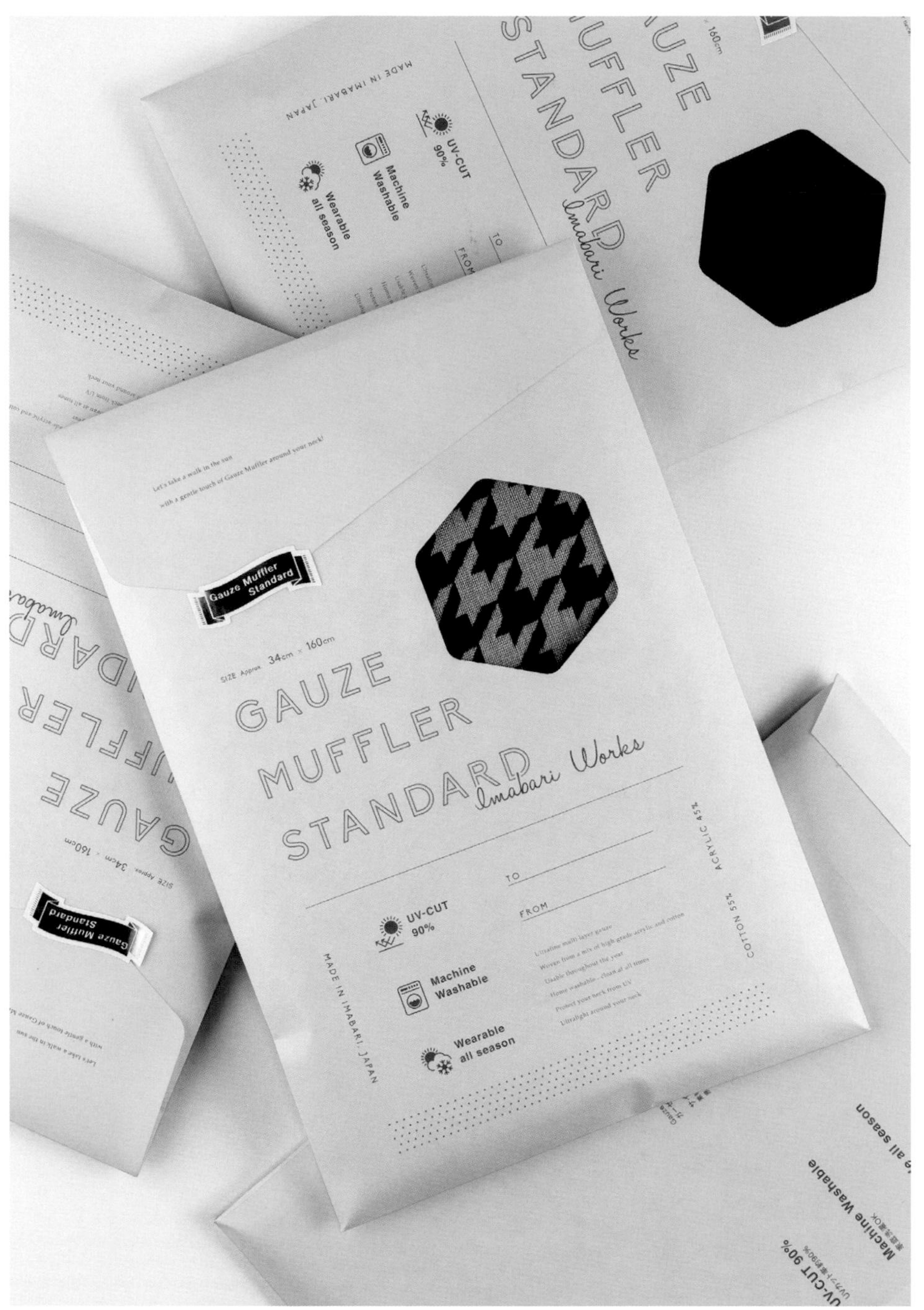

Gauze Muffler Standard

This packaging for Colorsville's standard "gauze mufflers" (scarfs) was inspired by the shape of an envelope. The small polygonal window was added to the package so that customers could see the color and feel the texture of the mufflers through it. Designer Koji Matsumoto changed the conventional shape of an envelope by altering the flap used to close the package. The color palette chosen promotes a soft and warm feeling, to complement the feel of the mufflers, and it is also suitable for both men and women.

Client
Colorsville Co., Ltd.

Design Agency
Grand Deluxe

Designer
Koji Matsumoto

Material
Paperboard

Size
200mm x 300mm x 20mm

Completion
2014

Gauze Muffler Standard
SIZE Approx. 34cm × 160cm
GAUZE
MUF

GAUZE
MUFFLER
STANDARD
UV-CUT 90%
UVカット率約90%
Machine Washable
家庭洗濯OK
Wearable all season
オールシーズンOK
Gauze Muffler Standard
ガーゼマフラースタンダード
サイズ：約34×160cm
Keep the water clean
colorsville

34cm × 160cm
ZE
LER
ARD
Imabari Works

Index

Published in Australia in 2016 by
The Images Publishing Group Pty Ltd
Shanghai Office
ABN 89 059 734 431
6 Bastow Place, Mulgrave, Victoria 3170, Australia
Tel: +61 3 9561 5544 Fax: +61 3 9561 4860
books@imagespublishing.com
www.imagespublishing.com

The Images Publishing Group Reference Number: 1274

Title: Fashion Packaging Now
Author: Huang, Chris (ed.)
ISBN: 9781864706802

For Catalogue-in-Publication data, please see the National Library of Australia entry

Printed by Everbest Printing Investment Limited., Hong Kong/China